The Open University

T192 Engineering: origins, methods, context

Part 2: Chapters 9–16

This publication forms part of the Open University module T192 *Engineering: origins, methods, context*. Details of this and other Open University modules can be obtained from the Student Registration and Enquiry Service, The Open University, PO Box 197, Milton Keynes MK7 6BJ, United Kingdom (tel. +44 (0)845 300 60 90; email general-enquiries@open.ac.uk).

Alternatively, you may visit the Open University website at www.open.ac.uk where you can learn more about the wide range of modules and packs offered at all levels by The Open University.

The Open University, Walton Hall, Milton Keynes MK7 6AA

First published 2016. Second edition 2018.

Edited and designed by The Open University.

Typeset by The Open University.

Printed and bound in the United Kingdom by Page Bros, Norwich.

ISBN 978 1 4730 2446 5

2.1

Contents

Part 2: Chapter 9   Design beginnings   I

Introduction   3

9.1   What is design?   5

9.2   Drivers for design   12

9.3   Designing for people   16

    9.3.1   People and variation   16
    9.3.2   Practical variation   18
    9.3.3   Numerical variation   19
    9.3.4   Using numbers to design   22
    9.3.5   Design variation and people   26

Reference   29

Solutions to activities in Chaper 9   30

Part 2: Chapter 10   Design contexts   **35**

Introduction   37

10.1   Design limits   38

    10.1.1   Conditions   38
    10.1.2   Constraints   43
    10.1.3   Considerations   44
    10.1.4   Putting this together   45

10.2   Boundaries and opportunities   47

    10.2.1   Boundaries of design   47
    10.2.2   Opportunities   49
    10.2.3   Designing for the future   52
    10.2.4   Using decision tables to sort information   53

10.3   Designing complexity and uncertainty   58

    10.3.1   Uncertainty and risk   59
    10.3.2   Uncertain structures: cathedrals and bridges   60
    10.3.3   Balancing uncertainty and risk   63
    10.3.4   Visual thinking   64

References   74

Solutions to activities in Chapter 10   75

Part 2: Chapter 11   Design approaches   **79**

Introduction   81

11.1 Design problems   82

    11.1.1 Problem framing   84

11.2 Creating solutions   92

    11.2.1 Scribbling and doodling to think creatively   92
    11.2.2 Getting creative   95
    11.2.3 Creative techniques and methods   98
    11.2.4 When you get stuck and when to move on   99

11.3 Sketching, geometry and triangles   101

    11.3.1 A quick introduction to diagrams   101
    11.3.2 Lines, angles and triangles   104
    11.3.3 Right-angled triangles   107
    11.3.4 Other types of triangles   113
    11.3.5 A triangle summary   115

Reference   117

Solutions to activities in Chapter 11   118

Part 2: Chapter 12   Design decisions   **123**

Introduction   125

12.1 Developing ideas into concepts   126

    12.1.1 Moving backwards to go forwards   126
    12.1.2 Design prototypes   128
    12.1.3 Strength by design   135

12.2 Developing concepts into detailed design   138

    12.2.1 Design evaluation   138
    12.2.2 Working out the details – a case study   142
    12.2.3 The process so far   150

12.3 Introduction to vectors   151

    12.3.1 What are vectors?   151
    12.3.2 Adding and subtracting vectors   158

Solutions to activities in Chapter 12   163

Part 2: Chapter 13   Design communication   **167**

Introduction   169

13.1 The need for communication   170

    13.1.1 Create and develop ideas   171
    13.1.2 Develop and analyse concepts   173
    13.1.3 Record and confirm proposals   175

13.2   Communication methods   177

    13.2.1   Common methods of design communication   177

    13.2.2   Common techniques in graphic communicaton   180

    13.2.3   Failure to communicate   184

13.3   Communicating analysis   186

    13.3.1   Using trigonometry with vectors   187

    13.3.2   Taking components of a vector   189

    13.3.3   Analysing forces: free body diagrams   194

Solutions to activities in Chapter 13   202

Part 2:   Chapter 14   Design processes   **209**

Introduction   211

14.1   Basic design processes   212

    14.1.1   The iterative design process   212

    14.1.2   Project design phases   214

    14.1.3   Types of design process phase   215

    14.1.4   Checkpoints: stage gates versus soft landings   217

14.2 Design process management   220

    14.2.1   Incremental innovation   220

    14.2.2   Design for manufacture   224

    14.2.3   Design for service   227

    14.2.4   Limitations   231

14.3   Analytical and design processes   232

    14.3.1   Dots instead of lines   233

    14.3.2   Iteration using numbers   235

    14.3.3   Iteration versus solving   238

Solutions to activities in Chapter 14   241

Part 2: Chapter 15   Design materials   **245**

Introduction   247

15.1   Material characteristics   248

    15.1.1   Knowing through experience   248

    15.1.2   Knowing through testing   254

    15.1.3   Knowing through experiment   257

15.2   Interpreting graphs: gradients   259

    15.2.1   Gradients of straight lines   259

    15.2.2   Calculating gradients   261

    15.2.3   Interpreting gradient   266

15.3 Modelling materials   271

    15.3.1 Intercepts and checking points   271

    15.3.2 Modelling shelves   274

    15.3.3 Being careful with knowing   275

Solutions to activities in Chapter 15   279

Part 2: Chapter 16   Design methods   **285**

Introduction   287

16.1 Material analysis   288

    16.1.1 Straight-line equations   288

    16.1.2 Drawing a line from its equation   292

    16.1.3 Finding the equation of a straight line   292

    16.1.4 Applications and practice   295

    16.1.5 Modelling the shelf   299

16.2 Analytical methods   301

    16.2.1 Words and definitions in engineering   301

    16.2.2 Strength under stress   303

    16.2.3 Take the strain   309

16.3 Engineering the future   313

Solutions to activities in Chapter 16   319

Acknowledgements   **327**

Index   **331**

Part 2: Chapter 9   Design beginnings

Introduction

Much of the world around you is designed in some way. Modern living relies on the products, systems and services created to support how we live. Design comes from the ability to think creatively – to be able to imagine 'what if …?' and come up with something that didn't exist before.

Some of the greatest human achievements have come from creative design engineering, allowing the realisation of some truly remarkable change in our world. Design engineering has helped to transform the environment, create incredible super-structures on land and sea, and even helped people travel to, and live in, space (Figure 9.1).

(a)   (b)   (c)

Figure 9.1 Examples of design engineering: (a) the Hoover Dam; (b) the Millau Viaduct; (c) the International Space Station

At the same time some of the smallest designs have enabled the biggest steps in the progress of humanity. The way people live has been changed by incremental advances in medicine, food production and many of the materials and devices people use on a daily basis (Figure 9.2).

(a)   (b)   (c)

Figure 9.2 'Small' design engineering innovations that have made huge contributions: (a) a disposable hypodermic needle; (b) a transistor; (c) Velcro fastening material

Design engineering has also developed many of the most important systems and services, from individual right up to global and universal scales. These systems have supported radical scaling up of human activity in a huge range of areas (Figure 9.3).

(a)   (b)   (c)

Figure 9.3   Examples of designed systems and services: (a) a standardised component system; (b) a distribution and transport system; (c) a satellite navigation (satnav) system and service

Design can be the fashionable, eye-catching products and images you probably think of. But design is also the least noticeable (and often most important) services and systems. This chapter will introduce you to some characteristics and drivers for design, some of which you might not have come across before, and start to explore how data can be used to inform design decisions.

9.1 What is design?

As soon as you read the word 'design' you probably formed some idea of what you think it is. It is a word that can be used in many ways and can mean different things to different people. Even in a specialised discipline like design engineering there are many different definitions and types of design activity. To complicate things further, design can be a verb or a noun: you can 'design a design'. So it is important to remove as much confusion and contradiction as possible when discussing anything containing the word 'design'.

This module introduces design in a particular way based on both theory and practice. It will include discussion of design but you will also be expected *to design* – to actually try techniques and develop skills that are useful in the process of designing. This practical approach to learning and practice is also at the heart of design engineering.

This section starts by discussing a few characteristics of design that you may not have come across before.

Design is more than aesthetics and appearance

It can be easy to think of design as only styling, fashion or the appearance of objects. You only have to look at the variety of similar products in shops to see that some design products have an obvious focus on appearance. External variations in kitchen appliance design often take place without actually changing the underlying product, in order to remain up to date or fashionable, or to fit in with other market drivers (Figure 9.4).

(a)   (b)   (c)

Figure 9.4 Aesthetic and external variation in products with the same underlying function

In this module, design is presented as much more than this – as something that is valuable as both a process and the outcome of that process. Good design brings aesthetic and functional elements together to create something that is greater than the individual parts. Many designers would argue that good design embodies *both* – the aesthetics are pleasing because of the utility, and the function is expressed in the appearance.

Consider bridges, for example, where the function of the bridge often relates directly to the shape of it – how the bridge looks is related directly to how it works. The Forth Rail Bridge is over 100 years old and fulfils its function by supporting very heavy moving trains using three balanced cantilevers. These cantilevers give the bridge its distinctive shape, and this shape is also aesthetically pleasing – it looks attractive (Figure 9.5). People have written books, poems and songs about this bridge – and it has also had cameos in film and computer games! The effect of this piece of design engineering goes far beyond solving the single problem of crossing water.

Figure 9.5   The Forth Rail Bridge demonstrates a practical and aesthetic solution to the challenge of designing a bridge

Good design is more than simply looks and aesthetics – the best design engineering is a result of blending both the aesthetic and the functional. As you will see in later chapters, this comes from blending different types of thinking and approaches in the process.

Design is more than products and objects

Some products are not much use on their own: they require other elements around them to enable them to work. For instance, your mobile phone wouldn't be much use without a whole range of supporting products and systems to enable it. These other elements are also designed.

Consider the design of the electricity supply system in the UK. In particular, think about the infrastructure that supports it (the power stations that generate the electricity, the wires that transport it, the substations along the route), the individual products used to access that system (sockets, wiring, light fittings), and then the service provided (energy companies, maintenance agreements). It would not be possible to design one without the other – the products depend on the system of electricity supplied, and the supply of electricity depends on the demand created by the products (Figure 9.6).

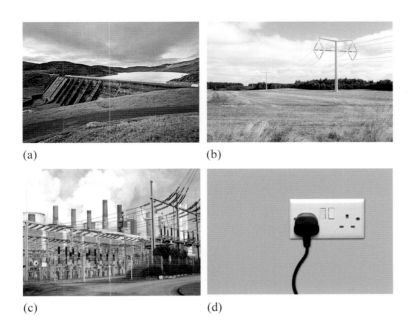

(a)   (b)

(c)   (d)

Figure 9.6 Some of the elements that make up the system of electricity supply in the UK: (a) hydroelectric dam; (b) pylons carrying transmission wires; (c) substation; (d) electrical socket and plug

Behind this simple relationship are an entire range of **products**, **specifications**, **systems** and **services** that are all required to ensure the consistent supply of electricity. Even the way in which these elements are used, a **process**, can be designed. These terms are defined below and in the glossary.

Design engineering terms

- **Product** – an object created to fulfil some function or purpose.
- **Specification** – a detailed description of the design and materials used to make something.
- **Process** – a series of events that are performed in sequence in order to fulfil some overall aim.
- **Service** – an activity or event provided in order to fulfil or support some specific need.
- **System** – a collection of elements that connect to form a coherent group that serves some purpose or function.

When the focus is only on the product itself, other elements around a design can sometimes be forgotten. Many design engineering companies now actively look beyond their products to design systems and services as well. For example, some lighting companies will now sell a 'service to provide light' rather than just individual light fittings. In doing so they provide a service to maintain (and even sometimes operate) a lighting system.

Design is more than simply creating a product – services, systems and processes can also be designed. Even when a design is simply for a product, the chances are it will require these other design elements to support it.

Design is not just for designers

Design takes place at every single stage in any project. Even the smallest design sub-task can be approached creatively, often leading to significant innovation and improvement when it is scaled up. In many world-leading product design companies, the design of apparently insignificant elements and components is given as much attention as the overall design because this can lead to other benefits.

In some cases the smallest components may have a significant effect. Take Trunki, for example, an internationally successful product that failed to get funding on the BBC television programme *Dragons' Den* due to the strap clip breaking during demonstration. Despite this failure, its designer continued with the product, realising that the problem could be overcome through further design and testing (Figure 9.7).

Figure 9.7   Children's hand luggage product Trunki

This is an extreme example of a small detail having a large consequence, but the lesson is important – you never know what detail might matter most. The principles of design can be applied usefully to *all* stages of a project and even beyond. The smallest detail in a project needs to be designed just as much as the overall project.

Design is much more than just solving a single problem

Problem solving is a significant motivation for design – you come across a problem and you want to solve it. But how do you know you are solving the right problem? What if what you do solves the original problem but creates another problem? Worst of all, what if solving a problem actually makes things worse?

A large part of good design engineering is about understanding and selecting the right sorts of problem to solve. In fact, the best design is about carefully shaping problems and framing them to generate a solution that improves more than the original problem. In some cases the solution that comes from the design process can have very little to do with the original problem but does much more. As Nigel Cross says in his book *Design Thinking* (2011), the best designers give the client something they didn't even know they wanted.

Good examples of this approach are the design innovations made by the company Tetra Pak (Figure 9.8). Each of these designs solves multiple problems at the same time to create a complete design – for example, the openings have to be reinforced for strength in storage and transport but also have to be easy to open. A potential solution to one of these conditions might lead to problems with the other, so solving both problems at the same time becomes important.

Figure 9.8 Examples of packaging designs that solve multiple problems to create successful design projects

In many ways solving individual problems is relatively easy if the resources are available. What is often far harder is solving the *right* problems with the *best* solution(s). Part of the skill of a design engineer is not only defining problems to solve but also working out *how* those problems might be solved. Being able to see problems from a range of different viewpoints and then distilling these is an important skill for the designer.

Design is not simply solving a problem – it is about selecting and framing the right problems. The best design goes beyond simple problem solving and creates something new.

Design is about thinking around the object

There is another way of thinking about design that makes it much more interesting and challenging. The job of the designer (and especially the design engineer) is to try to think of the things that no one else thinks of. Designing involves creating something new, and this means that it will have new consequences. Designers consider these consequences as well as the design itself because they know that this will lead to a more successful outcome – problems can be imagined before they become reality, and other opportunities can be taken advantage of.

Consider a product being designed for an extreme or challenging environment. If only the product itself is considered and the context is ignored, it's very unlikely the product will succeed. For example, in offshore design engineering, the nearest materials and backup are not very easy to access (Figure 9.9), meaning that the installation and operation of products really matters. The designer has to think about many different aspects of a design at the same time – installation, removal, repairs and maintenance, decommissioning – in addition to the artefact itself. When only the product itself is considered this almost always leads to other problems in the wider system, leading to costly failures and extended repair times.

Figure 9.9   An offshore oil platform, an environment where the design has to consider more than just the product itself

Design is not simply thinking about an object, it considers what is 'around' the object – the context, operation, repair, or replacement. The best design results in solutions that consider more than simply a static object.

Design is …

Some of the ideas presented above might be new to you and you might consider design in a slightly different way after thinking about them. A definition of design is not provided here because it is better for you to start to come to your own understanding of it in your own way. Before moving on, there are a few last characteristics of design for you to consider.

First, design is a *process*. It is something that people do with a specific aim or goal in mind. The process may not lead to a single perfect solution and part of that process might be to define what 'solved' means. But it is the journey that makes the difference. If you knew where the process was going to end up, then you wouldn't need to design in the first place.

Second, design makes use of creative and analytical attitudes, approaches and skills. Using only creative methods or only analytical methods in a design process rarely leads to successful projects. But by applying both, the design engineer can draw on the most effective methods to approach complex challenges.

Finally, design has a purpose and creates change. It is an inherently practical pursuit – it is not only theoretical or imaginary. The output from the design process is the creation or change of some aspect of the world around us.

As you work through this second part of the module, bear these three ideas in mind. You are expected to start to become a designer. In doing so you will be engaging in a process of analytical and creative activity – all with a view to making a change in the world around you.

9.2   Drivers for design

All designed objects or design projects have a reason behind them. Very often the reasons may seem quite obvious: to serve a function, to meet some specific need, or to be useful in some way. For most designs there is more than one reason, and some designs can have quite complex sets of motivations and drivers.

For example, there are a whole range of reasons for creating a plastic water bottle like the one in Figure 9.10 – as well as the obvious, functional reason of storing water. These reasons will have come from different sources, and will also vary depending on when in the design project the reason came about.

Figure 9.10   A plastic water bottle is the shape it is for more than simply the obvious, functional reasons

Activity 9.1

Pick an object near to you and list some reasons for it being designed the way it is. If you can't think of an object, then use the example of a plastic water bottle given in Figure 9.10.

Try thinking about: what the design does; how it does something; who benefits from it (and how/why).

From this activity you will probably have come up with a list of statements that were specific to the product you were considering. If you were to repeat the activity for a range of different products, you would come up with more reasons. But you would also start to see common patterns of reasons, and these reasons would be indicators of what people want and need from products. These are known as **design drivers**.

Here are a few examples of some common design drivers.

Common design drivers

- **To meet a need:** All people have certain basic needs such as shelter, food and warmth. Meeting these needs often requires creative design and problem solving. In addition, people require more complex systems such as healthcare, education, or access to other services such as telecommunications. Needs are often immediate reasons and very strong drivers for design – everybody has needs that have to be fulfilled.

- **To solve a problem:** Almost every time you come across a problem you use some sort of design process to create a new solution or workaround. Most problems are obvious and are identified when people encounter them. But some problems can be very complex, or might be only a symptom of an underlying problem. A creative designer can deliberately use *problem finding* and *problem framing* techniques to identify and develop potential designs.

- **To fulfil a desire or demand:** Desires and demands are perhaps less critical than needs or problems but they are still significant drivers and have arguably become much more important in modern lifestyles globally, as average living standards increase. These are usually psychologically or socially driven factors, such as the desire to have the same (or better) product as one's peers.

- **To improve something:** The need to improve something follows on from the driver of problem solving. Being able to do something better, faster or more reliably are all examples of improvement that can be significant drivers of design. In fact, much of modern product design and development is what is called **incremental design**, where small changes are made to existing products or systems in order to change them in some way. You will examine this process in greater detail in Chapter 14.

- **To respond to change:** Existing solutions to problems, needs or desires are not static – they tend to change as circumstances change. People's desire to have the latest technology or keep up with the latest fashionable trend is a strong driver for design change. Similarly, new technologies, manufacturing or other opportunities allow designers to update and recreate existing designs. Changes to environmental conditions, such as global warming, may also require a change of approach. Design is rarely a static thing.

- **Just because …:** Finally, it is worth including 'just because'. While it's true that very few design offices have the chance to simply design for the sake of it, some do engage in this speculative activity as part of their business. For example, Google and Apple both encourage staff to take time each week to work on personal projects, and many of these either inform future projects or become innovative products themselves. Of course, these individual design projects then have their own drivers, and being able to identify and explore these drivers is important.

Figures 9.11 and 9.12 show some examples of these design drivers.

In the list above, you might notice how similar many of the items appear at first. Quite often a project will have multiple drivers, and they may change over the course of the project.

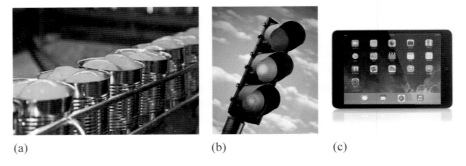

(a)   (b)   (c)

Figure 9.11   Examples of design drivers: (a) food production systems are driven by the human *need* to eat; (b) traffic lights solve the *problem* of controlling large volumes of traffic; (c) tablet computers are driven by people's *desire* for a particular type of device and interface

Activity 9.2

Go back through the reasons you identified for the design of the object you chose in Activity 9.1, and identify which design drivers you think best match each reason. For each reason and driver give a brief explanation of how they relate to each other.

There are no right answers to this activity – you will have a particular opinion and view of what matters most in your chosen design. What matters is how important you think each driver might be, and that you try to see other drivers of design that you might not have thought about before.

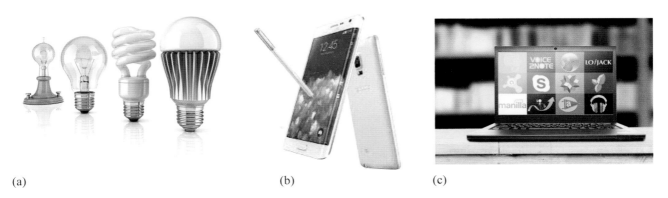

(a) (b) (c)

Figure 9.12 Examples of design drivers: (a) light bulb efficiency and longevity are driven by *improvement*; (b) mobile phones are constantly driven by technology *change*; (c) many online services and apps are driven *just because* the developers can create something quickly and test it

In Activities 9.1 and 9.2 you concentrated on products, but design drivers apply to system and service design as well. Most products also require consideration of systems or services to operate effectively. For example, the demand for electricity in the UK requires multiple elements to be designed: not just physical products (such as those shown in Figure 9.6), but also systems and services to organise and regulate the supply. Each of these aspects of a design project will also have particular drivers and it is important to keep these in mind when working on any design project.

A key design skill is the ability to recognise different types of design driver and use them to identify creative opportunities and possibilities. Whenever you come across a problem in real life, you have probably found a driver for design.

9.3   Designing for people

Everything that is designed comes into contact with people at some point. This is mostly through the use of a design, but people are also involved in less direct ways, such as manufacturing, installation or maintenance. Design failure very often occurs because of failures to take account of people. A consequence of the involvement of people is the complexity they bring. Just consider the numerous variations of any object around you. Why are there so many shapes of cup, of mobile phones or of cars? Why can one person seem to operate an object easily while other people find it hard? And why can't anyone solve the problem of comfortable seats on a train?

This variation and complexity arise from differences between individual people. People are not all the same and their behaviour is certainly not predictable. Here are a few key variations a designer might consider:

- People vary physically, meaning that design for people has to take account of a wide range of sizes, shapes and adjustments.
- People have different preferences and thoughts, meaning that what they feel about, and how they interact with, design varies considerably.
- People have a range circumstances and contexts (family, friends, employment, etc.).
- People have different experiences and knowledge, which means that a designer might have to make a range of assumptions.

All of these variations mean that designing for people can be a complex process. Dealing with this complexity is a central part of design. Later in the module you will look at these variations and complexities in greater detail, but this section starts by considering one obvious variation – the physical sizes of people. You will use this variation to explore how design can blend a variety of analytical and creative approaches to respond to design drivers.

9.3.1   People and variation

Start by considering how you would begin designing an object that has to 'fit' to people, such as a simple desk or table. People using it will vary in size and these differences might be quite extreme (at the time of writing, the tallest person recorded had a height of 2.72 m and the shortest woman alive is 628 mm tall). What sizes should you start with? Is a single height acceptable? If not, how many sizes might you need?

Activity 9.3

(a) What is the *difference* in height between the tallest recorded man (2.72 m) and the shortest living women (628 mm)? Calculate the answer in millimetres, then express this in metres to 1 d.p.

(b) What is the midpoint between the two extremes of height (the average of the two)? Would this be a sensible value to take as a starting point for a design?

Solving the problem of human variation is not a simple exercise. If you design a product to suit people at a particular height, you may then be limiting access for other people. Figure 9.13 shows a typical ticket machine in the UK. If you have used a machine like this, you might have wondered whether the designers took any account of human shape and sizes at all – or you might have found the machine comfortable to use. It all depends on your point of view.

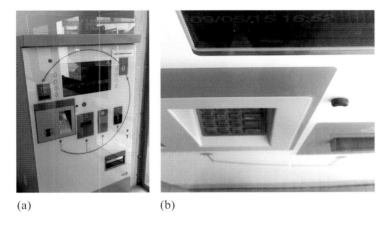

(a)   (b)

Figure 9.13   A common type of ticket machine in a UK train station: (a) a view of the machine from 2 m away; (b) a tall user's view of the keypad when standing at the machine. Note how difficult it is to see the keypad screen (from the tall person's point of view).

At some point decisions are required to be made about the properties of a design in progress. The ticket machine shown in Figure 9.13 had to be defined in terms of height, width and depth, and every component had to be located in relation to this to allow it to be manufactured. In making these decisions, however, you might solve the problem for some people but make it worse for others. Knowing how to think about difficult decisions like these can be useful as a designer. Because several different factors are involved, you need to use particular ways of thinking through this type of design problem.

9.3.2   Practical variation

One way to approach a design problem is to use your own knowledge and experience. You may not be a furniture, automotive or aeroplane designer but you probably have considerable experience of sitting down! Making use of this personal knowledge might seem trivial, but it is the start of all creative problem solving. The key is turning this personal knowledge into information you can use in any design process.

Activity 9.4

Measure the height from the floor to the top of your seat. Next, measure the height from the floor to the top of your desk or table where you study.

Make your measurements in millimetres and note them down somewhere for use in the next activity. Even if you don't usually study at a desk or table, find a place like this that you can use for this activity (and the next one).

Calculate the difference between these two heights in mm.

What you have done in Activity 9.4 is to measure something that already exists. You have an existing desk and you have given a value to a property of it. Now, when you talk to other people about your desk you'll be able to state the height in a way that they will understand.

Before you take this measured height as the perfect desk height, it is worth checking this assumption. Once again you will use a practical method to do this.

Activity 9.5

Adjust the height of your desktop by using accessible materials you have around you. For example, you could use a flat surface like a tray propped up on books, or a folder with some DVD cases underneath it. What you are looking for is some way to quickly and easily adjust a stable surface that you are able to use. If you have quite a high desk, then you might want to find a lower one, such as a table, to start the activity.

Try working on your desk at different heights, and note down how it feels to work at each height. (Is it more or less comfortable than the original height?) Once you have found a height that feels comfortable, take a note of the difference in height from what you were using previously.

Take a few pictures of your adjusted desktop. You will use these images in the online study resources for this week. A discussion of this activity will follow in the main text – but don't read on until you have tried it.

This technique is called **design prototyping**, where you create a quick physical mock-up of a design idea in order to test some aspect of that idea. It is exceptionally useful because it is quick and simple, and you get instant feedback on the problem you are exploring. Almost all design problems can be prototyped (even systems and processes) and this is a key method in any design engineer's toolkit.

The prototype you have just made can also provide two types of information. When you increased the height of your desk you might have noted whether it felt uncomfortable and whether this discomfort is acceptable or not. Or you might have compared two heights to see which one is more (or less) comfortable. You are no longer only measuring height; you are also making judgements about the desk at these heights. In both cases you now have new items of information, and they are of different types. The height of the desk is **quantitative** information, while what you think and feel about the new height is **qualitative** information.

The terms qualitative and quantitative were introduced in Part 1, Chapter 3, Section 3.1. Use the glossary to check your understanding of their meaning.

The height you are working with is fine for one person (you!) and it is possible to imagine that other people of about your own size might also be quite happy with that height. But the original problem was more general: what height should you use to design a desk to 'fit' people? In other words, you are interested in finding a height that many people will find comfortable, and one way to do this is to find out how many people might find a particular height comfortable.

To expand the problem beyond your own experience you need to use other techniques.

9.3.3 Numerical variation

When it comes to designing for large numbers of other people it becomes impractical to ask every individual what they think. But the same practical methods you have just used can be scaled up using statistical methods. For example, from Activity 9.5 you now have a desk height that suits you, and you might assume that most people of your size will also like that desk height. So now you need to know how many people are the same size as you. For that you need to make use of statistics.

Working with datasets

Datasets

A **dataset** is a collection of data, usually presented in the form of a table. In engineering, numerical data is particularly important.

The **range of a dataset** is the difference between its largest and smallest values.

It can be useful to distinguish between two different types of data:

- **Discrete data** is data that can take only certain values.
- **Continuous data** is data that can take any value (often over a particular range).

For example, metric screws are available in certain thicknesses and lengths. The dataset of screw lengths available might include 12 mm, 16 mm, 20 mm and 25 mm. It would not include 12.312 mm or other lengths in between these standard values. This is discrete data.

In contrast, a person's height can take any value (though you might reasonably expect it to lie between the two extremes quoted earlier!). The only restriction is the accuracy to which you choose, or are practically able, to measure it. This is continuous data.

Activity 9.6

Identify each of the following as discrete or continuous data:

(a) the number of students in a tutor group

(b) the distance from a person's home to the nearest bus stop

(c) the price of a ballpoint pen, in pence

(d) wind speed, measured in kilometres per hour.

Before carrying out a detailed analysis of any dataset, it is a good idea to examine the values to see if any patterns or unusual values stand out. You should never ignore data because it is different from what you were expecting, but if a dataset does contain surprising values, it is a good idea to question them in case a mistake has been made. You might look for the following:

- missing data – for instance, if you are given a table of data that has obvious unexpected gaps in it
- spurious precision – for instance, if a number is quoted to more significant figures than is plausible, or too few significant figures to be useful for the intended purpose
- dubious data, perhaps caused by a misplaced decimal point
- coded values, where the data provider may have used a code to indicate something, such as a missing value
- constraints – for instance, there may be some good reason why the data has to lie within a particular range
- the presence of outliers – single values that are very different from the rest of the dataset.

Having checked that your dataset looks valid, you can perform calculations on it. For example, it may be useful to find the average of a set of values.

You have probably come across the idea of an average before, and you may also know that there are different kinds of average. The most useful types of average are usually the **mean** and the **median**.

Average values: mean and median

Finding the mean of a dataset: To find the mean of a set of numbers, add all the numbers together and divide by however many numbers there are in the set.

Finding the median of a dataset: To find the median of a set of numbers:

- Sort the data into increasing (or decreasing) order.
- If there is an odd number of data values, the median is the middle value.
- If there is an even number of data values, the median is the mean of the middle two values.

These basic statistical tools are useful when it comes to designing for people.

Activity 9.7

Below are the heights of 15 people taken at random from the general population.

Heights (mm): 1671, 1817, 1763, 1733, 1722, 1745, 1773, 1778, 1725, 1696, 1689, 1718, 1735, 1705, 1734.

(a) Write down the minimum and maximum values in this dataset. Hence calculate the range of heights.

(b) Calculate the mean height, based on all the data values. Give your answer to the nearest mm.

(c) State the median height, based on all the data values.

(d) Compare the mean and median heights to your own height, and calculate the difference to each.

Before you move on from this activity, it is important to realise that this not just a theoretical exercise. The example height used in part (d) of the answer to Activity 9.7 produces a real value (44 mm) that can be used practically. As you saw in Activity 9.5, small differences (even smaller than 44 mm) can have a significant effect. It is important to be aware of what the values used actually represent when you use any mathematical methods in design engineering.

9.3.4   Using numbers to design

To move forward with the desk problem, you needed to know how many other people might be your height. You found a certain desk height acceptable and might reasonably assume this is a good size for everyone of the same height. But how might you find out how many other people are your height?

There are many sources of data on sizes, from the very general (such as people's heights) to the exceptionally specific (such as NASA's guide to the sizes of things in space). Two key sources where a range of human data and information can be found are the British Standards Institute (BSI) and the Health and Safety Executive (HSE). The data they provide about the size and shape of people is called **anthropometric data**, which consists mainly of physical characteristics and measurements. These data values are derived using statistical methods that allow generalisations to be made about human characteristics, which can be used to inform the design process.

Making use of these datasets and applying knowledge of how people interact physically with objects can be a complex process and is a discipline in its own right. **Ergonomics** is the study of physical aspects of the human body, such as size and mechanical performance, and how these can be applied to the real world. For example, in car design and manufacture, the design of a car interior has to take account of significant variation of human shape and size, and hence the range of adjustments that can be made to a car seat, seatbelt, steering wheel, etc. And that's before you consider how these adjustments relate to one another, or are operated mechanically.

One useful way of presenting data, which is particularly useful for anthropometric data, is to create a **histogram**. Histograms offer a convenient way of presenting data to make it easier to read for a particular purpose. Instead of using a continuous spread of data, you divide it up into 'buckets' (often referred to as 'bins' or intervals) and sort items into them. For example, you could think of it as a way of sorting people into height ranges and then working out what proportion of people are in each range. Bar charts are similar, but can be used to represent categories of things that aren't necessarily numerical.

Histograms and bar charts

Histograms are used to plot quantitative data, with ranges of data grouped into intervals. For instance, Figure 9.14 shows a histogram of 200 people using height ranges of 20 mm, with heights measured to the nearest 1 mm. Notice that the values on the horizontal axis are continuous – the first bucket goes from 1600 mm to 1619 mm, the second from 1620 mm to 1639 mm, and so on. The vertical axis shows percentages. The area of each bar represents the percentage of people whose height falls in that range, and the sum of all the areas would equal 100%.

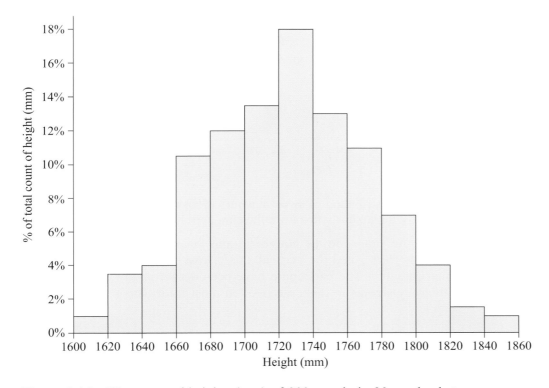

Figure 9.14 Histogram of heights (mm) of 200 people in 20 mm buckets

Bar charts can be used to group and count the frequency of anything, using categories that are not necessarily numerical. Figure 9.15 shows a bar chart representing a packet of sweets – sorting and counting the sweets according to flavour makes it possible to say something useful about how those flavours are distributed.

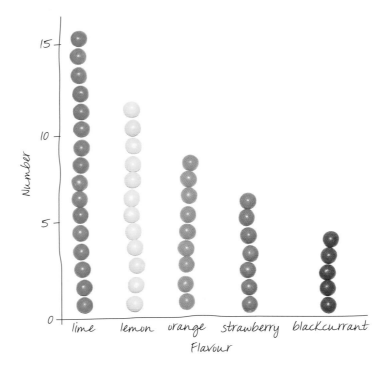

Figure 9.15   The distribution of sweet flavours in a single packet shown as a bar chart. Clearly the author's favourite flavours appear least often!

In Figure 9.15 the values on the horizontal axis (*x*-axis) represent a category − flavour in this case − and the vertical axis (*y*-axis) states how many sweets fell into that category. The bars could have been drawn in any order, but ordering them by size as in this case is often most informative.

Histograms and bar charts

Histograms:

- are used to show distributions of variables
- plot quantitative data, grouped into intervals, i.e. a number, or a range of numbers.

In a histogram:

- the bars appear in numerical order
- there are no spaces between the bars (unless the number of occurrences in a particular range is zero)
- the area of each bar represents a proportion, or percentage, of the total.

Bar charts:

- are used to compare variables
- plot categorical data, e.g. colour, flavour, gender, occupation.

In a bar chart:

- the bars can appear in any order
- there are spaces between the bars
- the height of each bar represents the quantity of interest.

Activity 9.8

Use the following height ranges and complete the table by counting how many people are in each bucket for the data given in Activity 9.7.

Height range (mm)	1600–1649	1650–1699	1700–1749	1750–1799	1800–1849	1850–1899
Number of people						

Which range would you be placed in based on your own height?

(If your height is above or below these ranges, then feel free to create additional ranges.)

In Activity 9.8 you found which height range contained most people. You will also have identified which bucket you were in based on your height.

For this data to be really useful you need a few more data points, and the ranges would be more useful if they were smaller, as in Figure 9.14. Based on the data in Figure 9.14, 18% of the population are in the 1720–1739 mm bucket. This means that 18% of people are between 1720 mm and 1739 mm tall. Another way to write this is by using a tolerance symbol (±), so in this case the tolerance is (to a good approximation) 10 mm above or below 1730 mm. This can be written as 1730 (±10) mm.

Activity 9.9

In Activity 9.5 you worked out your new perfect desk height. Now assume that this desk height is directly related to your own height.

Use the data in Figure 9.14 to work out:

(a) Which bucket does your height fall into? Write this bucket as a value with a tolerance.
(b) What percentage of the population is in that same bucket (i.e. what percentage might be satisfied with your desk height)?
(c) What percentage of the population of 200 people is outside that bucket (i.e. what percentage might not be satisfied with your desk height)?

From this activity it seems that quite a few people might not be entirely happy with your specific desk height. A next step might be to work out a bit more accurately what sort of height ranges would be acceptable to suit as many people as possible.

But there are a few big assumptions in what you have just done.

First, it was assumed that there is a link between a person's height and their preferred desk height. This might not be a valid correlation – arm length or sitting height might give a more appropriate relationship. Or there might not be a reliable human measure to use in this instance.

Second, it was assumed that 20 mm is a suitable division for the buckets in Figure 9.14. It is possible that people in both the 1720–1739 mm and 1740–1759 mm buckets have exactly the same preference, and that 40 mm buckets would be appropriate. However, since Activity 9.5 showed that anything less than a 20 mm change didn't make a noticeable difference, a 20 mm range in height seems quite reasonable.

It is no trivial matter to physically design something for people to use. The ergonomics of design engineering can be a very complex aspect of design, but simply being aware of people's sensitivity to physical variation can be useful as a designer. Even better, perhaps, is to realise that placing people at the centre of any design process can help you to tackle difficult 'human' design problems.

9.3.5   Design variation and people

As you have seen, designing for the 'average' or majority in a population means you often ignore other large parts of the population. This can have a particularly significant effect on particular population groups that lie outside the average groupings, such as children, older people or wheelchair users. One way of approaching this is to design in order to suit as many people as possible, or even for *all* people in any population. This is known as **inclusive** or **universal design**.

Taking this approach for the desk example, the challenge is to create a surface that is suitable for as much of the population as possible. This then becomes the new **design driver** – to solve the problem of a desk that is adjustable to suit a wide range of users. This changes the original design question, but it also expands the potential user market. Remember, you started considering only your own height and preference (a market of 1 person) – designing for a wider range of the population automatically means creating a more accessible product for *all* users of that design. In fact, most desks attempt to do precisely this and have adjustable feet to ensure that they are adaptable to as wide a range of people as is reasonably possible.

But physical variation is not the only human issue a designer must consider – the attitude and thinking of people is also a hugely important area of study. Like ergonomics, this is almost a whole discipline in itself, called **human factors**. It deals with how people think, react and interact with products, systems and services. As with ergonomics, it is essential to recognise how important this can be for the success of any design. Research shows that the way people *feel* about a design has a huge impact on how they use that design – whether they persist with it, use it correctly or simply ignore it.

Take your desk height as an example. If the desk were to be fully prototyped using different materials, you might feel very differently about each height depending only on the material. Some research even shows that your very posture changes depending on how much you like your desk!

Similarly, the design of instrument and control panels for complex systems has to consider how people read, use and interact with them – it only cannot consider functional requirements. Modern cockpits in large commercial aeroplanes, for example, are designed specifically to take account of how people use and interact with the instruments; Figure 9.16 shows an example. Designing with the user in mind throughout the process is known as **user-centred design**.

Figure 9.16 The cockpit of a large aeroplane, demonstrating the complex interfaces between the instruments, controls and people

By placing the user of a design at the centre of the design process, the focus of the project shifts from what is often a static perspective (considering certain aspects only) to a more active view of design (how certain aspects work in the real world). Unfortunately, changes in aeroplane design came only after a series of major failures, where it was recognised that changing the way information was presented to pilots would allow them to make better decisions. The lesson from this is simple – never ignore the user in any design project.

This section has guided you through a short design process. It started with a general exploration of desk height; you then made use of direct knowledge, then tried something to test your ideas and finally checked what you did. If you were to repeat this process and improve the starting question, you would be able to repeat and improve what you did each time. This repetition and improvement is known as **iteration**, and it is the essence of design – starting somewhere, thinking about it, doing something, then checking it, and repeating the whole cycle until it works the way it needs to.

At each stage you also used a range of types of thinking and processes, both analytical and creative, to 'think through' the problem one step at a time. Each time you did this, what you found informed the next stage in the process – all with the overarching aim of responding to the original question posed. Design is not simply doing one thing or applying one kind of approach – it is a process that incorporates a range of skills, attitudes and approaches.

Reference

Cross, N. (2011) *Design Thinking*, London, Bloomsbury.

Solutions to activities in Chapter 9

Solution to Activity 9.1

Your answer will depend on what object you chose. Check that you came up with reasons that considered: what the design does; how it does something; who benefits from it (and how/why), and so on.

The following reasons are for the example of the water bottle:

- to contain water
- to drink water from easily and quickly
- to be a good size and shape to be held in a hand
- to work immediately and without breaking, spilling or leaking
- to be a cheap solution for the person using it
- to be a cheap product to manufacture for the company
- to have sufficient strength and structural integrity to resist loads due to stacking while on display, in storage and during transportation
- to be readily compacted for ease of recycling.

Solution to Activity 9.2

As before, the water bottle is used as an example. Your own answers will be different from the examples below because you will have started with different reasons and probably a different object. Look especially for those drivers that you might not have thought of initially. (Note that the table continues on the next page.)

Reason from Activity 9.1	Design driver
To contain water	Problem – this is the basic problem of storing water in a way that doesn't leak.
To drink water from easily and quickly	Need – this is the basic need – to drink!
To be a good size and shape to be held in a hand	Desire – this is something that is desirable, but it's not absolutely essential.
To work immediately and without breaking, spilling or leaking	Improve – bottle design is changing all the time and some are better than others at reducing spills.
To be a cheap solution for the person using it	Change – it perhaps responds to new ways of manufacture? Or new materials?
To be a cheap product to manufacture for the company	Need or desire – not sure, it depends on the company's driver?

To have sufficient strength and structural integrity to resist loads due to stacking while on display, in storage and during transportation	Problem – this is the problem of moving the bottles around without breaking them.
To be readily compacted for ease of recycling	Improve – this helps make the bottle production more sustainable.

Solution to Activity 9.3

(a) The difference is found by subtracting the shortest from the tallest. Both heights need to use the same units before subtracting.

First, convert 2.72 m into mm (2.72 m $\times$ 1000 = 2720 mm)

Then subtract: 2720 mm $-$ 628 mm = 2092 mm

So the difference in height is 2092 mm

Convert this to metres, by dividing by 1000: 2092 mm $\div$ 1000 = 2.092 m

This is equal to 2.1 m, to 1 d.p.

Unit conversions and rounding were covered in Part 1, Section 1.3. You can find more practice examples in the online study resources.

(b) To find the midpoint you could halve the difference between the two heights and add it to the smaller height. Adding the two heights together and dividing by 2 will give the same result and is the usual way to find an average.

Average height = (2720 mm + 628 mm) $\div$ 2 = 1674 mm, or 1.7 m to 1 d.p.

Without more information this would not be a sensible value to take as a 'typical' height. You need to know more about the distribution of heights, not just the extreme values, to make that judgement.

As it happens, 1.7 m is not too far from the average height of some groups of people, but you cannot be sure of this without more information.

Solution to Activity 9.4

For example, a typical desk might be 758 mm above the floor, and the seat 540 mm above the floor.

The difference between these two heights is 758 mm $-$ 540 mm = 218 mm.

Solution to Activity 9.5

Here is one person's answer.

I used DVD cases to prop up a folder. This did actually change the way I wrote notes quite dramatically. At a higher height (about 3 DVD boxes) it felt a lot more comfortable.

Higher than this and it felt a bit strange – not comfortable for my shoulders and arms.

Here's a picture of the notes I took:

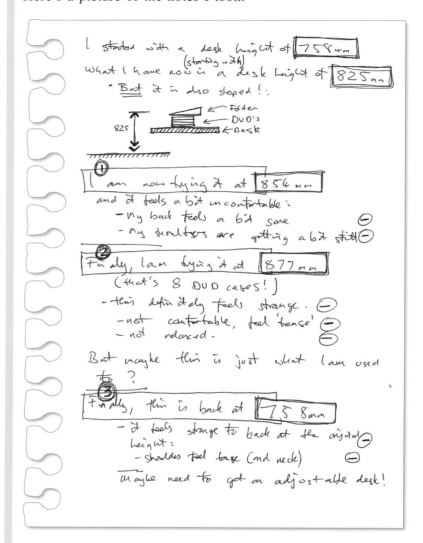

As I went through these tests I measured each one as a full height from the floor. But I could easily have measured the difference between the desk and the height of the folder. I might even have measured it in DVD cases – one case is about 16 mm, and I used 4 of them (4 × 16 mm = 64 mm).

This all suggests I might not have my desk high enough – a bit of a problem considering it's screwed to the wall … I might need to come up with a creative solution to that as the next problem.

Solution to Activity 9.6

(a) Discrete – you can have only a whole number of people.

(b) Continuous.

(c) Discrete.

(d) Continuous (though if you used the Beaufort scale to measure wind speed the data would be discrete).

Solution to Activity 9.7

(a) Minimum = 1671 mm, maximum = 1817 mm.

Range = 1817 mm − 1671 mm = 146 mm.

(b) To find the mean value, add the 15 different values together and divide by 15. All heights are in mm.

1671 + 1817 + 1763 + 1733 + 1722 + 1745 + 1773 + 1778 + 1725 + 1696 + 1689 + 1718 + 1735 + 1705 + 1734 = 26 004.

Mean height = 26 004 mm ÷ 15 = 1734 mm (to the nearest mm)

(c) Putting the heights in order gives (in mm): 1671, 1689, 1696, 1705, 1718, 1722, 1725, 1733, 1734, 1735, 1745, 1763, 1773, 1778, 1817.

The median is the middle value, which is 1733 mm.

(d) The answer to this part will depend on your own height. The example answer given below is based on a height of 1690 mm.

The mean is 1734 mm, making the difference 1734 mm − 1690 mm = 44 mm.

The median is 1733 mm, making the difference 1733 mm − 1690 mm = 45 mm.

Solution to Activity 9.8

Height range (mm)	1600–1649	1650–1699	1700–1749	1750–1799	1800–1849	1850–1899
Number of people	0	3	8	3	1	0

Solution to Activity 9.9

The answers to this will depend on your own height. In these example answers a person of 1762 mm height has been used.

(a) 1770 ($\pm$10) mm bucket (because 1762 mm is within the 1760–1779 mm range).

(b) 11% (estimated from the vertical axis (y-axis) on the histogram in Figure 9.14).

(c) The percentage outside this range can be found by either adding up all the other percentages (a very slow process) or subtracting 11% from 100%, to give 89%.

Part 2: Chapter 10   Design contexts

Introduction

Design is necessarily a complex activity. As you saw in the previous chapter, the complexity that people bring to any project can make what appears to be a simple task much more difficult.

Being able to deal with complexity in an engineering context is important. This chapter will discuss the extent and boundary of this complexity as well as introducing a few tools and methods to help deal with it.

Dealing with complexity comes with experience and practice, and it can take some time to develop the attitude required to do this without feeling overwhelmed. At the same time, making sure you don't simplify too soon or too much also matters. The challenge for the designer in this process is to find the 'sweet spot' in between these two extremes.

10.1 Design limits

You came across some of the complexity involved in design in the previous chapter when you considered the height of a desk. This was only a single factor in what was quite a limited consideration of this as a design project. In real-life projects the range of factors that have to be taken into account can be quite large. For example, 'designing a house' can mean many different things, as Figure 10.1 illustrates.

(a)   (b)

Figure 10.1 (a) The tallest house in the world – 27 storeys (Mumbai, India); (b) an example of a small house. They are both technically houses but each has had very different conditions, constraints and considerations applied.

In the desk height example in the previous chapter you saw examples of things you either *had* to take account of or could *choose* to take account of. At no point was the question asked whether a flat surface needed to be used as the desk! This was simply assumed to be an absolute requirement of the project – something that it could not do without.

Every project has a set of these different types of variable. Knowing the differences between them and being able to map them out can help inform both the process and the design itself. This module will use these three categories:

- **conditions** – things that have to be applied to a project
- **constraints** – things that limit or control what can be done in a project
- **considerations** – things that are important and might have an impact on a project.

10.1.1 Conditions

When there is no choice about something in the design process, it is referred to as a condition on the design. Conditions are not simply options to consider in the design; they are necessary criteria that must be met, often as legal requirements. Most conditions arise for obvious reasons – for instance, to protect people or to protect the environment. For example, electrical goods have to be designed to comply with certain basic performance characteristics for safety reasons, and these are set out in various laws, often backed up by 'standards', depending on the situation of use.

Many conditions are simply common sense but it is surprising how often they can be missed or forgotten in the design process. It is the responsibility of the designer to be aware that these conditions may exist and how they may apply in a particular discipline.

Legislation and regulations

The law provides the 'top' level of conditions in most countries. In the UK, legislation comes in the form of Acts of Parliament that set out what is illegal and unlawful. Complying with the law is a necessity in the UK, and most people understand the need for laws, and accept their application.

What can be slightly harder to understand is the full set of legislation that exists – a list that is continually growing and developing. Being aware of the legislation that most affects your own discipline is important, and there are some pieces of legislation that affect almost all disciplines in design and engineering.

For example, in the UK the Disability Discrimination Act 1995 (UK Parliament, 1995) protects the rights of disabled people and can have an impact on the design of products, services and systems, as well as the places where people work or where services are provided. As you saw in the previous chapter, conditions can be re-framed in different ways when designing new products, but it is important to know that there is legislation in this area too.

Figure 10.2 The UK government legislation website (2016)

Legislation in the UK can be found on the UK government legislation website (Figure 10.2). It is unrealistic to plan to be aware of every piece of legislation and all the amendments, but being aware of the most relevant legislation in your own discipline or area of interest is important. Similarly, being able to think creatively about the possible impact of legislation on a project is also useful.

Activity 10.1

Pick one of the following pieces of legislation. Write down two or three points about how it might affect a particular area of engineering that you are interested in. Base your answer on the introductory text provided below – there is no need to look up the legislation. Use your own thinking and common sense to set out general points you think might be relevant.

- **Data Protection Act 1998**

  'An Act to make new provision for the regulation of the processing of information relating to individuals, including the obtaining, holding, use or disclosure of such information' (UK Parliament, 1998).

- **Energy Act 2013**

  'An Act to make provision for the setting of a decarbonisation target range and duties in relation to it; for or in connection with reforming the electricity market for purposes of encouraging low carbon electricity generation or ensuring security of supply; ...' (UK Parliament, 2013).

- **Environmental Protection Act 1990**

  'An Act to make provision for the improved control of pollution arising from certain industrial and other processes; ...' (UK Parliament, 1990)

You do not have to go into a lot of detail – this exercise is about trying to imagine (quickly) the possible impact of a condition on a design process. Later stages in the process verify whether or not the impact is 'real' or relevant.

After legislation come regulations. Regulations are rules that usually arise from primary legislation or that are created by a recognised group, such as local government, professional institutions or trade bodies. These tend to be more detailed than the primary legislation, covering specific rules or matters that connect what happens in practice to the law. As such, they tend to be a bit more discipline-specific.

An example of regulations are the Building (Scotland) Regulations 2004, created by the Scottish Government under the Building (Scotland) Act 2003. These regulations give the necessary detail on how to meet the legal requirements in the legislation itself (see the box below for more on this).

Legislation, regulations and standards – a mini soap opera

Sometimes finding out precisely how legislation comes about or is applied can depend on the discipline you work in. Very often the route from legislation to what actually matters at a practical level can be slightly convoluted.

For example, in construction in Scotland, legislation about safety in buildings ultimately leads to very specific guidelines on what electrical equipment is acceptable, how this is to be installed and even who can install it. But how these guidelines came about is a slightly longer story …

The full story is that the Building (Scotland) Act (UK Parliament, 2003) sets out provision that buildings have to be safe. It also allows the creation of regulations by Scottish Ministers to ensure this safety in specific areas. This is what it actually says:

> 1 Building regulations
>
> (1) The Scottish Ministers may, for any of the purposes of:
>
> (a) securing the health, safety, welfare and convenience of persons in or about buildings and of others who may be affected by buildings or matters connected with buildings,
>
> … make regulations ('building regulations') with respect to the design, construction, demolition and conversion of buildings and the provision of services, fittings and equipment in or in connection with buildings.
>
> *(UK Parliament, 2003)*

This doesn't really help at all in terms of giving a design engineer much useful, tangible information.

So you need to track down the Building (Scotland) Regulations 2004. These regulations (and their amendments, as well as procedural amendments) give more detail on the standards by which buildings will be judged to be safe, such as structural stability, fire safety and (of interest here) electrical safety:

> Electrical safety
>
> 4.5. Every building must be designed and constructed in such a way that the electrical installation does not –
>
> (a) threaten the health and safety of the people in, and around, the building; and
>
> (b) become a source of fire.
>
> *(Scottish Parliament, 2004)*

What you need to know as an electrical engineer or design engineer for electrical products in construction is that there are Technical Standards that are deemed to meet the requirements of the Regulations (and thereby comply with the law in the first place).

The *Technical Handbook 2015 Domestic* contains a lot more detail on what can and can't be done when dealing with electrical installation in houses. In particular it refers to British Standard BS 7671: 2008, and this is really the document that you need as an electrical design engineer in construction disciplines.

Most electrical designers and engineers working in construction will know about the *Technical Handbook* (also known as 'The Regs') – it's what everyone in the UK works to for most building design projects. But fewer people know just how complicated the route from legislation to what you actually need to do is.

Standards and specifications

As with legislation, many standards operate at a national level, and in the UK the British Standards Institute (BSI) is responsible for the creation and maintenance of national standards, as well as integration of those standards with European Standards where appropriate. These standards cover a wide range of topics, from materials and objects through to processes and systems. Many of the main standards a design engineer in the UK would use come from this source.

Other bodies or institutions can set standards as a means of determining whether someone or something meets a particular set of criteria. Very often it can be useful to agree common criteria, such as technology specifications (DVD data formats or USB connection specifications). For example:

- The *UK-SPEC* (Engineering Council, 2014) is a set of standards that are created and maintained by the Engineering Council, UK. They provide standards by which registration with the Engineering Council can be achieved, thus demonstrating a person's 'competence and commitment' to the profession.

- The specification for USB 3.0 is maintained by the Universal Serial Bus Implementers Forum (USB-IF), a group of manufacturers. This common specification allows a range of products to be designed to a common standard of connection to other devices.

As with legislation there will be certain standards and other key documents that relate to your own sub-discipline in engineering. Ensuring you stay up to date with the most relevant documents is an important aspect of professional practice.

10.1.2   Constraints

Design constraints limit or control what is possible within a project. Unlike conditions they are not necessarily stated directly, but they have a similar effect by setting boundaries within which a design project has to operate.

There are three constraints that apply to almost all design projects, which are considered here as examples – cost, quality and time.

- **Cost** – the most common constraint on any design is that of cost. No project budget is infinite, and being able to design within cost constraints or conditions is a necessity for every single design project. The type of costs can vary for different projects – for example, they may refer to the material, manufacturing or operating costs. How a project measures and uses cost is vital to understanding the scope of that project.

- **Quality** – most designers want their project to be of high quality but there are limits to what can be achieved within the resources available. Similarly, different projects might have different levels of quality requirements for different markets and conditions. For example, a washing machine in a laundrette has a different set of criteria for the quality of parts from those of a domestic machine.

- **Time** – the final basic constraint is that of time, a constraint that also applies to every aspect of design engineering. Simply put, the design and development of a project cannot go on forever – at some point it has to come to a conclusion, meaning that there is a limit to what can be achieved. Once realised, a project will then be subject to time in terms of operation and use, perhaps through wear and tear, repair or maintenance.

These three constraints are well known in design and are sometimes referred to as the 'project management triangle' because they relate to one another directly (Figure 10.3). For example, you cannot reduce the cost of a project without affecting the other variables, time and quality (you will either have less time to complete the project or the quality will have to be lowered).

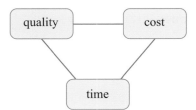

Figure 10.3   The 'project management triangle', showing the relationship between the standard project constraints of time, cost and quality

This relationship is perhaps easier to understand if you use the 'fast, good, cheap' version of the triangle shown in Figure 10.4. Each of the three oval shapes in the diagram represents one of the words fast, good and cheap. The three ovals overlap to form a triangle. Where two shapes overlap, an additional shape is created from the overlap, but there is no point where all three ovals overlap. The diagram intends to show that you may, at most, achieve any two of the three outcomes, but not the third. For instance, if you achieve good and cheap, then it's unlikely to be fast!

Figure 10.4   Alternative version of the 'project management triangle'

In addition to these basic constraints, there are others that will be specific to individual disciplines in engineering or even particular circumstances and contexts in projects. As with conditions, being aware of potential constraints in your own area of interest is important.

Activity 10.2

Note down some examples of constraints you can identify in the contexts below – each of these is a real design engineering context. Try to state the constraint and the effect it might have on the design itself.

Remember, you are simply using your own knowledge, experience and common sense to generate these considerations. As with any real project, the consideration might start as a simple observation and then move to a condition. For example, in the pram design industry there will be a very heavy focus on who will be buying the product, and this will affect the design.

(a) Offshore drilling rig pumping station (consider the environment – how will that constrain a design project?)

(b) High-performance engine testing laboratory (consider the very specialist nature of this project – how will that affect the design?)

(c) Baby buggy or pram design (consider the end user(s) of this product – how will this constrain the design project?)

(Remember that constraints are different from conditions in that they are not 'made up' – they are already there.)

10.1.3   Considerations

As you saw in Chapter 9, there are other considerations that a designer has to take into account in any project. Very often these considerations relate to people, or to the circumstances in which the project is placed. They can vary significantly, will not all have the same importance, and can even change during the course of the design process.

In fact, the considerations that matter most for any design project change regularly and are usually what a designer is working with at any given point in the process. For instance, with the desk example in the previous chapter, the average height, comfort and ergonomics of people were considerations that led to conditions for the design (that it had to have a height that was adjustable in some way).

The list of considerations you could apply to any design can be as long or as short as the project requires, and it often comes down to how much information can be retained at any one time. Being able to judge which are the most important to the project becomes vital – good choice of considerations almost always leads to good design solutions.

Different design situations will also have very different design considerations. For example, the design of a chemical processing plant will necessarily focus more on operational and practical issues than on appearance and aesthetics. On the other hand, a major new river crossing has to consider the visual impact of the crossing in its physical and social context.

Part of the design process is dealing with these considerations – identifying them, prioritising them and then deciding on whether they have been 'properly' considered. Each consideration is most likely to be a compromise with other considerations or constraints.

Considerations do not all have the same importance, or even the same importance at the same times – for instance, taking account of someone's height at a desk is potentially more important than what materials are currently fashionable for desk design. So an important skill for any designer is to be able to identify and prioritise such considerations.

10.1.4 Putting this together

In the previous chapter you were introduced to design drivers, starting and directing a project in a particular way. Design projects are designing for people and that introduces a further range of complexity, mostly considerations. In this section conditions and constraints have also been added.

It's worth trying to visualise how all this fits together, because these different factors can make the process of design quite a complex one. At times the number of issues a designer has to consider can seem impossible to deal with. At other times it may seem that the limitations being imposed make it difficult to design creatively. It's a bit like squeezing toothpaste from a tube (Figure 10.5) – to get all of the toothpaste out, it's no use squeezing in only one place (the paste just ends up somewhere else). To get the best out of any design process, all the different factors have to 'squeeze' together.

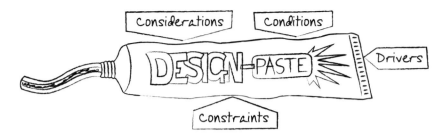

Figure 10.5   A visual metaphor for the design process – a toothpaste tube being squeezed

Before continuing, there are a few important points to make about this complexity.

First, it is very rare that you can meet all of the considerations and conditions perfectly. Very often, some of them contradict others – for example, the financial constraints of a project might be in conflict with the need for a certain level of quality. Much of design engineering is about finding the *best* solution, not necessarily the perfect one. Being able to negotiate, compromise and optimise competing variables is an important design skill.

Second, there are opportunities to manipulate all of these elements. Conditions can be turned into constraints or even considerations, depending on how the design is approached. For example, the focus of the desk height problem in the previous chapter could be changed – if the driver for the design is a market need for reading, then this is a very different activity from writing. It might be possible to reframe the problem and apply a very different set of conditions, constraints and considerations. This is a method considered in a later chapter.

Finally, as with any complex task, designers need some way to help approach this complexity in order to be able to move forward. Being able to prioritise which factors matter more than others, in which circumstances and when, becomes important. You might be surprised how well you are able to do this by simply using common sense and a bit of creative thinking. With practice and experience, working with these factors becomes second nature. Of course, in order to tackle them more effectively, it helps to have a few tools and methods to use. The online study resources introduce some of these tools and give you a chance to learn and make use of them.

10.2   Boundaries and opportunities

In the previous chapter you were introduced to the possibility that design is not simply about products on their own; even simple objects can be considered in a wider context in the design process.

As a design engineer you will often have to consider much more than the design object itself, and to explore the wider contexts of a project. One context that is becoming increasingly important is that of the **design lifecycle** – the effects of the design from creation, through manufacture, to end of life and even beyond.

10.2.1   Boundaries of design

The start of a design necessarily requires some resources. You came across this at the start of Part 1, where the ideas of craft, one-off production, mass manufacture and bulk production were introduced. For physical products, these resources are mainly the raw materials, other products, time, energy, manufacturing, etc., required to create the object that is delivered to market. Being involved in the manufacturing process as a designer can have a significant impact on a product.

Very often simple changes to a designed object can lead to significant advantages in the market. For a mass manufactured item, such as the ballpoint pen you saw in Part 1, changes to how it is manufactured might lead to significant overall savings. For example, you might be able to make the body of the pen thinner without seriously affecting its strength. The amount of material saved in a single pen would be trivial, but once multiplied by thousands or millions it could make a substantial difference.

At smaller scales of production, changes to a design can still have a significant effect on resources and manufacturing. In low and medium volume design and manufacture, such as fashion design, decisions around specific details have various implications but usually one or two of these will take priority in any decisions made. For example, the connection detail of a strap to the bag shown in Figure 10.6 was clearly considered in terms of aesthetics, structure, manufacturing, material and possibly a few other factors. Looking at the detail, it appears that the aesthetics and function of this junction were the priorities here. These decisions will then affect the resource costs and manufacturing of the product. But at some point a decision will have been made to consider these and ensure that there was a balance between what was needed for the design and what was realistically possible within the constraints.

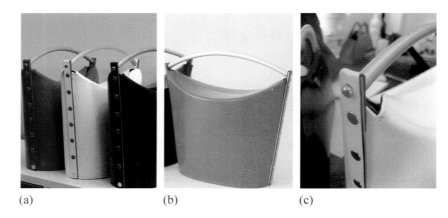

(a)   (b)   (c)

Figure 10.6   Low-volume design and manufactured products (a) and (b); connection detail (c)

Achieving this balance is critical because what every designer wishes for is a successful outcome. As you have seen, there are many criteria by which the success of a design can be measured, but some apply in general. For example, the take-up and use of a design is a key measure of its success.

This consideration of the implications of design decisions applies not just to the manufacturing stage. The end of a design's life can come about in a range of ways – from simply breaking or wearing out, through to becoming obsolete or unfashionable. What happens after this point depends on a range of factors, not least of which is the way in which the product was designed in the first place.

Some products are designed to be easily repairable, in order to extend their lifetime. This can also have an additional benefit to companies manufacturing the original product by extending their business to include spare parts, maintenance or even greater levels of replacement.

Of course, the opposite is also true. Some product designs have only a limited life expectancy, through failure during use, or lack of compatibility and support. This is known as **planned obsolescence** and, together with cheaper manufacturing generally, it became prevalent in the latter part of the twentieth century. In recent decades, and with improvements in mass manufacturing techniques, planned obsolescence has become a business strategy for some companies, leading to changes in consumer behaviour. The long-term sustainability issues caused by companies supplying (and society demanding) more than can be supported sustainably are now starting to be recognised. As with everything in design, it is the balancing of these competing tensions that is key to success.

Without achieving such a balance, a design will never become an **innovation**, the successful introduction and spread of a new product, system or service in a market. The challenge when considering these issues is that the designer has to think about more than the product itself.

Reuse, repurpose and recycle

The reuse, repurpose and recycle framework is a useful guide for considering how the sustainability of a product may be improved.

- **Reuse** – by maintaining the product's life and continuing its original use. This involves the least resources by repairing or replacing parts.

- **Repurpose** – by changing the original function, purpose or market of the product to extend its lifecycle. This might involve more resources through significant adaptation or change.

- **Recycle** – by breaking down the constituent elements and reusing them as materials only. This involves the greatest use of resources through the destruction of the original product.

This subsection has focused on products, but systems and process designs also have such lifecycles. For example, the design and engineering of a traffic control system will still have products and resources as its inputs, and it will have an end-of-life sequence. Different systems will require different types and amounts of resource, and it is critical to consider the lifecycles of these.

10.2.2 Opportunities

You may be reading this and thinking that the list of issues identified so far is huge – maybe too much for a single design engineer to deal with. But thinking creatively around these problems can lead to new opportunities. These newer ways of thinking about design are now quite common in leading design and engineering companies, allowing new designs, markets and even whole business opportunities to emerge.

This is achieved by recognising that the design itself is not an isolated entity – it exists because of the design drivers introduced in the previous chapter, it is subject to the constraints and considerations introduced here, and it will persist way beyond the drawing board or computer of the designer.

Considering the complete design lifecycle – from inputs and inception all the way through to the end of life – introduces a new set of opportunities and considerations. You can see this through an example, by considering the use of a particular class of materials: plastics.

Plastics are generally easy to process, are extremely versatile, and have replaced many alternative materials that are far more expensive to produce. Many of them are also very durable – they last a long time. Used appropriately, they can be a very attractive material. Paradoxically, their low relative cost and ease of use has led to them being used as a disposable material, and their longevity can lead to other problems in the lifecycle – particularly after use.

In recent years people have become much more aware of some of the downsides of using plastics. Synthetic plastics are often made from oil, a non-renewable resource. Although almost all plastics have the potential to be recycled into new plastic products, there are many barriers to this – financial and logistical, as well as technological – and much material that could be recycled is not. Waste plastic can also be used as fuel, just like the oil it is derived from, but here too the difficulties associated with collecting, sorting and transporting material make this hard to justify when the raw material is itself so inexpensive. The result is that, even with good progress towards better recycling infrastructure, much of the UK's plastic waste still ends up in landfill.

In an alternative approach, there has been significant progress in developing biodegradable plastics over recent years, both by adding degradable components to synthetic plastics like polyethene and by developing truly biodegradable materials based on biopolymers such as starch. However, most plastic remains extremely durable and can take centuries to degrade in the environment.

When not disposed of properly, plastic can pose a significant problem in terms of pollution. Many of the plastics commonly used for packaging have densities that are lower than that of water – so these plastics float rather than sink in the sea, and currents and tides can cause them to accumulate in unexpected places (Figure 10.7). This is a reminder that possible consequences for other countries need to be considered when making design decisions. A product might be recycled in some countries, but not in other parts of the world that lack the facilities to do so.

Figure 10.7   Plastic waste on a tropical island

During the design process, and in this case in the choice of materials, designers make choices that can adversely affect people in other countries and far into the future. This can lead to ethical issues, for instance sending recyclable plastics to China or electronic equipment to Africa for disposal, which can have an impact that the original designer was unaware of.

As oil prices fluctuate, and environmental concerns grow, priorities are slowly changing. The steady increase in recycling infrastructure has enabled far greater quantities of plastic (along with other materials) to be recovered. This has been driven in part by government policy, with increasingly ambitious targets for the recycling of plastic packing (from 37% in 2013 to 57% in 2017 in the UK) (Source: RECOUP, 2016). The extension of charging for disposable plastic carrier bags to all parts of the UK in 2016 is an example of using legislation and policy to influence behaviour.

Another approach is to use information to modify behaviour – targeting the largest audience possible to try to have the greatest effect. For instance, simple standardisation of recycling symbols helps people to distinguish between different plastics that can be very similar in appearance: some examples are shown in Figure 10.8.

Symbol	Acronym	Full name and uses
 1	PET	Polyethylene terephthalate – fizzy drink bottles and frozen ready meal packaging
 2	HDPE	High density polyethylene – milk and washing-up liquid bottles
 3	PVC	Polyvinyl chloride – food trays, cling film, bottles for squash, mineral water and shampoo
 4	LDPE	Low density polyethylene – carrier bags and bin liners
 5	PP	Polypropylene – margarine tubs, microwaveable meal trays
 6	PS	Polystyrene – yoghurt pots, foam meat or fish trays, hamburger boxes and egg cartons, vending cups, plastic cutlery, protective packaging for electronic goods and toys
 7	Other	Any other plastics that do not fall into the above categories, e.g. melamine, which is often used in plastic plates and cups

Figure 10.8 Standard recycling symbols in the UK (the names of the polymers stated here are those commonly used in this context; for example, 'polyethylene' rather than 'polyethene')

The durability of plastics can be turned to an advantage with the right infrastructure in place. Certain plastics can be recycled and used in a number of applications where wood has traditionally been used, such as street furniture and building materials. This material has significant advantage over wood but has some way to go to replicate the other qualities that wood possesses.

New product materials like this often provide the raw material for design project ideas. For a designer, and especially a design engineer, being aware of new developments such as this can be useful. What could you do with a synthetic wood replacement?

Activity 10.3

A synthetic wood replacement comes in standard timber sizes, can be made to look like wood, and although not quite as strong as wood in some ways, is close enough. It can be treated like timber in other important ways too: it can be sawn, cut and shaped using exactly the same type of hand and power tools.

Imagine you are asked to come up with some product ideas using elements of this material that are 50 mm × 75 mm × 1500 mm. What sorts of ideas would you come up with?

Spend about 20 minutes thinking about (and sketching out) an example of an outdoor product made from this material, for example for a garden, street furniture, or playground equipment.

10.2.3 Designing for the future

Despite admirable progress in the reuse and recycling of materials, there remain particular problems with some very scarce materials. The problem of diminishing oil reserves is well known, but may be thought trivial compared to some other material limitations. Supplies of rare earth minerals and metals, some of which are necessary for electronics components, are becoming particularly limited.

Because of these resource issues, design projects that use resources more efficiently and effectively have an increasing advantage commercially. Some companies now actively utilise design as a method of achieving longer-term market benefits by looking at how they manufacture, distribute and even operate and decommission projects. This shift in focus to the design lifecycle allows opportunities for greater innovation to take place.

For example, Phillips Lighting is a company that sells light. That is, a building owner or user will agree a specification of lighting they want in their building, and Phillips will provide that – all the fittings, power, controls, repair, replacements, etc. This is an example of a whole service product, similar to the model used by Rolls-Royce for its A380 engine, which you will come to in Chapter 14. Advantages of this approach are that significant sustainability can be achieved over much longer periods of time – it is not in the interest of Phillips to install poor-quality fittings only to have to replace them after a short time.

It is important for any designer to be as aware as possible of the consequences of what they design. This can be exceptionally difficult to achieve, but there are certain basic steps that every designer can take to consider at least some aspects of the impact a design project will have in a systematic way. Two tools that can help you to think about this complexity are decision tables and visual mapping – the former will be introduced in the next subsection, and the latter in the online study resources.

10.2.4 Using decision tables to sort information

A decision table can be used to compare two sets of conditions or parameters. This can be an extremely useful tool to deal with lots of information efficiently. A decision table can help with making a design decision in a way that ensures you consider each option against a consistent set of decision criteria (say, conditions). In reality everyone has their own preferences, but this method ensures that each option gets equal treatment, without being too biased.

For example, Table 10.1 shows a decision table set up to consider three design options for a new bus shelter (in horizontal rows) against three decision criteria that apply to the design (in vertical columns). The criteria were selected as suitable ones for this stage in the design process. Figure 10.9 illustrates the three design options in the form of rough models, based on early sketch ideas.

Table 10.1 A decision table that compares design options (vertical) against decision criteria (horizontal)

		Decision criteria		
		Ease of construction	Ease of maintenance	Aesthetically pleasing
Options	Option A – Roof garden			
	Option B – Slopy shelters			
	Option C – Curvy roof			

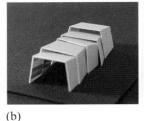
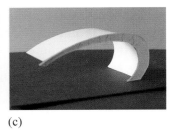

(a)   (b)   (c)

Figure 10.9   Three design options for a bus shelter: (a) Option A – 'Roof garden'; (b) Option B – 'Slopy shelters'; (c) Option C – 'Curvy roof'

For each option, the designer might then assign a value and make notes in each cell of the decision table, so that the three options can be easily compared. Table 10.2 shows an example of a completed decision table for the options above, where each option has been given a number between 0 and 3 against each of the decision criteria, using a scale where a higher number means a better match.

Table 10.2   The completed decision table that compares the design options in Figure 10.9 against the decision criteria

		Decision criteria		
		Ease of construction	Ease of maintenance	Aesthetically pleasing
Options	Option A – Roof garden	**3** (simple vertical and horizontal slabs)	**0** (planting requires additional maintenance)	**2** (greenery is always good!)
	Option B – Slopy shelters	**2** (hard to set out)	**1** (difficult junctions)	**3** (visually interesting – nice contrast in street)
	Option C – Curvy roof	**1** (structure is difficult to make!)	**3** (with self-clean polymer, could be easy)	**3** (visually interesting – again, nice contrast in street)

Using a decision table like this allows the designer to quickly compare ideas and proposals. In this case a simple comparison of overall scores would suggest that Option C is the best fit to the decision criteria. This may not be the whole picture, as some criteria may have higher priority, or other factors not included here may need to be considered. But the decision table provides a powerful way of thinking through the advantages and disadvantages of each design in a systematic way.

In reality, such tables may be quite sketchy and less formally presented. Figure 10.10 shows the original version of this decision table in the designer's sketchbook.

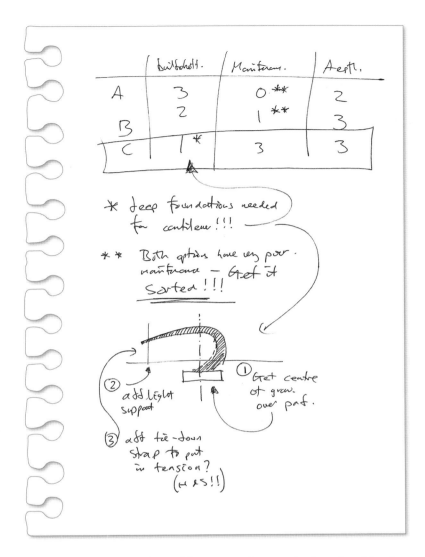

Figure 10.10 Decision table extract from a design sketchbook

Note that in this sketch it is not only the decision table that matters. Additional notes and diagrams have been added to explore different aspects of the design. For example, the designer has noted that there is a challenge with the structure of Option C and has sketched out three options that could be considered to deal with this issue.

A final point about this method is that it is often enough to use the process to bring out preferences and decisions in the design process. You might find yourself tweaking the numbers a little bit to get the answer you really want. This is absolutely fine as long as you are aware of it!

Activity 10.4

Construct a decision table based on your thoughts about three different pairs of footwear that you own, or would like to own. Focus on one particular type, such as fashion shoes, sports shoes or work-wear.

Pick your own design criteria and number scale, and add a few notes to explain any important issues you think of that are important to the design.

Example of a decision table in use – the MET matrix

The previous discussion introduced the idea that the end of life of a plastic product can vary. Most modern product designs will contain multiple materials and this can make the end of life of the product quite difficult to envisage. Being able to set all the issues out and then apply some means of analysis – and to be able to do this efficiently and effectively – is an essential skill in any design process.

A useful tool to do this is the 'MET matrix', where MET stands for materials, energy and toxicity. The MET matrix is a form of decision table that allows a series of factors to be considered along a project lifecycle. Table 10.3 shows a blank MET matrix with the columns representing stages in the project lifecycle (in order from left to right). Set against these are the three factors – materials, energy, toxicity – and points about each can be entered into each cell. For example, you could consider what materials are required to manufacture something (top left cell) or how toxic something is to decommission (bottom right cell).

Table 10.3 A blank MET matrix, which allows the mapping of elements (vertical) against the project lifecycle (horizontal)

		Project lifecycle (time)			
		Materials supply and manufacture	Transport and distribution	Use and maintenance	End of life
Elements ('things')	Materials				
	Energy				
	Toxic emissions and waste				

The level of detail in each cell can depend on the stage of the project – for some complex projects the material element might have several sub-elements, and for some projects one of these cells might be a full report.

You can see an example of an outline MET matrix below, based on an analysis of paperback book lifecycle in the USA (Table 10.4).

Table 10.4 Example MET matrix analysing a paperback book lifecycle in the USA

| | | Project lifecycle (time) | | | |
		Materials supply and manufacture	Transport and distribution	Use and maintenance	End of life
Elements ('things')	Materials	**New paper**: can use wood pulp; cotton, linen (depends on quality required) **Cover**: composite material which may contain wood pulp, polymers, inks, halogenated hydrocarbons	**Packaging**: cardboard, plastics, paper (possibly wood)	None	**Paper**: biodegradable and recyclable as raw material **Cover**: not recyclable, compostable (contains polymers and toxins)
	Energy	**Creation**: energy mix required for material processing – paper, inks, card, glues **Manufacture**: energy mix for printing and binding	**Storage**: building heating and operation energy. **Transport**: fuel / energy – varies (depends on transport mode)	Very low	**Recycling**: moderate energy use
	Toxic emissions and waste	**New paper**: requires 'washing' and 'cooking' (sodium hydroxide and sodium sulphide) **Recycled paper**: contains chlorine (from bleaching)	**Transport**: depends on transport mode – e.g. diesel emissions	None	**Cover**: if burned, can release dioxins: EXCEPTIONALLY HAZARDOUS **Ink**: can contain carbon black and heavy metals which re-enter the environment if placed in landfill

As you look at this example, don't worry too much about the detail provided – more important is to realise that the matrix itself is a useful way of checking each aspect of a lifecycle. Decision tables, a MET matrix and other similar visual tools can make a significant difference to how you think about complex projects.

Visual mapping is considered in the online study resources. You may like to take a look at this now, if you haven't already done so.

10.3   Designing complexity and uncertainty

All this complexity and information may seem overwhelming, and to be honest, it is. James Webb Young in his book on producing ideas famously said that designers are special generalists – that a designer has to know a bit about everything (Young, 2003). This can be particularly true in design engineering, and sometimes the level of knowledge required can be quite daunting. The number of elements in any product design can also seem intimidating when they are all set out (Figure 10.11).

Figure 10.11   Many products are made up from a wide range and number of complex components

There are ways of dealing with this complexity that can be useful to remember, so consider the following points as you read the rest of this section.

First, designers use a variety of tools to help them to tackle problems. Sketching, diagramming, making lists, using decision tables or mind maps, making models – these are all ways of either storing and working with ideas 'outside' of your head or helping you think about a problem. You have already come across a few of these tools, which allow you to take a complex problem area and try to make sense of it by mapping it into smaller parts. Look out for these tools as you work through the rest of Part 2, and be aware that you will find some tools more useful than others.

Second, designers make use of embodied knowledge. This is knowledge gained directly from experience of how materials and products operate in real-world contexts. You came across this in the Pont du Gard case study at the beginning of Part 1 – you 'know' something because you have experience of something and are confident about using that experience. For example, children learn about centre of gravity when stacking things on top of one another. This knowledge is just as useful when applied to toy blocks as it is to the tallest structures – ignore it in either situation and things fall over!

Finally, designers are able to deal with uncertainty. This can be general uncertainty at the start of any project, where no one is certain about what might be required or the parameters within which it must be delivered. Or it might be the specific uncertainty of a well-defined problem that no one knows the answer to. In each case the designer acts slightly differently, but the attitude that goes with it is the same – uncertainty is not something to be afraid of, but it does have to be approached carefully and managed well.

You have already come across some tools to help with thinking about complexity, and more will be introduced in later chapters (along with some embodied knowledge). Before that, this section takes a quick look at dealing with uncertainty and risk.

10.3.1   Uncertainty and risk

Dealing with uncertainty is often the hardest thing for designers to overcome as they start their careers. Many have come from an education system that insists there is only one (usually correct) answer to any problem. As you saw in Chapter 9, this is simply not true – for some design problems there is no single right answer.

The process of design should generally aim to move from greater uncertainty to lesser uncertainty – the early stages of a project can be full of uncertainty, while later stages can be more fixed. However, in all design projects it is not known how a design will perform until it is completed, tested and then used. Each design project is a response to a new situation – it would not be design otherwise. Designers face uncertainty in all they do and try to reduce it by:

- using models to predict how designs will behave
- using research and analysis to establish what is unknown
- testing aspects of a design to eliminate or reduce uncertain issues
- using experience gained from the performance of previous designs for similar problems.

As experience (of success and failure) increases and predictive models become more accurate, the inherent uncertainty in design decreases. A well-established technology that is matched to a well-established context has little uncertainty. In these circumstances designers have the task of creating variations and modifications on the basic design.

Once a design solution is well understood, the production of variant designs becomes a mature business, where ingenuity goes into making the processes as efficient as possible. *Managing* design becomes more important than the fundamental activities of innovation and design. In the building industry the creation of a new fast-food restaurant may use the same well-established rules all over the world. Similarly, some types of automotive and electronics factories have become almost standard items. The machines and assembly lines can be established from a greenfield site in less than two years. Design uncertainties in these cases are low, but other uncertainties of unpredictable markets and competition remain.

These types of design are relatively standard and they are a form of **incremental innovation** – design that comes about from small changes. Very often these changes are in response to particular design drivers, such as user demand. The other side of this is **radical innovation** – design that comes about from a single, large change. This usually happens when a brand new technology (or a radical new way of using existing technologies) becomes available.

For example, consider the mobile phone. The initial design was a radical innovation since the technology was being used in a very different way. But since then many of the changes have been incremental innovation, usually responding to either technology improvements or market demands (Figure 10.12).

Figure 10.12   The mobile phone is an example of both radical and incremental innovation

Many larger design companies will spread the risk of producing designs across a number of products, ensuring a mix of incremental and radical innovations if they can. Today's innovative products are the basis of tomorrow's variant designs, but to produce such innovation the boundaries of what is already known have to be pushed slightly.

10.3.2   Uncertain structures: cathedrals and bridges

The world of large structures provides good examples of radical innovation and the risks and uncertainty involved. Some of the cathedrals in existence today are the survivors of designs produced by secret guilds of masons hundreds of years ago. Flying buttresses (Figure 10.13) were a design innovation that looked beautiful and allowed tall walls with large windows to be built. The function of the flying buttresses, and the decorated finials on the top of the verticals, is to keep the internal forces inside the stone so that all elements are in compression, or pushing against one another. Stone is very

Tension and compression were introduced in Part 1, Chapter 1.

good at resisting compression but very poor at resisting tension forces. The simple arch also makes use of this property of stone to span spaces in bridges and vaults, as you saw previously with the Pont du Gard.

(a)

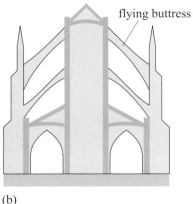

flying buttress

(b)

Figure 10.13   (a) Flying buttress on the Monastery of Batalha, Portugal; (b) a diagram cut through a cathedral showing the flying buttresses

There were other methods of achieving the same effect of tall walls and large windows. Iron reinforcing bars could be placed in the walls to resist sideways forces. In some medieval cathedrals you can see both methods used, literally side by side. On the outside, public, wall of the building there are buttresses and plenty of ostentation but on the interior, private, side there are fewer, less ostentatious buttresses and more iron reinforcing within the walls.

It is worth noting that parts of cathedrals *did* fall down. In the early years of using these new methods, several cathedrals failed, often quite spectacularly. Beauvais Cathedral partially collapsed in 1284, only 12 years after it was completed, as a result of pushing these new methods to their limits (and, arguably, skimping slightly on materials and not completing the entire structure).

Such failures contributed valuable knowledge to subsequent designers and deliver a valuable message – designers (and engineers) learn a lot from failure, allowing future designers and engineers to use this knowledge creatively. These lessons and technologies are still in use today in buildings such as the Sagrada Familia in Barcelona (Figure 10.14). This incredible structure is also built from stone, using the same principles and techniques pioneered hundreds of years earlier (with a few lessons learned along the way).

Figure 10.14   The nave ceiling in the Sagrada Familia, Barcelona

Nonetheless, it is perhaps better to see such failure in testing or models rather than the real thing. Dealing with the uncertainty of failure matters during the design stages.

The first large suspension bridges in China, constructed several hundred years ago, used principles that were subsequently seen in the bridges built by Thomas Telford (1757–1834) and Isambard Kingdom Brunel (1806–1859) in the UK in the 1800s. These later engineers rapidly pushed to the limits the available materials and the scientific understanding of their day. There was a great deal of uncertainty in their designs, although they had the benefit of some scientific analysis and could build simple theoretical models of how structures might behave. Brunel, for example, applied elements of numerical modelling to the business of building bridges.

Telford and Brunel were in competition to build a bridge to cross the Avon Gorge at Clifton in Bristol (Figure 10.15). Both proposed a design based on a suspension bridge. Telford's proposed design used two towers built up from the riverbed. Brunel commented sarcastically that he had not thought of building towers from the sand of the riverbed when there were good rock buttresses to build on.

(a)

(b)

Figure 10.15   (a) Brunel's Clifton Suspension Bridge; (b) Telford's design for the suspension bridge

Telford's design was more cautious than Brunel's, so the towers had to be closer together because the span that could be achieved was more limited. The cost of Telford's towers was much greater, but the structural uncertainty in his design was less. Put another way, it had a higher safety factor. Nowadays the analysis of a suspension bridge is routine; the relationships between the cost of towers and the **tensile strength** of the main wire ropes are well understood. Tensile strength describes the resistance of a material to breaking when tensile, or pulling, forces are applied to it – it's a measure of the maximum stress a material can withstand under tension. The properties of the relevant materials are known in great detail.

However, there is still uncertainty. The London Millennium Footbridge, a suspension bridge over the River Thames (Figure 10.16), was found to behave in erratic ways after it was opened to large numbers of pedestrians in June 2000. The structure was quite flexible, and the motion of people crossing it could cause it to sway. The swaying of the bridge made it alarming to use: it was closed for repairs within days and opened later with a modified design that has been trouble-free for many years.

Figure 10.16   The London Millennium Footbridge

Interestingly, the Clifton Suspension Bridge was not finished in Brunel's lifetime because of a shortage of money. Innovative design is not necessarily financially profitable; it can be a risky and uncertain business. One of the main responsibilities of any designer or engineer is to ensure that this risk and uncertainty is dealt with at the right time – ideally in the design and testing stages of any project.

10.3.3   Balancing uncertainty and risk

Innovation has been identified as a critical component in business success. However, innovation involves uncertainty and risk. The imperatives for companies to move away from the routine to new contexts and new technologies are now very strong. However, the tendencies of many designers are to reduce uncertainty. They tend to be more like Telford than Brunel, in the case of the Clifton Suspension Bridge. As you have discovered, designers cannot escape uncertainty but that does not stop them trying to minimise it where possible. To maintain a balance between exploring new possibilities and staying within the bounds of known and understood designs, companies try to create a 'culture of innovation'.

Activity 10.5

Write down two examples (each) of radical and incremental innovations from designs around you.

The radical innovations do not have to be recent, or even a product – they can also be a part of another design.

Tim Brown has been a key figure in design and innovation, and in 2012 held the position of chief executive officer at IDEO, a leading design consultancy that has played an important role in increasing understanding and improving design practice in a broad range of industries. Brown comments:

> My message for business leaders is always, if you want to be more innovative, if you want to be more competitive, if you want to grow, you can't just think about what your next product's going to be or what your technology's going to be. You have to think about the culture that you're going to build that allows you to do this over and over and over again.

> *(Brown, 2009)*

As with many of the other concepts you have come across so far, it is the balancing of risk and uncertainty in order to innovate that is the valuable activity.

10.3.4   Visual thinking

In the previous sections, maths was used in a few places, perhaps without you realising it. In design engineering the most efficient and effective way to do something is always sought, whether this is to solve a problem, move to the next stages or simply find out what you need to know. Complex analytical problems can be turned into (for example) visual problems – and this provides you with an additional set of tools in your maths toolbox. This subsection offers a few examples, and provides an opportunity to revise and extend your maths skills.

Visualising fractions: concrete mixing ratios

In Part 1, Chapter 2 you used fractions and percentages as a way of describing things using numbers. For example, if you stretch a material, it will change its shape, and knowing the percentage change can tell you about the qualities of that material.

A very similar tool is to use **ratios**. Ratios are used to relate quantities to one another and are a convenient way of communicating fractions.

For example, bronze is an alloy of copper and tin, so to form bronze you need some of each. The proportions required can be stated as a ratio as follows:

- 90% copper and 10% tin
- 9 parts of copper and 1 part of tin
- 9:1 copper to tin.

Each of these is equivalent – the last one is arguably easier to write, and to use practically in some situations.

As another example, a material very commonly used in civil and construction engineering is concrete. Concrete is made up from cement, sand and gravel, and is usually specified in terms of the ratios of volumes of these materials. The ratio of these elements to one another affects the final strength of the concrete. A 'weak' concrete mix will contain more sand and gravel (i.e. less cement), whereas a 'strong' concrete mix will usually contain more cement. Both weak and strong concrete mixes have important uses. Strong concrete is important where it must bind to other materials, resist water or deal with forces in particular ways. Weak concrete is useful where a softer, cheaper (but still inert) material is needed, such as for filling cavities in structures.

Ratios are used to state how the concrete is to be composed, like a recipe for concrete. For example, a 1:2:3 mix will have 1 part cement, 2 parts sand, and 3 parts gravel. This can be written as:

- 1 part of cement, 2 parts of sand, and 3 parts of gravel
- 1:2:3 cement, sand, gravel.

Again, these are different ways of writing the same thing.

In this case ratios are useful for both accuracy and convenience – if the 'recipe' is followed, you can be confident about the strength of the concrete that will result. More importantly, a ratio does not require specific units of volume – the numbers can be anything – cubic metres, shovel loads, or buckets – making it straightforward to measure and mix any required amount of concrete on a construction site.

One way to work with ratios is to use a visual method. For example, you can think about the concrete mix above by visualising buckets as shown in Figure 10.17.

Cement   Sand   Gravel

Figure 10.17   A visual representation of the ratio 1:2:3 in concrete

From the figure it is clear that there are 6 parts in total – cement is 1 part out of 6, sand is 2 parts out of 6, and gravel is 3 parts out of 6. To put it another way: one-sixth $\left(\frac{1}{6}\right)$ of the mixture needs to be cement; two-sixths $\left(\frac{2}{6} \text{ or } \frac{1}{3}\right)$ needs to be sand; three-sixths $\left(\frac{3}{6} \text{ or } \frac{1}{2}\right)$ needs to be gravel.

This then allows you to measure and order material for a required volume. You can take that volume, divide it by the number of parts and then multiply it by the appropriate ratio for each material to find the volume of each individual material that is needed.

> ### Example 10.1   Mixing concrete
>
> You are making a general 2:3:5 cement, sand, gravel mix for a pavement edging. You have to make $0.75\,\text{m}^3$ of concrete in total. How much of each material is required?
>
> #### Solution
>
> Total 'parts' is:
>
> $$2 + 3 + 5 = 10.$$
>
> Portions of each material are:
>
> $\left(\frac{2}{10}\right)$ cement
>
> $\left(\frac{3}{10}\right)$ sand
>
> $\left(\frac{5}{10}\right)$ gravel
>
> Volumes required are:
>
> Cement: $\frac{2}{10} \times 0.75\,\text{m}^3 = 0.15\,\text{m}^3$
>
> Sand: $\frac{3}{10} \times 0.75\,\text{m}^3 = 0.225\,\text{m}^3$
>
> Aggregate: $\frac{5}{10} \times 0.75\,\text{m}^3 = 0.375\,\text{m}^3$
>
> (Note that the total volume is $0.15 + 0.225 + 0.375 = 0.75\,\text{m}^3$.)

So ratios are a convenient way of communicating and calculating in some situations, and you can use visual methods to think about and work with them.

Here is a summary of the key techniques for working with ratios – this is also included in the *Handbook*. There are practice questions in the online study resources.

Working with ratios

Finding a ratio equivalent to a given ratio

Multiply or divide each number in the ratio by the lowest common factor.

If possible, a ratio is usually written in its simplest form, where the numbers are integers that can't be cancelled any further.

For example: the ratio 6:3 can be simplified by dividing each number by 3 (the lowest common factor), to give 2:1. So 6:3 is equivalent to 2:1.

Comparing ratios of two numbers

Write each ratio in the form 'number:1' and compare the numbers on the left.

For example: the ratio of copper to tin in bronze alloys can vary. If the ratio of copper to tin in bronze type A is 23:2 and in bronze type B it is 32:3, which alloy contains the highest proportion of copper?

The ratios can be written as $11\frac{1}{2} : 1$ for bronze type A and $10\frac{2}{3} : 1$ for type B. This makes it much easier to see that bronze type A contains more copper.

Calculating a quantity from a ratio

1   Calculate the sum of the numbers in the ratio.
2   To find the portion of the quantity corresponding to each ratio number, divide the number by the sum and multiply by the quantity.

For example: since $5 + 2 + 3 = 10$, the ratio 5:2:3 divides 1250 into

$$\frac{5}{10} \times 1250 = 625$$

$$\frac{2}{10} \times 1250 = 250$$

$$\frac{3}{10} \times 1250 = 375$$

respectively.

Activity 10.6

One type of lead-free solder is a tin (Sn) and silver (Ag) mix. It has good material strength properties, and by varying the amount of silver, specific solders can be used in specific contexts to optimise the amount of material required.

- 19:1 Sn:Ag solder is a good general purpose solder for copper and stainless steel pipes.
- 24:1 Sn:Ag solder is sometimes used to solder elements in food equipment.

(a) Which of these solders contains the greatest proportion of silver?

(b) If you had 100 g of each solder, how much tin and silver would you have in total?

(c) Another way of writing solder ratios is based on fractions of 100 (like a percentage). For example, the first mix would be written as $Sn_{95}Ag_5$, where the small numbers represent the ratios out of 100. Write the second solder ratio in this form.

Keeping concrete warm

For a small project, using buckets of material to mix concrete is absolutely fine. But large-scale projects, or those where the material performance is absolutely critical, require more attention. The concrete supports for the replacement Forth Road Bridge, for example, were made from poured concrete. But this concrete could not simply be thrown together using a few cement mixers (Figure 10.18).

Figure 10.18   Forth Road Bridge replacement under construction in 2015, showing the three main support towers being constructed from concrete

Concrete gains its strength through a chemical reaction that binds the cement to the particles of sand and gravel. During this process (called curing) the mixture loses water and gives off heat. This means that the shape of the concrete (specifically its surface to volume ratio) and the surrounding temperature have a direct impact on how long it takes to cure and gain strength. Large volumes of concrete can take *years* to cure fully, meaning that the design of the structure has to take this into account. The concrete in the Hoover Dam was going to take so long to cure (about 100 years) that refrigeration pipes were installed during construction to cool it faster.

If concrete dries too quickly, it can do so unevenly, which leads to movement, shrinkage and cracking that can weaken the final structure. Similarly, if it gets cold too soon, the reaction can slow down and even stop, so that the cement does not bind to the particles fully. Other materials and chemicals can be incorporated to affect this reaction – slow it down, speed it up, 'artificially' increase the temporary or permanent strength, etc. It is even possible to add material that allows concrete to become transparent!

Maintaining the perfect conditions for moisture content and temperature is therefore important – something that can be quite difficult on an exposed project like the Forth Road Bridge.

In recent decades many improvements have been made to the materials, specifications, systems and processes around the installation of concrete. Each of these innovations has a design engineering background, highlighting the importance of understanding the entire process of any project.

Visualising equations: using sketching to do algebra

In structural engineering the shape of structural elements is very important. You will look at this in greater detail in a future chapters, but in preparation, have a look at the shapes in Figure 10.19.

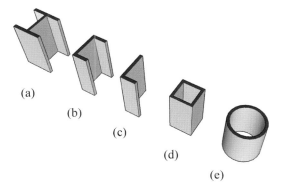

Figure 10.19   Some standard structural steel sections: (a) I section; (b) C section; (c) L section; (d) square hollow section (SHS); (e) circular hollow section (CHS)

These are all common shapes for structural steel elements and are made by rolling and pressing hot (but not molten) steel. Each shape has particular properties due to the material and how its shape is used to transfer forces in a structure.

An important way of considering these properties is through the area of the material when the shape is cut. This is known as the **cross-sectional area** and is shown as red in Figure 10.19. For a steel section this area is vital in working out its basic strength and predicting how it will perform when a force is applied to it from different directions. Many handbooks and standard product tables will provide this information, but being able to work out the cross-sectional area is a useful engineering skill and will help you to gain confidence in making your own formulas and working with units.

Working through the calculation of the cross-sectional area for a square L section shows how sketching can help you to think about algebra. The first step is to set out what you know as a diagram. You know the shape and are given two sizes – the breadth and the thickness of the metal. The depth of this particular shape is the same as the breadth so that will simplify things nicely. The sizes can be represented as letters: b for breadth and t for thickness (Figure 10.20).

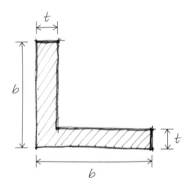

Figure 10.20   A square steel L section

Starting from the basic shape, you can sketch out a few ideas of how it could be divided up into smaller areas to work out a formula for the total cross-sectional area (Figure 10.21).

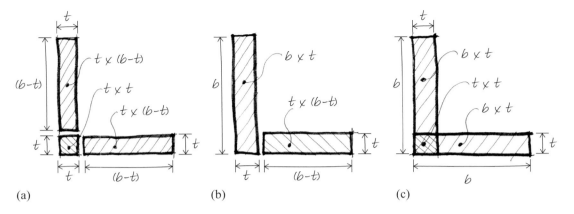

Figure 10.21 Alternative ways of breaking up the starting shape to create a formula for the total area. The gaps between areas have been left to show the shapes clearly.

You can then use these sketches to start to work out the areas of the different sections and then the total area itself. Using each figure in turn:

Figure 10.21(a)

$$
\begin{aligned}
\text{Area 1} &= 2t(b - t) \\
&= 2bt - 2t^2 \\
\text{Area 2} &= t^2 \\
\text{Area 1} + 2 &= 2bt - 2t^2 + t^2 \\
&= 2bt - t^2 \\
&= t(2b - t)
\end{aligned}
$$

Figure 10.21(b)

$$
\begin{aligned}
\text{Area 1} &= bt \\
\text{Area 2} &= t(b - t) \\
&= bt - t^2 \\
\text{Area 1} + 2 &= bt + bt - t^2 \\
&= 2bt - t^2 \\
&= t(2b - t)
\end{aligned}
$$

Figure 10.21(c)

$$
\begin{aligned}
\text{Areas 1 and 2} &= bt + bt \\
\text{Overlap} &= t^2 \\
\\
\text{Area 1} + 2 - \text{Overlap} &= 2bt - t^2 \\
&= t(2b - t)
\end{aligned}
$$

Some of these calculations may look quite complicated for such a simple shape, and that is the important point – there is more than one way to approach this. It is absolutely fine to sketch out different possible approaches and then to select the one you find most straightforward. In fact, the chances of making a mistake are greatly reduced if you use a simpler method.

What you have done here is to create a general mathematical equation for working out the area of this shape, so that you don't have to start from scratch the next time you need to do this. The next step is to check it and then use it.

Activity 10.7

Use the formula $t(2b - t)$ to work out the cross-sectional area of a square L section where $b = 125$ mm and $t = 12$ mm.

Then use any one of the formula diagrams in Figure 10.21 to check this answer.

Realising that you can create, manipulate and modify formulas like this is a useful skill so look out for opportunities to practise this throughout the rest of Part 2. Give it a try now with the next activity.

Activity 10.8

Find a general formula to calculate the total cross-sectional area of a square hollow section (SHS) using the dimensions given in the figure below. Try not to use a method that relies on subtracting the smaller square from the large one – try to split up the perimeter shape into smaller shapes first. Then check this formula by finding another way of expressing the area.

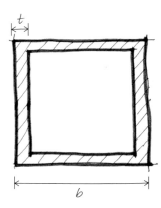

As you worked through the previous activity, your working may have been quite different from that shown in the answer. This is absolutely fine – as long as it gets to the right answer! The aim of this section is to show you that there are various ways to think about and do maths. The online study resources show you ways of writing out these problems that you might find useful, and demonstrate that the way maths is applied in professional settings is not too far away from what you have been doing here.

References

Brown, T. (2009) 'IDEO's Tim Brown: how to build a culture of innovation', CBS MoneyWatch, 23 September 2009 [Online]. Available at www.cbsnews.com/8301-505125_162- 51345772/ideos-tim-brown-how-to-build-a-culture-of-innovation/ (Accessed 16 July 2013).

Engineering Council (2014) *UK-SPEC: UK Standard for Professional Engineering Competence*, London, Engineering Council.

RECOUP (RECycling Of Used Plastics Limited) (2016) 'UK Packaging Recycling and Recovery Targets' [Online]. Available at http://www.recoup.org/p/204/uk-packaging-recycling-and-recovery-targets (Accessed 5 July 2016).

Scottish Parliament (2004) Building (Scotland) Regulations 2004.

UK Parliament (1995) Disability Discrimination Act 1995.

UK Parliament (1998) Data Protection Act 1998.

UK Parliament (2003) Buildings (Scotland) Act 2003.

UK Parliament (2013) Energy Act 2013.

UK Parliament (1990) Environmental Protection Act 1990.

Young, J.W. (2003) *A Technique for Producing Ideas*, New York, McGraw-Hill.

Solutions to activities in Chapter 10

Solution to Activity 10.1

Here is one possible response:

'I used building services engineering as my area of interest and chose the Energy Act 2013. As a building services engineer this would mostly affect me in terms of how I design systems for buildings – my clients are very likely to be asking about this. The points I might need to think about are:

- The products I specify and use to design the heating and cooling systems for buildings might need to change – to have better energy ratings, to have better control systems, or to have better information provided about them to my clients.

- Low-carbon electricity generation might be a growing market that I could make more use of – perhaps suggesting the installation of small power generation or designing a provision for this in future.

- I might need to demonstrate compliance with this legislation or some other guidance that follows it – this could be similar to the EU Energy Labelling system. It's likely I should spend time finding out about this, which would contribute to my personal development.'

Of course there are many possible responses to this question. Whichever area of engineering you chose, it is likely that at least one of the three examples of legislation would be relevant (and often more than one), and you should have been able to suggest two or three specific points that would need to be considered.

Solution to Activity 10.2

(a) **Offshore drilling rig pumping station**: the location will impose many constraints – for instance, it must be possible to transport all the necessary materials, components and people required for construction and operation to the location of the pumping station, and the pumping station must be able to withstand long-term exposure to salt water and potentially severe weather conditions.

(b) **High-performance engine testing laboratory**: there will be safety constraints here (tests can fail), as well as constraints on the working space – for instance, enough room for the test equipment, and high standards of cleanliness. There may also be constraints in terms of access – who can work on the project.

(c) **Baby buggy or pram design**: much of this will be covered by conditions (for safety, structural integrity, etc.). But some constraints might be a particular price point for the product or a particular style or fashion that fits a market demand. There will also be constraints in terms of designing for specific user groups, and they might have very particular demands (which will most likely be converted to design conditions).

Solution to Activity 10.3

Here are a few examples of products currently available.

Solution to Activity 10.4

Your design criteria are likely to depend on what sort of footwear you chose. For instance, if you considered walking boots, then 'comfortable', 'waterproof' and 'non-slip soles' might be important. For a beach holiday or a night out, the important criteria are likely to be different.

Solution to Activity 10.5

Here are a few suggestions.

Radical innovations:

- smartphone (when it first came out)
- voice recognition technology on a laptop
- microwave technology in microwave ovens
- folding plugs/miniaturised high-voltage components.

Incremental innovations:

- pen
- keyboard
- word-processing software
- recycled paper in a sketchbook.

Solution to Activity 10.6

(a) Both solders have their mix in the form x:1. So the one with the most silver will be the one with the lowest proportion of tin. Hence 19:1 Sn:Ag has the highest proportion of silver out of the two.

(b) For 19:1 there are a total of 20 'parts'. To use these parts to calculate the weight, multiply by 5 g (100 g divided by 20 parts):

$19 \times 5\,\text{g} = 95\,\text{g}$ tin

$1 \times 5\,\text{g} = 5\,\text{g}$ silver

For 24:1 there are a total of 25 'parts'. As before, use these to work out weight by multiplying by 4 g (100 g divided by 25 parts):

$24 \times 4\,\text{g} = 96\,\text{g}$ tin

$1 \times 4\,\text{g} = 4\,\text{g}$ silver

In total, therefore, there are $5\,\text{g} + 4\,\text{g} = 9\,\text{g}$ silver and $95\,\text{g} + 96\,\text{g} = 191\,\text{g}$ tin.

(c) You can use the values derived in part (b) directly, since they add up to 100.

If 19:1 is written $Sn_{95}Ag_5$, then 24:1 is written as $Sn_{96}Ag_4$.

Solution to Activity 10.7

Substituting $b = 125$ mm and $t = 12$ mm into $t(2b - t)$, gives:

$$= 12\,\text{mm} \times (2 \times 125 - 12)\,\text{mm}$$
$$= 12\,\text{mm} \times (238)\,\text{mm}$$
$$= 2856\,\text{mm}^2$$

Check: using the first diagram (Figure 10.21(a)).

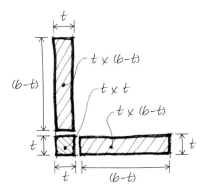

Three areas: $t(b - t) + t \times t + t(b - t)$

$$= 12\,\mathrm{mm}(125 - 12)\,\mathrm{mm} + 12\,\mathrm{mm} \times 12\,\mathrm{mm} + 12\,\mathrm{mm}(125 - 12)\,\mathrm{mm}$$
$$= 1356\,\mathrm{mm}^2 + 144\,\mathrm{mm}^2 + 1356\,\mathrm{mm}^2$$
$$= 2712\,\mathrm{mm}^2 + 144\,\mathrm{mm}^2$$
$$= 2856\,\mathrm{mm}^2$$

Solution to Activity 10.8

As with the L section, there are a few different ways you could do this.

One way is to take two 'long' sides of area bt and two 'short' sides of area $t(b - 2t)$, as follows:

$$
\begin{aligned}
\text{Long sides} \;&=\; 2bt \\
\text{Short sides} \;&=\; 2t\,(b - 2t) \\
\text{Total} \;&=\; 2bt + 2t\,(b - 2t) \\
&=\; 2bt + 2bt - 4t^2 \\
&=\; 4bt - 4t^2 \\
&=\; 4t\,(b - t).
\end{aligned}
$$

A more straightforward approach is to use an overlap method, using four 'long' sides, bt, and then subtracting four overlaps of t^2 to give:

$$
\begin{aligned}
\text{Long sides} \;&=\; 4bt \\
\text{Overlaps} \;&=\; 4t^2 \\
\text{Total} \;&=\; 4bt - 4t^2 \\
&=\; 4t(b - t).
\end{aligned}
$$

This provides confirmation that the other method was also valid.

If you did subtract the small square from the large square:

$$
\begin{aligned}
\text{Outer square} \;&=\; b^2 \\
\text{Inner square} \;&=\; (b - 2t)^2 \\
\text{Total} \;&=\; b^2 - (b - 2t)^2 \\
&=\; b^2 - \left(b^2 - 4bt + 4t^2\right) \\
&=\; b^2 - b^2 + 4bt - 4t^2 \\
&=\; 4bt - 4t^2 \\
&=\; 4t(b - t).
\end{aligned}
$$

This also gives the same result.

Part 2: Chapter 11 Design approaches

Introduction

This chapter looks at two of the most important activities in design – setting up good problems and then thinking creatively about solutions to those problems. These activities are often closely related due to the iterative nature of design. It is very common for a designer to move between solutions and problems continuously as a project progresses.

Throughout this chapter a lot of emphasis is placed on visual thinking and using a sketchbook to expand your thinking and ideas. As you go through this part of the module, make as much use of your sketchbook as you can to help with your study. There is further advice in the online study resources.

11.1   Design problems

Everybody is surrounded by problems in their everyday lives. Very often they go unnoticed, because people often change their behaviour in response to a problem without even realising it. Problem solving is a very human activity that everyone engages in to a lesser or greater degree. But some problems go beyond the individual's capacity to work around them and these then become important drivers for design, as you saw in Chapter 9.

Some problems are quite simple to identify and state; these are known as **well-defined problems**. These problems tend to be very specific and quite detailed – for example, you might be designing a child's toy but have the specific task of designing a particular part, say a hinge, and this will have quite easily defined conditions (safety, durability, material choices, and so on).

Some design problems are very difficult to state or might have very complex drivers and conditions. These are known as **ill-defined** (or **complex**) **problems**. For example, a broader system problem, like traffic management, will require solutions that address multiple users, technologies and even social conventions.

Most real-world problems lie between these two extremes, and being able to identify when a problem is well- or ill-defined is essential in any project. One of the difficulties with many initial design problems is that they are presented as being the 'right' problem and are rarely challenged. Any project benefits from exploration of the initial problem to ensure that it is a 'good problem' for the project to solve. As you saw in Chapter 10, there are very rarely single, right solutions to any design problem, and this also applies to the problems themselves: there is no perfect problem.

Here are a few common 'problems with problems':

- The initial problem is considered from only one perspective, meaning that solutions might ignore other (potentially vital) perspectives.

- The initial problem is not really a problem – it is actually a symptom of a deeper problem, meaning that solutions are not really addressing what needs to be solved.

- The initial problem is poorly understood or there isn't enough information, meaning that there is a chance that the wrong problem will be solved.

As an example of this, consider the 'problem' with opening canned food. To get to the food inside the tin can, a can-opening device is required. Traditional can openers can be difficult to use for many people. They also have to be purchased, washed, replaced, etc. So the can ring pull was designed to avoid this, theoretically allowing someone to open a can of food using only the ring pull attached to the can (Figure 11.1).

Figure 11.1 A food can with a ring pull opener

In practice, these ring pulls require quite a bit of manual dexterity and strength to operate, making them unusable for a large section of the general population. People adapt to this problem by using other tools, such as kitchen knives – possibly resulting in more people being admitted to hospital due to accidents in the kitchen!

This, in turn led to the design and manufacture of the 'can opener lifter' to make it easier to operate the ring pull (Figure 11.2). So the question is, has the real problem of the problem been met here? Or is yet another plastic object just another solution to a symptom of a deeper problem?

Figure 11.2 A food can being opened by the ring pull opener using another product

There is an important relationship between finding a *good problem* and then finding the best solution to that problem. Very often these two activities happen at the same time – as you develop a solution to one problem, you might realise that another problem is actually more important and then change direction slightly to deal with that. Or, it may be that the emerging solution offers a different set of opportunities than the original problem allowed for. As any design project develops, the problem and solution develop at the same time.

Activity 11.1

Consider this mini problem for a child's electronic toy:

> How might you store batteries to prevent them falling out but to also allow relatively easy access for replacement?

Is this a well-defined or ill-defined problem? Or some combination of both?

Note down some reasons for this.

Getting a project off to a good start by considering the problem itself before trying to find a solution can be very difficult when you start out as a designer, since the natural instinct is to solve what is in front of you. But with experience comes the realisation that time spent framing a problem is well worth it over the course of a project.

11.1.1 Problem framing

Problem framing is a method of focusing on a problem area. It is a way of considering a problem in a particular way, or from a particular point of view. You are changing not the problem itself, but the way you see the problem. This has similarities with setting conditions or considerations on the problem.

What you are trying to do when you frame a problem is to focus on a particular part of the problem (or the context), or to see the problem from a different perspective. This allows the problem to be stated in a particular way, which you can then start to think creatively about.

The problem framing process introduced here is:

- First, explore the problem – be aware of as much of the problem as you possibly can.
- Second, focus the problem – filter the information you gathered to prioritise what matters and what doesn't, and to focus on the problem in particular ways.
- Third, generate a problem statement(s) – summarise the process by creating a brief statement of the problem. This will be the starting point for generating solutions.

This cycle of exploring the problem and then narrowing it down can be repeated as many times as is useful to progress a design project. By repeatedly expanding and then contracting the focus of a problem, the designer aims to find a series of 'good' problem(s). This is also referred to as 'divergent' and 'convergent' thinking in the design process (Figure 11.3).

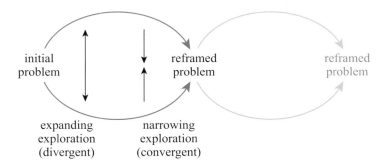

Figure 11.3   The divergent–convergent model of problem exploration where the initial problem is opened up and explored, then focused into a second problem statement

This basic method of framing (and reframing) can be used formally or informally. Formally, it can be used to generate full project requirements or specifications, either at the early stages of a project or at key stages in the design process.

But the process is more commonly used informally and quickly. As you design, you regularly evaluate what you do against a range of criteria, and many of these will be problems framed in a particular way. For example, you might quickly sketch an idea and then wonder what it's like from the perspective of three or four different types of user. Based on such considerations, you might then accept or reject the idea being developed. When you do this you are actually assessing problem frames, and the outcome might even be the rewriting of the problem itself.

As mentioned previously, people do this naturally all the time – you come across a problem and want to solve it, usually from your own point of view (and sometimes it might come as a surprise to find that somebody else has come up with a different solution to the same problem). So, as you look at the steps in the framing process (explored below), bear in mind that you probably already know this – you just might not be aware that you know it!

Problem exploration

The first step in exploring a problem is to become more familiar with the problem by gathering information and generally getting involved in it. This is often referred to as **design immersion** – quickly absorbing information around a particular subject or problem area.

Some sources of information for any project are:

- conditions, constraints and considerations that apply to the project (you looked at some of these in Chapter 10)
- your own experience and knowledge – do not underestimate how much you know about a subject
- desk research – looking through magazines and journals, online sources, books, and other standard sources of information

- observation of the problem, either directly by actively engaging in the problem or indirectly by observation, sketching or other recording
- **ethnographic studies**, such as interviewing people (users or stakeholders), exploring the habits and behaviour of groups, etc.

As you can see, there are a lot of potential sources of information, so designers approach this in a particular way. Using a range of sources in a general way to become more knowledgeable and aware of the information around a problem is always useful. After this, certain patterns or themes might emerge – or gaps in knowledge might become apparent.

To help with this process, methods such as mind mapping or sketching out patterns in the information are important. For example, Figure 11.4 shows some early research into a product design project where the designer has mapped out alternative products from their own research. These individual bits of information and knowledge have started to arrange into patterns that might say something useful about the problem.

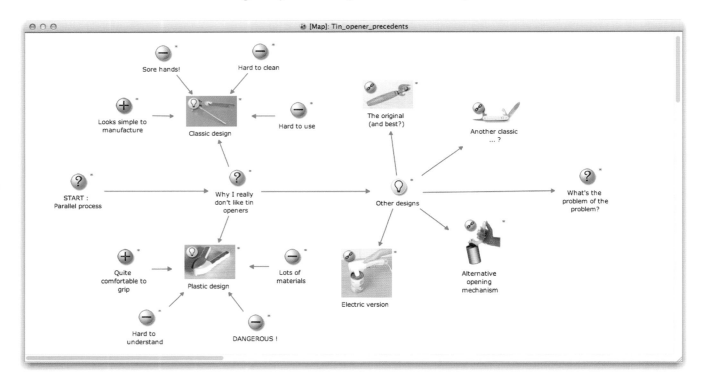

Figure 11.4   An example mind map collecting information around a single product. Question marks have been used to represent questions, light bulbs to represent ideas or sources of inspiration, and link icons for looking at existing products. Pros and cons are shown by plus and minus signs, and queries are shown by question marks.

As a designer, you are not looking for things you already know; you are looking for things that you didn't even know you didn't know!

Problem focusing

When you have a lot of material relating to a problem, it can be difficult to know where to start working with it. **Mind maps**, which are introduced in the online study resources, are a type of diagram used to visually organise information around a particular topic or concept. They provide one tool for dealing with complex information, but they allow only a certain amount of sorting to take place. To really investigate a problem in detail, you need other tools.

One of these is the **5W and 1H approach**, which you may have come across before.

The 5W and 1H approach to problem framing

The letters stand for what, where, why, who, when and how – all words that can be associated with a problem to ask particular questions. For example:

- What is the problem? What is the nature of the problem? What are the things associated with the problem?
- Where is the problem? Does it have a specific physical place? A social or online place? Can you point to the problem?
- Why does this problem exist? Why has it not been solved? Why does it persist?
- Who has the problem? Who knows about the problem? Who doesn't know about it, but should?
- When does the problem happen? When does it not appear? When do people find it a problem?
- How is the problem expressed? How does it appear? How do I know it's a problem?

The point in doing this is not to find specific answers to these questions but to explore the problem itself. The problem of the desk height from Chapter 9 was opened up by asking 'Who has this problem?' (or, 'For whom might a solution for this be useful?'). By focusing on different questions around a problem, you can get to know the problem better and perhaps even reshape it to become a better problem.

Another useful technique here is to use a three-frame cartoon to create a story from a single point of view. To do this, draw three rectangles, pick a focus point (one of the '5W and 1H') and sketch a story. For example, Figure 11.5 shows a three-frame cartoon using the questions 'who' and 'how' for a particular type of mobile phone user – someone who is not confident with new technology. The designer has tried to imagine what this user will see when they enter a phone shop and then drawn that as a story.

Figure 11.5 Three-frame design cartoon exploring *who* and *how* a certain type of user experiences buying a new phone. In this example, the experience of the shop itself and the confusion of information is the focus of attention.

This technique of imagining design 'stories' allows a designer to quickly explore alternative points of view in any project. By considering the mobile phone from the point of view of a particular user, a series of different products and services can emerge. Figure 11.6 shows two products that came about from considering the mobile phone from the perspective of a particular user – one who is not confident about using the advanced features of modern mobile phones.

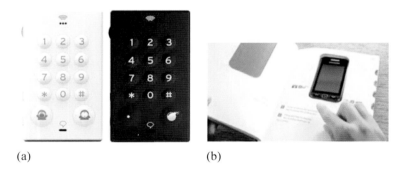

(a)   (b)

Figure 11.6 Two different approaches to considering a particular user for a mobile phone: (a) 'John's Phone', a mobile phone with simple functionality and interface; (b) the 'Out of the Box' concept for starting up with a new mobile phone

Again, the point of this approach is to explore and know more about the problem. With the phone example, what it identified was a **good problem**: some users find setting up and using a mobile phone very complicated. This problem, it turns out, represents a huge market of users.

And this is just one perspective on this product. Refocusing a problem by using different users and stakeholders (such as manufacturers, suppliers, or anyone involved in the lifecycle) provides an alternative framing of that problem.

The lesson here is clear – finding good problems can lead to new ideas and even new markets.

Problem statement

What you are aiming for by framing a problem is to create a single problem statement that can be worked on in the next stage of the process. Ideally you want this to be as complete as possible, but you must also be aware that it could change at some point in the future. Such change is absolutely fine because it should be change that is positively impacting on the design project.

A good problem statement summarises and gives some context to the problem. In doing so, it can influence the direction solutions may take – but without limiting this activity by being too specific or fixed.

Here are a few examples of problem statements (P1, P2, etc.) using the desk height example from Chapter 9:

- P1 – How might we solve the problem of poorly adjusted desk heights?
- P2 – Come up with creative methods of helping people correct their desk heights.
- P3 – Design a product that allows any user to adjust their desk working height.
- P4 – Design a desk that can be adjusted to provide two or three heights for someone reading.
- P5 – Design a writing desk that can be adjusted easily by any user to any height they wish.

These problem statements may seem quite similar but they do all have very different prompts – some are more open-ended, others are quite specific. They should all be seen as starting points for a number of creative sessions that will provide as many different options and ideas as possible – they are not a brief or specification, although they usually are developed into this. Creating several problem statements in this way can also help the overall problem framing process.

For example, P1 could involve a solution that looks at adjusting people's behaviour, not just the desk itself. Or it might involve considering what people do at desks and designing something that removes the need for a desk (Figure 11.7).

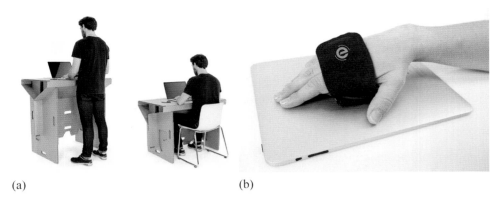

(a)   (b)

Figure 11.7   Alternative solutions to the basic desk height problem: (a) a standing desk; (b) a hand holder for tablet computer or e-reader

Similarly, P2 could lead to a service provided by another company to assess a workspace, and P3 could result in a second product to augment the desk itself, or you could even consider this as an e-book reader. That's three problem statements that don't necessarily even involve designing a new desk.

Once you have some good problem statements, you can go on to try and work on them. Before you do that, there are a few final points to make about problems.

The process of researching and framing problems gives designers another tool to manage risk and uncertainty. By being more aware of a problem context, you are simply better informed, leading to reduced risk from unknowns. Then, by developing multiple views of problems you are spreading the risk of solutions by having different options to consider.

Finding and exploring problems is an excellent way of moving forward. Very often a design problem can seem too complex to even start dividing it up into smaller parts, so having a way of approaching problems themselves can really help in dealing with this complexity.

Alternative problems provide alternative opportunities. As you saw with the mobile phone example, entirely new markets can be uncovered by thinking about problems from different perspectives. More accurately, existing design drivers are discovered when you explore problems.

A designer gets into the habit of thinking about problems in a particular way – they rarely take a problem as it is presented superficially. Exploring, focusing and shifting your perspective on problems will lead to better problems to solve and give the project more ideas and solutions to work on.

Activity 11.2

Generate several problem statements for the problem identified in the cartoon shown in Figure 11.5.

You might find it useful to look at the problem statements P1–P5 to help you with this. Alternatively, think about starting a few statements with the phrases:

- How might we …
- Design a …
- Come up with ideas to …

11.2   Creating solutions

After exploring and generating good problems, it is finally time to get creative and think about solutions. This is perhaps what most people think of when they imagine a designer at work – someone being creative for most of their time, perhaps using only blank paper and a pencil to draw whatever comes into their head. In reality, creativity is more about hard work and developing ideas, not simply waiting for ideas to emerge.

In fact, waiting for ideas to come is often the very worst way to think creatively! Like any other thinking skill, creativity is a process that can be developed. The more you practise it, the better you get. All it takes is a little preparation and practice – so take every opportunity to practise and try the creative methods presented here.

James Webb Young in his book *A Technique for Producing Ideas* (Young, 2003) noted that preparation is essential to being creative. There are a few key habits and attitudes that anyone can develop to improve their creative thinking immediately.

If you don't do something with your ideas, they don't exist. It's as simple as that. So get into the habit of acting on your ideas, and get into the particular habit of using some means of recording your ideas.

This is where keeping a sketchbook or design diary comes in useful, but to get the most out of it you have to use it. This is similar in some ways to the learning log you have already been using, but it is also very different in that it should be for immediate ideas and thinking – not just self-reflection and deliberate consideration. Being able to *quickly* draw an idea is an essential skill for any designer.

11.2.1   Scribbling and doodling to think creatively

One of the greatest scribblers in history was Leonardo da Vinci (1452–1519). He doodled helicopters and anatomical studies, noted down shopping lists, and simply sketched whatever seemed to come into his head. Figure 11.8 shows his sketches of a geared water mill, someone riding a horse, and someone blowing a trumpet in the ear of another person!

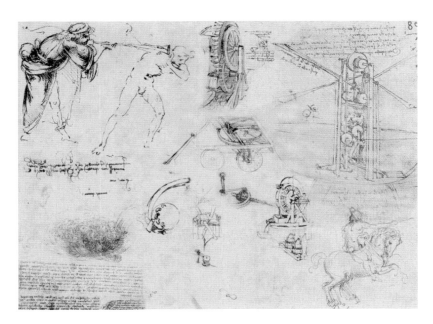

Figure 11.8 A few examples of Leonardo da Vinci's sketches

Leonardo is generally regarded as one of the greatest artists to have lived, but his sketches also reveal another side of his thinking – a person who was curious about the world and who liked to tinker and play with ideas. Looking at some of his sketches here, it is clear that the quality was far less important than the ideas. Clearly there is a strong relationship between sketching and creative thinking.

But (and this is very important) it is not the quality of the sketches that matters – it is the ideas and thinking behind the scribbles. Have a look at the diagram in Figure 11.9 – this is a sketch by another very famous thinker, and if you look carefully you can just make out a double helix with shapes crossing from one helix to the other. This is the original sketch for the structure of DNA – the biological polymer that carries information essential for life – by one of its discoverers, Sir Francis Crick.

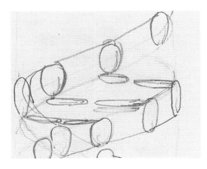

Figure 11.9 Francis Crick's sketch of the structure of DNA

What matters in a sketch is not the artistic quality – it is the idea behind the shapes. For Crick, this was simply a way to work out the problem of the structure of DNA – sketching it allowed him to *think* about it.

The sketchbook is one of the main tools of any designer because it is a completely empty space within which any ideas can be sketched and tested out. You have already seen several examples of sketches, and in each of these the principle was the same – to quickly create an idea that can then be evaluated, worked on further, or developed in another sketch.

You can also think of sketching as a way of getting ideas out of your head. You can hold only so much in your head, and the design process is complex: so being able to do some of the hard work on paper is useful. At a practical level, you simply cannot keep very many ideas in your head, so being able to transfer them to a relatively cheap storage medium (paper) is a very efficient way of thinking creatively.

You may feel more comfortable with writing descriptions in words, and it is absolutely fine to mix text with sketches (very often a few words here and there really augment a sketch). But using text alone is not always a viable option. See Figure 11.10 for an example – imagine how many words it would take to describe all the options in this picture sufficiently that someone else would know what you meant!

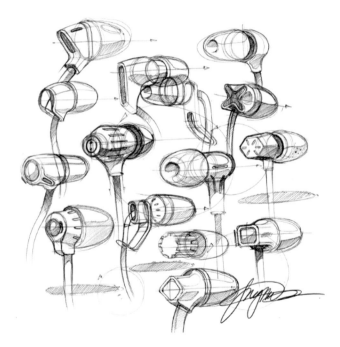

Figure 11.10   Sketches of lots of different options for headphone ear buds

A final benefit of sketching is that you can share ideas very quickly with other people. In the early stages of a design project this can be especially useful when combined with some of the other tools you have come across, such as the decision matrix.

So get into the habit of sketching creatively as a way of:

- getting your ideas out of your head and onto paper
- making and trying versions of ideas
- sharing your ideas with other people.

Don't be worried about the quality of your scribbles and notes. A sketchbook is your tool for thinking. Your scribbles are your own way of doing things. Remember how the discovery of the structure of DNA was aided by sketching – it isn't a beautiful drawing, but it is still one of the most amazing scribbles in history.

And that really is the secret to sketching creatively – you only have to scribble. Even just doodling geometric shapes can help you think creatively (Figure 11.11). The more you scribble and doodle, the better you get at doing it and at thinking using sketches.

Figure 11.11   Page from a sketchbook showing geometric doodles

Activity 11.3

Take a few minutes to scribble and doodle in your sketchbook. Draw some:

- circles, spirals and swirls
- boxes, nets and lines
- repeating patterns and wallpaper!

Note: this activity does not contain any feedback.

11.2.2   Getting creative

For many people, creativity can be quite intimidating, and many people do not view themselves as creative. Part of the problem is that many people consider creativity as having to come up with something radically new and (usually) quite amazing. But the reality is that most creative practice is something quite different.

First, most creative design is actually simply a lot of work: trying lots of ideas, evaluating them, changing them, etc. You will look at this part of the design cycle in the next chapter but you can already see this when you look at any sketch – the sketch is certainly not the final design. There is a lot of work between coming up with an idea and making that idea into a concept.

Second, creativity in design is not only about making something different, it is about making something useful and valuable. Take Chindogu, for example. This is the Japanese 'art' of making novel devices that have a function but that are essentially useless at the same time – as in Figure 11.12. Products such as trousers with a picnic table sewn in, or a hat that prevents noodles slapping a person's face as they eat are (by definition) very new. But that does not necessarily make them useful – functional and useful are not the same thing.

Figure 11.12   A Chindogu design that demonstrates that novel ideas are not always capable ideas

Creativity in a design context requires that there is also some aspect of usefulness to what is being created. This is not to say that fantastical ideas are not good – they can be very useful – but they have to be used in a particular way. Once again, creativity in design is not just about having an idea – it's about developing that idea into something that can be realised.

Finally, a lot of design creativity is incremental, where small ideas or changes to an existing design are made to improve it. In fact, most creative design is a form of incremental creativity – for most design challenges you do not have to start from the very beginning each and every time. Many of the greatest achievements in design engineering are actually small changes to an existing product or system that improve it significantly. These changes may be driven by any of the design drivers introduced in Chapter 9. For example, new materials, technology and manufacturing techniques have enabled significant developments to be made to prosthetic limbs over the last few centuries (Figure 11.13).

PERFECTING THE PROSTHETIC LEG
How incremental innovation works for patients

Eucomed
Medical Technology
www.eucomed.org

c. 1800 ....> c. 1920 ....> Today

Figure 11.13 Images of the incremental development of an above-knee prosthetic leg

Approaching the creative design process as a form of incremental innovation can also be used as a specific design strategy – either to generate new products in different ways or to work on a single project before it is released. For example, the Brompton folding bicycle (Figure 11.14) went through several incremental iterations and changes as it was being developed. In many ways the design process for this product was one of incremental change and prototyping.

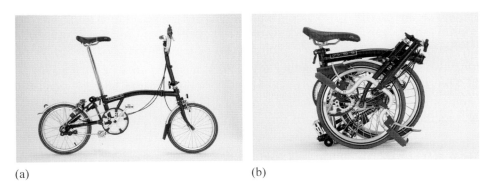

(a)   (b)

Figure 11.14 The Brompton folding bicycle in its (a) unfolded and (b) folded configurations

Some companies actively develop their products incrementally to create **product families** – products that come from a similar source but have slightly different variations. Working creatively within a framework such as this is just as important (and difficult!) as starting from scratch with a blank piece of paper.

You will explore incremental innovation and product families further in Chapter 14, but for now it's time to get creative.

11.2.3   Creative techniques and methods

The following techniques and tips are just a few examples of ways to think and design creatively. Different people have different preferences for how they go about it, so it is important to be aware of which of these approaches work best for you (even if you don't like to use them).

Set a challenge

Start with a single challenge and come up with several ideas to meet that challenge within a given time period. A good way to start this is to use a problem statement or similar prompt. Often 10–20 minutes is a good time period – you can always circle good ideas and work on them later or have another session. It's also a good idea to actually tell yourself this: 'I am going to spend 15 minutes coming up with ideas on how I might solve …'.

Follow a thread of ideas

If one idea doesn't work and you have no other ideas, then develop it further. In fact, create several more ideas along a chain of thinking based on that idea. Don't worry about creating options that might seem very similar when using this technique – perhaps different colour options might make a difference (but it is the difference that you want to play with, not just the colour).

A different perspective

You came across different perspectives in the previous section when you considered the '5W and 1H' method of exploring problems. This can also be used when you are thinking creatively about something. If you find yourself running out of ideas, pick one you already have and ask the '5W and 1H' questions about it – try to spot other ideas as you ask these questions.

Merging

Putting two or more things together can sometimes lead to a new creative idea. The trick is to mix *ideas*, not objects – if you just mix objects, you may get something like the butter stick (Figure 11.12). So put a couple of your ideas together and see what third thing might come out of that.

Let it digest

Human brains like to operate in particular ways to avoid using too much energy. This means you can get into habits of thinking where you rely on existing connections and ideas. One way to generate new connections is to simply try to stop thinking about a creative problem and let your 'subconscious' do the work for a while. This is known as 'incubation' in creative thinking, and the more you tell yourself to not think about something, the better your ideas will be!

Be ridiculous

When you are starting to repeat ideas, try thinking of the impossible and fantastical. The more implausible the better – in fact, go one step further and try to think of ways to do the opposite of what you are trying to achieve. Again, the point is that you come up with different ideas as you do this.

Quantity not quality

Produce lots of ideas and do not worry about their quality. More ideas are better in order to encourage and develop creative thinking. Having more ideas also gives you lots of options to consider or different directions to take your creativity in another iteration. The quality of the ideas is not important because it is the process of thinking that actually matters. Each idea that you think is a failure will contain something that is useful to the design process.

Random input

If you feel yourself getting stuck, think of any object or subject and apply it to the problem. You can use it for inspiration, merge it with an existing idea, scale it, cut it up, use parts of it, etc. It's not just about using the random object literally – if the object makes you think of something else, then that's exactly what it's supposed to do. To choose a random object, you can just close your eyes, move your head and use the first thing you see when you open your eyes.

Tell a story

Focus your creative thinking by telling a story, as you did with the problem focusing and three-frame cartoon technique – all you have to do is add another few frames to show how the story might end. This relies on focusing on what the subject of the story needs, not the solution itself. For example, with the mobile phone in Figure 11.5, the last frames of the story might show a solution and – more importantly – how the person in the story was satisfied by that solution.

Use other people

Asking other people can give you lots of new ideas – even if they don't come up with anything new themselves, very often just speaking to someone else can make you think of new ideas. Of course, asking them to come up with ideas themselves can lead to other ideas too. When you do this, try the following 'rules':

- Don't criticise any idea (the activity is to get ideas down, not assess them yet).
- Build on the ideas of others.
- Do it quickly and stop as soon as the ideas start to dry up.

11.2.4 When you get stuck and when to move on

At some point you will find yourself getting stuck or having trouble coming up with ideas. This is perfectly normal and it happens to every designer at some point. When you find yourself staring at a blank piece of paper waiting for ideas to come to you, it's probably time to do something else.

One of the difficulties is that when someone is expected to come up with creative ideas, they can sometimes 'freeze'. This is a recognised cognitive process in the brain and it can take a lot of experience and confidence to be able to deal with it. As with most things, the best way to do this is simply by practising – the more you do it, the better you will get at it.

When you do get stuck, try these techniques:

- Stand up and walk about a bit, then return to the problem.
- Pick up one of the 'failed' ideas you had earlier and *make* it work – nothing is impossible in your head …
- Go and do something completely different – preferably physically different: go for a walk, do some gardening, ride a horse, or carve fish from carrots.
- Go and stare at clouds, water, fire or trees. The chaotic motion of these objects affects our perceptual systems slightly differently than random motion.
- Bed, bath or bus – there is a reason why you often come up with ideas in the bath or as you are about to go to sleep: your brain is 'defocusing', meaning that different connections can be made in your mind.

Activity 11.4

Have a go at sketching some creative solutions to one of the problems below. Do *not* worry about the quality of the sketches (the quantity of ideas is far more important). Use a mixture of words and images if you want.

Set a timer for 60 seconds. Come up with and sketch quickly as many ideas as you can for one of the following problems:

- Design a means of adjusting a desk to certain fixed heights.
- Design a mouse trap that does not kill the mouse.
- Design a cup-holder to fit on a bicycle.
- Design a device for crushing tin cans for recycling.

Having creative ideas for solutions is only the start of coming up with a solution. Turning a creative idea into a developed concept requires a lot of further work, which is the subject of the next chapter.

11.3   Sketching, geometry and triangles

This section extends some of the visual thinking that was introduced in previous chapters to show how it can be used in analysis as well as for communication. As you work through this section, try to draw as many of the ideas and concepts as you can. This is to give you some more practice at creating diagrams, but it might also help you to think of the concepts in a new way or simply to remember them more easily.

11.3.1   A quick introduction to diagrams

At the start of this chapter, one useful purpose suggested for sketching was to carry out an analysis of a design idea. Sketching was also introduced as a way of generating new ideas. There are many different types of sketch, and one in particular that is very useful in design engineering – the **diagram**.

A diagram is slightly different from a sketch in that it usually has a very specific purpose, or a set of information contained in it. For example, compare the two images in Figure 11.15.

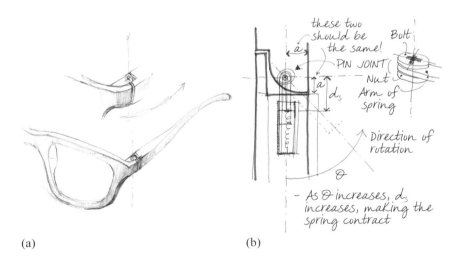

(a)   (b)

Figure 11.15   Examples of (a) a sketch and (b) a diagram of the same detailed part of a product design

These are both representations of the same thing, but they look very different and serve very different purposes. Figure 11.15(a) might be useful to show someone what something will look like, but Figure 11.15(b) allows specific information to be analysed or communicated. This is particularly useful in a design engineering context where quick analysis is useful to make decisions. Many of these decisions rely on the specialist knowledge of a number of people in a design team, and being able to share a sketch of a single problem is a very effective and efficient way of communication between people.

Many engineering offices have some version of a **calculation sheet** – a sketchpad designed to set out diagrams and calculations in the same place. This recognises the unique relationship between diagrams and maths in design engineering. You came across this in the previous chapter when you looked at using equations to work out the cross-sectional area of structural components. This same principle applies in even the most complex of projects, where it can still be more efficient to sketch out ideas and options rather than relying on words alone.

Figure 11.16 shows a more explicit use of a technical diagram to explore the forces acting on a structural beam. Diagrams that show the forces acting on an object are often referred to as **free body diagrams**, which you will learn more about later. This is an example of a situation where dividing a complex problem into smaller problems becomes a very efficient process. Each part of the diagram can represent a particular problem, which is then solved analytically using mathematical tools.

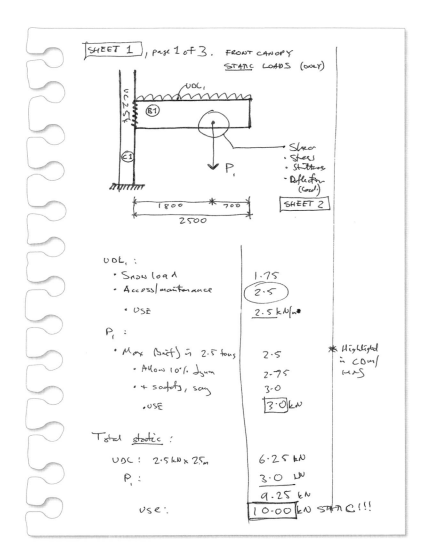

Figure 11.16 Example of a specific engineering diagram, showing how a diagram, text and calculations are mixed to create an effective method of thinking about and communicating a problem

Using diagrams like this helps in three main ways:

- it clarifies a problem by setting it out logically and cleanly – dividing it into other clear problems when necessary
- it makes checking and error identification easier, whether this is your own process or checks carried out by other people
- it reduces problems and errors of communication with other people, allowing them to contribute to the process.

To make best use of diagrams, it helps to know some of the conventions used for drawing them. You will look at graphic communication conventions in the next chapter, but first you need to know something about geometry.

As you work through this next subsection on geometry, use it to have a go at sketching in a bit more detail. Even if you are confident about using the concepts, try to sketch each idea as practice in setting out diagrams – imagine using these diagrams to communicate the idea to someone else.

11.3.2   Lines, angles and triangles

In later chapters you will need to use geometry as a method of analysis in design engineering. Much of this geometry concerns lines and angles. This subsection starts with a brief summary of some key definitions and principles of geometry. You have probably come across these ideas before, but it may be a while since you have used them. Have a look at this summary, and if you feel you need some revision, then use the maths practice examples in the online study resources.

A **point** marks a position but has no size. Figure 11.17 shows six points: *A*, *B*, *C*, *D*, *E* and *F*. Two points can be joined by a straight line, such as *AB*. Strictly speaking, a **line** extends infinitely far in both directions, and *AB* is just a portion of that line – a **line segment**. In this module the general term 'line' will be used to mean either of these things.

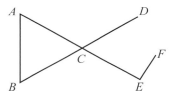

Figure 11.17   Points and line segments

Angles are measures of rotation and can be measured in **degrees**. There are 360 degrees (written as 360°) in a full turn, and therefore there are 180° in a half-turn and 90° in a quarter-turn or **right angle**.

A **plane** is a flat surface that extends infinitely far in all directions. For example, a flat piece of paper is part of a plane.

The names given to different types of angle are shown in Table 11.1.

Table 11.1 Types of angles (these angles are also defined in the T192 glossary)

Angle	Diagram	Description
Acute angle		Greater than 0° and less than 90°
Right angle		Equal to 90°
Obtuse angle		Greater than 90° and less than 180°
Straight angle		Equal to 180°
Reflex angle		Greater than 180° and less than 360°

Some useful principles involving angles are summarised below.

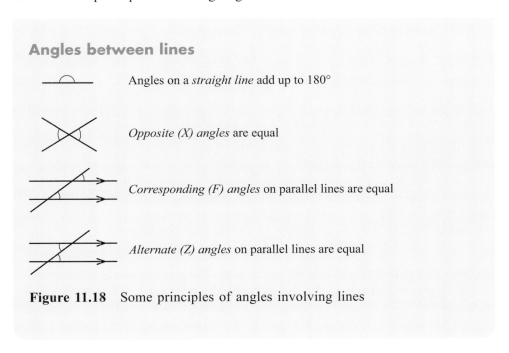

Angles between lines

Angles on a *straight line* add up to 180°

Opposite (X) angles are equal

Corresponding (F) angles on parallel lines are equal

Alternate (Z) angles on parallel lines are equal

Figure 11.18 Some principles of angles involving lines

Triangles are two-dimensional shapes with three sides and three internal angles, for instance *ABC* in Figure 11.17. Some particular types of triangle are given special names, as defined below and illustrated in Figure 11.19.

Angles in triangles

- The interior angles of a triangle always add up to 180°.
- The angles in an **equilateral triangle** are equal (and each is equal to 60°).
- The base angles in an **isosceles triangle** are equal; the apex angle is different.
- A triangle with one angle equal to 90° is known as a **right-angled triangle**.

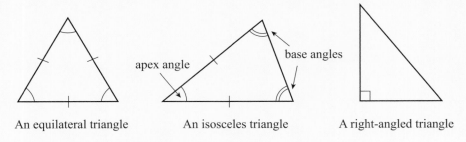

An equilateral triangle   An isosceles triangle   A right-angled triangle

Figure 11.19   Different types of triangle. The small lines drawn perpendicular to some sides of a triangle indicate that those sides are equal in length.

You may encounter any of these triangles in engineering, but right-angled triangles are particularly useful for analysing problems.

Two other terms you may come across in connection with triangles, or indeed any geometric shape, are **congruent** and **similar**.

Two shapes are said to be congruent if they are the same size and the same shape. They may be moved, flipped or rotated, but if you imagine cutting them out, you would be able to arrange the two shapes so that they fitted exactly on top of each other. For instance, assuming your feet are both the same size, the soles of your shoes are congruent in shape. The wheels of the Brompton folding bicycle in Figure 11.14 are also congruent.

Two shapes are said to be similar if they have the same shape (flipped if necessary), but not necessarily the same size. Their measurements (length, height, depth, etc.) may not be the same, but they will be in the same proportion to each other. For instance, the sizes of sheets of the A series of paper (A4, A3, A2, etc.) all have exactly the same proportions (Figure 11.20).

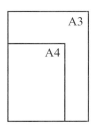

Figure 11.20 Sheets of A4 and A3 sized paper, showing that the proportions of the sides remain constant

Two triangles that are similar will contain the same three angles.

11.3.3 Right-angled triangles

In a right-angled triangle, the angle between two of the sides is equal to 90°. Another way of describing this is to say that the sides are **perpendicular** to each other. Any line that is at right angles to another line can be described as a perpendicular.

Figure 11.21 shows a right-angled triangle. The longest side, which is always the side opposite the right angle, is called the **hypotenuse**.

In general, this module will use the notation shown in Figure 11.21 for labelling triangles. The vertices, or points, of a triangle are labelled A, B and C. The side lengths are labelled a, b and c in such a way that A is opposite a, B is opposite b, and C is opposite c. This convention can be used for any triangle, whether or not it includes a right angle.

For this triangle the length of the hypotenuse is c.

The theorem named after the Greek philosopher Pythagoras (570–495 BCE) is one of the most well known in mathematics and involves the relationship between the sides of a right-angled triangle. There is evidence that the relationship was known well before this time, but Pythagoras may have been the first to provide a rigorous proof.

Pythagoras' theorem

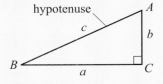

Figure 11.21 A right-angled triangle showing the convention used for labelling points and sides

For a right-angled triangle, the square on the hypotenuse is equal to the sum of the squares on the other two sides.

For example, for the right-angled triangle in Figure 11.21,

$$a^2 + b^2 = c^2.$$

The converse of Pythagoras' theorem is also useful:

If a triangle has sides of lengths a, b and c with $a^2 + b^2 = c^2$, then the angle opposite the side of length c is a right angle.

Activity 11.5

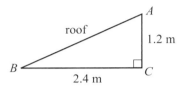

(a) If the figure above represents a cross-section of a garage roof spanning a gap (BC) that is 2.4 m wide, with maximum height (AC) 1.2 m, find the length of the roof (AB). Give your answer in m, to 1 d.p.

(*Check*: imagine the situation, does your answer seem sensible?)

(b) If the maximum height of the roof is increased to give a new roof length of 3.0 m, by how much was the height of the roof increased? Give your answer in m, to 1 d.p.

(*Check*: imagine the situation, does your answer seem sensible?)

Trigonometry

In the roof example above, a more useful method of approaching the problem might have been to consider the pitch of the roof – the angle it makes with the horizontal. Trigonometry is a branch of mathematics that provides methods for using triangles to find unknown lengths and unknown angles. You will start here by considering the relationships between the lengths of the sides and the angles within right-angled triangles.

As an illustration, consider the right-angled triangle shown in Figure 11.22. It has two acute angles as well as the right angle. Start by focusing on just one of these acute angles, the one marked θ (theta) in the diagram. For this purpose the sides have been labelled differently, to emphasise the relationships between angles and sides that apply in right-angled triangles.

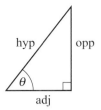

Figure 11.22   A right-angled triangle with chosen angle θ

One of the sides of the triangle is the hypotenuse (the side opposite the right angle), and you can distinguish the other two sides by using the fact that one of them is **opposite** the chosen angle θ, while the other is **adjacent** to it. The sides of the triangle have been marked hyp, opp and adj accordingly, for 'hypotenuse', 'opposite' and 'adjacent'.

Now look at Figure 11.23, which shows three triangles 'similar' to the triangle in Figure 11.22. (Remember that similar triangles are the same shape and include the same angles, but are not necessarily the same size.) So all four triangles have the same three angles. The sides of these triangles are also marked hyp, opp and adj in relation to the angle θ.

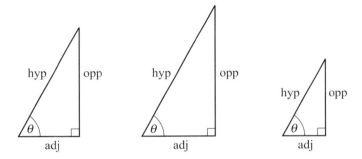

Figure 11.23   Three right-angled triangles similar to the triangle in Figure 11.22

The crucial fact that forms the foundation of trigonometry is that if you find the ratio of the lengths of two sides of a triangle and also the ratio of the lengths of the corresponding two sides of a similar triangle, then you will always get the same answer. So scaling a triangle does not affect the ratio of the lengths of any two of its sides. This fact applies to all similar triangles, not just right-angled ones, but for now only right-angled triangles will be considered.

This means that for each of the triangles in Figure 11.23, the ratio of the lengths of the opposite and adjacent sides has the same value. The same is true for the ratios of the lengths of the other pairs of sides. These three ratios are the key to solving problems involving the relationships between lengths and angles in right-angled triangles, and they are given the special names below.

Trigonometric ratios

Suppose that θ is an acute angle in a right-angled triangle in which the lengths of the hypotenuse, opposite and adjacent sides are represented by hyp, opp and adj, respectively, as in Figure 11.22.

The **sine** of the angle θ is

$$\sin \theta = \frac{\text{opp}}{\text{hyp}}.$$

The **cosine** of the angle θ is

$$\cos \theta = \frac{\text{adj}}{\text{hyp}}.$$

The **tangent** of the angle θ is

$$\tan \theta = \frac{\text{opp}}{\text{adj}}.$$

A popular method of remembering these definitions is to take the initial letters from the equations

$$\sin = \text{opp} \div \text{hyp}, \quad \cos = \text{adj} \div \text{hyp}, \quad \tan = \text{opp} \div \text{adj}$$

to make the acronym

SOH CAH TOA.

Some people find it helps to invent a mnemonic to remember the acronym SOH CAH TOA (Some Of Her Children Are Having Trouble Over Algebra is one example), but the easiest way to remember the acronym is probably just to treat it as a word, and read it: so-ca-toe-a. The acronym tells you the sides used in each ratio, and which side is divided by which. For example, SOH tells you that to find the sine of an angle in a right-angled triangle, you divide the length of the opposite side by the length of the hypotenuse. In a practical problem the lengths will probably have a unit associated with them and it is important (as always) to convert lengths to the same unit before finding the ratio.

Using a calculator for trigonometry

Before trying some examples, make sure you know how to use your calculator to work with trigonometric ratios. The sine, cosine and tangent functions are likely to be clearly marked as 'sin', 'cos', and 'tan'. You also need to make sure that your calculator is in the right 'mode' to measure angles in degrees (not 'radians' or 'grad', which are alternative ways of measuring angles that are not covered in this module). The order in which you need to put in the angle and press the function key will depend on your calculator.

Check that you can use your calculator to give the following answers:

$$\sin 30° = 0.5, \quad \cos 30° = 0.8660\ldots, \quad \tan 30° = 0.5774\ldots$$

You also need to be able to use your calculator to find the angle that has a particular sine, cosine or tangent. For example, if you know that $\tan \theta = 0.75$, what is θ? What you are looking for is known as the **inverse tangent**, or **arctangent**. The button on your calculator will be labelled as 'tan^{-1}' or 'arctan' (if you are using a calculator on your computer, you may have to press the inverse key, labelled 'Inv', to reveal this option). Check that you can use your calculator to give the right answer, which is written like this:

$$\tan^{-1}(0.75) = 37° \text{ (to the nearest degree)}.$$

Your calculator should also have buttons for calculating **inverse sine** (**arcsine**) and **inverse cosine** (**arccosine**); make sure you can find these.

Try this activity to check that you are confident in using basic trigonometric ratios. Additional straightforward questions are provided in the online study resources if you need more practise before moving on to the practical problems below.

Activity 11.6

An Electronic Distance Measuring device (EDM) is used in civil and structural engineering to measure distance and angles. Such a device is used to measure information, as shown in the figure below, and this information can be used to work out the height of the building.

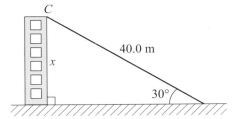

Calculate the height of the building using only the information provided and the appropriate trigonometric ratio.

Solving problems with trigonometry

There are many design engineering problems that can make good use of trigonometry to analyse and solve them. For any problem it is always worth trying to create a diagram to set out the problem visually. This is useful even if it only helps you sort the problem out in your head.

Example 11.1   Television transmitter masts

Television transmitter masts can be stabilised using steel cables to prevent them moving too much in the wind. Imagine you are dealing with a mast that is 30.0 m high and has 4 cables stabilising it. Each cable is 12.0 m away from the base and is connected to the mast two-thirds of the way up.

How much steel cable will be required in total?

Solution

First, sketch a diagram to help you set out the problem: Figure 11.24. Here, the cable is drawn as attached two-thirds of the way up the mast and the height to that connection is given (the problem is being 'solved' as it is drawn).

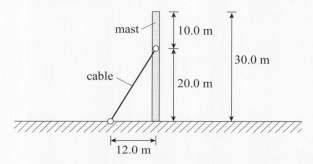

Gives a triangle of:

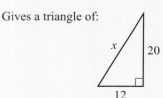

Figure 11.24   Diagram of the transmitter mast problem

Then do the calculations. Because this is a right-angled triangle you can use Pythagoras' theorem:

$$x^2 = 12^2 + 20^2$$
$$x^2 = 544$$
$$x = \sqrt{544}$$
$$x = 23.324$$

So, one cable is 23.324 m long (to 3 d.p.). For all 4 cables, therefore, you would need 23.324 m × 4 = 93.295 m (to 3 d.p.). Since the initial data is given to 3 s.f., an appropriate final answer for the length of cable required would be 93.3 m to 3 s.f.

In this example, notice that two diagrams were generated – one to illustrate the problem and then another that extracted only the really important information to solve a part of the problem. This helped set out what was known and what was unknown about the problem, as well as the general thinking around the problem.

Activity 11.7

Imagine you are working on a cable stay bridge – a bridge similar to the Millau Viaduct shown in Chapter 9.

You are analysing part of a bridge section with three cables that are connected to the vertical support and bridge deck based as shown in the figure below. The vertical support and bridge deck are at right angles to one another.

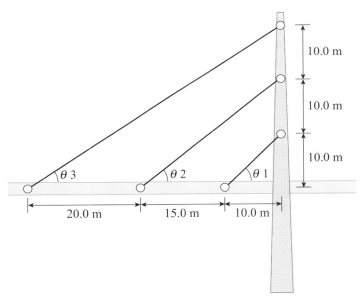

(a) What is the total length of cable used (to 2 d.p.)?

(b) What are the angles between the cables and bridge deck ($\theta 1$, $\theta 2$, $\theta 3$)? (Note: remember that the inverse of a trigonometric ratio is used to find an angle.)

11.3.4 Other types of triangles

Of course, not all triangles are right-angled triangles. You may need to deal with other situations, and there are some more general rules that can be applied to *any* triangle.

Figure 11.25 is a reminder of the notation that will be used to label the points and the sides for a general triangle. The angles at A, B and C can be shown as $\angle A$, $\angle B$ and $\angle C$, or just by A, B and C.

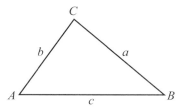

Figure 11.25   How to label a general triangle

In the previous chapter you saw how splitting up a complicated shape into simpler shapes can be used to construct a formula that describes the area of the more complicated shape. Using the same principle, a general triangle can be divided into two right-angled triangles – which you know how to deal with – as shown in Figure 11.26.

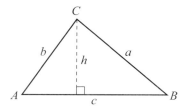

Figure 11.26   A general triangle with a perpendicular added, to give two right-angled triangles

By applying the trigonometric relationships you already know to each of the right-angled triangles in Figure 11.26, you can deduce two useful relationships that are valid for any general triangle: the sine rule and the cosine rule.

The details are not included here, but if you want to know how these formulas are obtained, you can find out in the online study resources – or you may want to accept the challenge of working it out for yourself. As a general rule, you will not be expected to be able to derive mathematical formulas in this module – or even to remember them, since they are all in the *Handbook* – but you do need to know how to use the formulas to solve problems.

Sine and cosine rules

The sine rule can be used if you know one side length of a triangle and the opposite angle, and one further angle or side length.

Sine rule

$$\frac{a}{\sin A} = \frac{b}{\sin B} = \frac{c}{\sin C}$$

or, equivalently,

$$\frac{\sin A}{a} = \frac{\sin B}{b} = \frac{\sin C}{c}$$

The cosine rule can be used if you know the lengths of two sides and the angle between them.

Cosine rule

$$a^2 = b^2 + c^2 - 2bc \cos A$$

$$b^2 = c^2 + a^2 - 2ca \cos B$$

$$c^2 = a^2 + b^2 - 2ab \cos C$$

Activity 11.8

The diagram below shows a building of unknown height x m, and the values of two angles between the horizontal and lines to a point C on the top of the building, measured from points A and B that are 100 m apart.

Use the sine rule to find the distance BC, and hence deduce the height of the building, both to the nearest metre.

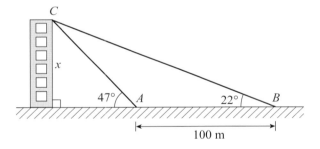

11.3.5   A triangle summary

Here is a useful summary of the equations you can use to solve problems involving triangles, and when you can use them.

In order to solve a problem involving a triangle, you need to know two angles and one side length, or one angle and two side lengths, or three side lengths.

You have seen four methods of finding unknown lengths and angles in a triangle:

- Pythagoras' theorem
- the trigonometric ratios sine, cosine and tangent

- the sine rule
- the cosine rule.

Start by sketching a diagram showing the known measurements and identifying the ones you need to find out.

Use the following decision tree (Figure 11.27) to write down an equation relating the unknown quantity (the thing you are trying to find out) to some, or all, of the known quantities.

Put the values in (taking care over units) and solve the equation.

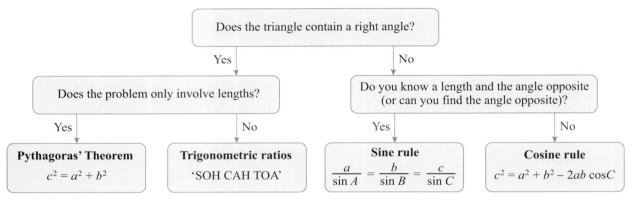

Figure 11.27   A decision tree showing methods of solving problems involving triangles

Working on problems involving geometry is a very useful way to develop your own skills and approaches to design engineering problems generally. In the online study resources there are more design engineering problems that you can use to practise using these methods.

Reference

Young, J.W. (2003) *A Technique for Producing Ideas*, New York, McGraw-Hill.

Solutions to activities in Chapter 11

Solution to Activity 11.1

This could be seen as both, depending on how you considered it.

There is no single right answer, but read through the comments here and see how they compare to the way you viewed the problem.

Well-defined:

This could be a well-defined problem as long as you know what 'relatively' means here. As a designer you might take the decision that this means 'difficult enough to prevent a child taking it off but a reasonably common way of securing things for an adult'. In that case you might use a screw on the battery cover and see that as a simple solution to a simple problem.

Ill-defined:

This could also be an ill-defined problem. What age is the child? Imagine a game controller where the batteries might need to be removed regularly – a cover secured by screw might be very annoying in this case. Similarly, you might decide that you want the design to be as inclusive as possible, meaning that you need to make it easy to operate for as wide a range of people as possible.

In reality:

It is likely to be both – but not at the same time!

Most likely it would start as ill-defined if the design was in the very early stages, and become increasingly well-defined as the project continued. You will come across this type of development in the next chapter.

Solution to Activity 11.2

There are many different responses you could have made to this. The following are given as examples to help you think about your own statements.

- P1 – How might the problem of too much information in phone shops be solved?
- P2 – Come up with creative methods of helping people find a new phone if they don't know what they need.
- P3 – Design a process that allows a customer to find out what they need in a phone.

- P4 – Design some information layouts that clearly explain particular facts and issues.
- P5 – What is the best way to understand what customers are unsure about?

Solution to Activity 11.4

As with any sketching activity, there are no right or wrong answers, but have a look through the following points and use these to think about your own solutions:

- See how many ideas you came up with. If it was only one or two, then spend another few minutes trying some of the techniques listed in the text to help you generate ideas.
- If you have a lot of very different ideas, have a think about whether your ideas were all relevant to the problem or if they were really just random and different. If it was the latter, you might want to think about how you can make that work better in future sessions (for instance, by giving yourself a more specific goal to work towards).
- If you have a lot of similar ideas, think about whether these are developments of ideas or just the same idea repeated. If it was the latter, you might want to try some of the other idea generation tips in the text.
- Above all, check that you are trying to sketch and set out your ideas visually. The more you do this, the better you will get at it (and the better your ideas will be).

Solution to Activity 11.5

(a) In this case, $a = 2.4$ m, $b = 1.2$ m, and the length of the roof is c. Units have been omitted here and in some later solutions for clarity, but remember to include appropriate units in your final solution.

$$c^2 = 2.4^2 + 1.2^2 = 5.76 + 1.44 = 7.20$$
$$c = \sqrt{7.20} = 2.68\ldots$$

The length of the roof is 2.7 m to 1 d.p., which seems like a reasonable answer.

(b) In this case, $a = 2.4$ m and $c = 3.0$ m. Representing the new height of the roof by b, $2.4^2 + b^2 = 3.0^2$.

Rearranging the equation,

$$b^2 = 3.0^2 - 2.4^2 = 9.00 - 5.76 = 3.24$$
$$b = \sqrt{3.24} = 1.80.$$

The height of the roof has been increased from 1.2 m to 1.8 m, so the increase in height is 0.6 m. Again, this seems a reasonable result.

Solution to Activity 11.6

The values you have are one angle $\theta = 30°$ and the hypotenuse of the right-angled triangle formed hyp = 40.0 m. You wish to find the size of the side opposite the angle.

This means you can use the trigonometric ratio $\sin\theta = \frac{\text{opp}}{\text{hyp}}$ as follows:

$$\sin(30°) = \frac{\text{opp}}{40.0}$$
$$\frac{1}{2} = \frac{\text{opp}}{40.0}$$
$$\text{opp} = 20.0.$$

Hence the height of the building is 20.0 m.

Solution to Activity 11.7

(a) For each cable you can apply Pythagoras' theorem to calculate the lengths.

$$a^2 + b^2 = c^2$$

where c will be the cable length in m, and use the dimensions given to define a and b:

First (shortest) cable: $a = 10.0$ m, $b = 10.0$ m

$$c = \sqrt{10^2 + 10^2}$$
$$= \sqrt{200}$$
$$= 14.14 \,(\text{to 2 d.p.})$$

Second (middle) cable: $a = 20.0$ m, $b = 25.0$ m

$$c = \sqrt{20^2 + 25^2}$$
$$= \sqrt{1025}$$
$$= 32.02 \,(\text{to 2 d.p.})$$

Third (longest) cable: $a = 30.0$ m, $b = 45.0$ m

$$c = \sqrt{30^2 + 45^2}$$
$$= \sqrt{2925}$$
$$= 54.08 \,\,(\text{to 2 d.p.})$$

The total length of cable needed is $14.14 + 32.02 + 54.08 = 96.16$ m.

(b) For each angle, you can use the trigonometric identity $\tan\theta = \frac{\text{opp}}{\text{adj}}$ and the inverse, as follows.

First (shortest) cable:

$$\tan\theta = \frac{\text{opp}}{\text{adj}} = \frac{10}{10} = 1$$
$$\tan^{-1}(1) = 45°$$

Second (middle) cable:

$$\tan \theta = \frac{\text{opp}}{\text{adj}} = \frac{20}{25} = 0.8\ldots$$

$$\tan^{-1}(0.8) = 38.7°$$

Third (longest) cable:

$$\tan \theta = \frac{\text{opp}}{\text{adj}} = \frac{30}{45} = 0.666\ldots$$

$$\tan^{-1}(0.66\ldots) = 33.7°$$

Solution to Activity 11.8

In triangle ABC, the angle A is $180° - 47° = 133°$, so angle C is $180° - 133° - 22° = 25°$. In this triangle, the side length opposite the angle C is known, so to find the distance BC, use the sine rule in the form

$$\frac{a}{\sin A} = \frac{c}{\sin C}.$$

Rearranging this gives

$$a = \frac{c \sin A}{\sin C} = \frac{100 \sin 133°}{\sin 25°} = 173.053\ldots$$

So the distance BC is 173 m, to the nearest metre.

Finally the height x satisfies the equation $\dfrac{x}{BC} = \sin B$, so

$$x = BC \sin B = 173.053\ldots \times \sin 22° = 64.82\ldots$$

Hence the height of the building is 65 m to the nearest metre.

Part 2: Chapter 12   Design decisions

Introduction

There is no single, simple process for taking an idea and turning it into a functioning design. Different projects may require different processes for the design to emerge – some may require many phases of activity before the ideas can develop fully; others might have to focus much more on the technical solution to a very strong creative idea.

But all projects have a point at which they have to move from very open-ended creative activity to a more focused set of activities to realise those ideas. Managing the design process to ensure that activities are balanced to get the best results is a critical skill. You will look at overall management of the design process in Chapter 14.

This chapter focuses on the important process of developing a concept, evaluating it and then moving to the next stage – detailed design. You will also be introduced to vectors as another powerful analytical tool for design engineering.

12.1   Developing ideas into concepts

In the previous chapter you saw that ideas are only the start of the creative part of the design process. An idea has to be developed into something that can be tried and tested to see whether it responds to the problem statement or original design driver(s). This testable idea is called a **design concept**, and the stage of the design process where this takes place is often called the **concept design stage**.

In developing a design concept it will often be the case that some ideas work and others do not; some ideas require a lot of time and effort to make them work, and others seem to design themselves. In reality most designers move between coming up with ideas and developing designs as the project progresses, in a process that is very similar to the way in which problems and solutions evolve together, as you saw in Chapter 11.

A key step in this process is one that may seem counter-intuitive at first – the designer has to be comfortable with failure and be prepared to sometimes go backwards in order to make progress.

12.1.1   Moving backwards to go forwards

Thomas Edison (1847–1931) prototyped and created hundreds of filament light bulbs in order to develop solutions that worked effectively. This meant that he created hundreds of failed attempts to solve this problem (Figure 12.1). In design and innovation it is usually the success that is remembered, not the hundreds of failures and all the effort that goes into them. IDEO, an internationally recognised design practice, has a motto that asks staff to: 'Fail early and often to succeed sooner'.

Figure 12.1   Thomas Edison famously said 'I have not failed. I've just found 10 000 ways that won't work'

Unfortunately, the word 'failure' in engineering has a particular definition when it comes to mechanics and structures! The type of failure meant here is quite different: it is an attempt to solve a design problem that did not lead to a successful solution. However, just because a design has failed to generate a solution, it does not mean the idea is of no use. The 'failure' will now inform the designer about the nature of any future solution.

As a quick example, look back to Chapter 10 and the bus shelter ideas shown in Figure 10.9; you will notice that they are all quite different. This is a very deliberate part of the early process where the designer wants to consider as many different ideas as possible.

The ideas that are rejected at this stage are 'failures' in the sense that the designer has decided they are not suitable to continue with. But they are also important pieces of information in terms of what has been learned about the project. In some particularly complex projects, especially when there is a general lack of good information to support the project, this process of elimination is the only way to move a project forward.

This approach to failure can also be thought about as part of the design process. Simply put, sometimes you have to retrace your steps and go backwards in the design *process* in order to make progress in the design *project*.

This is one of the reasons why so much emphasis has been placed on sketching ideas – it is usually more cost-effective to draw a few sketches than it is to go ahead and make a risky final version that you only think might work. In other words, having the ability and flexibility to fail at the sketching stage is simply an efficient way to proceed with a design project.

This can be a difficult attitude to adopt if you have been educated to think of there being only a single, correct answer to a problem. As you have already seen, this is not the case in complex design problems, and one of the ways of investigating and experimenting with many imperfect solutions is to simply try them and see what happens.

If the design process were to be simplified to a single sentence it would be that last point: design is trying lots of different things to see what happens, picking the best one(s) and trying more things.

Of course, you cannot do this endlessly. The experience of the design engineer goes into design process management as well as the design itself. That is, the progress of the design project matters just as much as the focus of the design. A badly managed design process rarely leads to good design. This is where prototyping and evaluation become useful tools in the process.

Recognising the value of failure is an idea that can be applied in many other areas of life as well, including your studies – don't be afraid to try things out and make mistakes, as it is often the very best way to learn.

12.1.2   Design prototypes

Even an experienced designer cannot be entirely certain that what they sketch will work precisely how they imagine it. To reduce this uncertainty, the designer needs to try to imagine as much as possible about the concept – what will go right, what will go wrong, and what might happen by accident. Sometimes a designer might be looking for something specific; at other times they might simply be looking to see what might appear. You came across this in Chapter 9 with the desk height activity – this was a simple exploration to find something out, which then turned into something specific.

A useful aid in these explorations is the **design prototype**. A prototype is a physical model (or mock-up) of the solution being tried, which can be explored and tested directly. Prototypes can range in complexity, size and detail but they all have one thing in common – they are used to test and try out aspects of the design project.

An example of prototype use in the design process is given in Figure 12.2, where a medical instrument has been prototyped very quickly and then used to communicate with the users of that instrument. This allowed the designer (IDEO) to discuss the requirements with the user directly and (more importantly) observe the user trying to communicate their needs. Having a prototype to experiment with and adjust immediately allows this communication to happen more effectively.

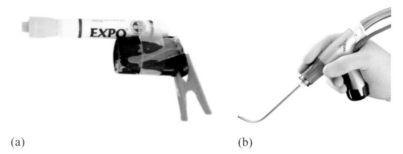

(a)   (b)

Figure 12.2   (a) IDEO's rough prototype; (b) the finished instrument

Prototypes can also be used to communicate particular things to other people, perhaps a client or another design team member. For example, Figure 12.3 shows a structural prototype for the Forth Rail Bridge – a physical mock-up of how the real thing would work, used to communicate and demonstrate a particular aspect of it. (You can see how the Forth Rail Bridge turned out in Chapter 9, Figure 9.5.)

Figure 12.3 Photograph showing a mock-up of the balanced cantilever principle behind the Forth Rail Bridge

It is important to note that prototyping is a particular form of modelling a concept quickly with a very specific purpose. Prototyping is not about making a beautiful representation of a design; it's about making a physical sketch to evaluate the design in some way or to learn something about it. The communication in the medical instrument example above (Figure 12.2) was a two-way discussion between designer and client to develop the project.

Now it's your turn to experiment with shape and form to create a structure. In the next activity you will make a structure out of paper. In doing so you will learn through experience what it is to succeed through failure!

As you go through this activity, try to really experiment with the material by allowing it to get close to failing. Try to find the boundaries of this failure – don't just make it collapse but look for points where it is near to failure. Even better, try to think about what is happening at the failure point. You do not have to understand this mathematically or technically – all you have to do is use what you see in front of you.

Activity 12.1

Your brief is to design a structure to support a single can of beans (or other canned food) between other cans using only a sheet of paper. (Note that the activity continues on the next page.)

The entire structure must be on a flat, level surface and the supported can must be above this surface.

You may use up to 5 cans of beans and 1 sheet of A4 paper.

You may use the materials in any way at all – cans can weigh things down as well as hold things up.

Try as many different ideas as you possibly can – make good use the techniques introduced in Chapter 11 to help with this.

Do not be afraid of failure – in fact, go for as many failures as you can to test out the limits of the material.

For each idea, take a photo of your structure before and after you add the load. Try to quickly rate each one structurally before you try it.

Afterwards, think about how the main forces were 'travelling' through your structures and how that may have led to each succeeding or failing.

Note: the discussion of this activity will follow in the main text – but don't read on until you have tried it.

This activity allows you to really focus on the performance of a material (paper) as part of a structural system (along with the cans). It also forces you to optimise the material properties of paper, and you may have discovered quite a few subtle things as you did this. It's worth exploring some of these further because the principles involved can be scaled up to real structures, as you will see. (These structures will be referred to as 'bridges' in this discussion as they all bridge a gap between cans.)

Simple suspension structure

In the first example, Bridge A (Figure 12.4), the solution is not particularly elegant but it meets the brief.

Figure 12.4   Bridge A, a can supported using a hanging sheet of paper. This relies on the friction between the cans at the sides, which in turn relies on the weight of the upper cans.

The paper is simply hanging between the other cans to form a bridge, relying on the weight of two cans to hold it in place. You can probably see that the most likely way for this bridge to fail would be for the paper to slip sideways from between the cans. The fact that it doesn't tells you that there is a balancing sideways force that is stopping the paper from slipping. This is generated by the weight of the upper can pressing the paper onto the lower can, increasing the friction between them. These frictional forces prevent the paper from moving.

This basic type of hanging structure has been used for thousands of years and is known as a **simple suspension structure**. Most of these bridges use anchors at either end instead of weight placed on top, but the principle is similar – the loads acting on the suspension bridge have to be resisted by the material at either endpoint. Failure to balance these forces results in failure of the overall structure – usually quite dramatically.

Figure 12.5   The Arroyo Cangrejillo Pipeline Bridge, Catamarca, Argentina – a simple suspension bridge

Scallop shell

The second example, Bridge B (Figure 12.6), shows the paper folded to form a 'concertina' shape (technically known as a scallop shell structure). This gives the paper additional depth that it did not have before it was folded.

Figure 12.6   Bridge B, a scallop shell beam structure, showing how increasing the effective depth of the paper can significantly change how the structure responds to a load

In this case the paper does not sag significantly under the weight of the load, and there is no significant sideways force pulling the paper away from the sides. The weight is supported by balancing 'internal' forces within the paper bridge: the weight pushes down on the bridge and the supports react to this force (with an equal and opposite force once the structure has settled into an equilibrium position). The bridge resists these forces internally through its material properties and shape. One of the forces in the bridge is an elastic force going across the ridges – the concertina structure is acting rather like a stiff spring. If this bridge were to fail, it would probably be because the 'spring' collapsed.

Changing the shape of the structure here has changed its overall strength. The depth of the structure is now the distance between the top and bottom of the folds – not just the thickness of the paper. This new depth is known as the **effective depth** of the structure. This is a significant engineering principle that is used in many areas of engineering, allowing far greater loads to be applied to materials without significantly increasing the *amount* of material. You can see this principle in action in profiled metal or corrugated cardboard, as shown in Figure 12.7.

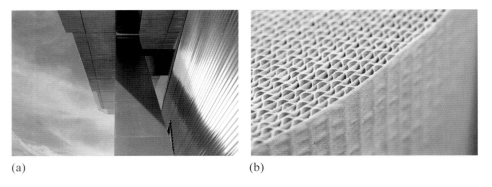

(a)   (b)

Figure 12.7   Applications of effective depth to gain strength in a material: (a) profiled metal cladding; (b) corrugated cardboard

Vaulted structure

The third example of a paper structure, Bridge C (Figure 12.8), shows a paper barrel vault structure. As with Bridge B, this increases the effective depth of the structure by folding the paper into a shape that distributes the load to the cans at either side. This bridge relies on a combination of internal tensile and compressive forces and frictional forces – a possible failure mechanism could be to push the cans at the side apart.

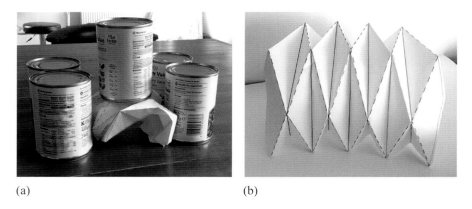

(a)   (b)

Figure 12.8   Bridge C, a paper barrel vault support, which increases the effective depth of the paper by changing the geometry of the paper through folding

In this example, distributing the load across many triangles is very important. A poorly distributed load might cause one of the triangles to fail, which may then cause its neighbours to fail, and ultimately cause the whole structure to fail. So the individual triangles each have to support part of the load, and they all have to work together as a complete structure. You can see this principle in action in another building example in Figure 12.9, where the entire external envelope of the building is a structural surface composed of individual structural elements, in this case hexagons.

Figure 12.9 The Eden Project – an example of a structural surface that distributes the loads it carries

Circular cross-section column

The fourth example, Bridge D (Figure 12.10), shows a paper tube created to sit across the four base cans, which easily supports the top can. This 'bridge' is acting like a column and the load is transferred through the paper tube directly to the ground. The shape of the paper maximises the amount of material available to resist the weight of the load – i.e. all of the paper is being used along its entire length. This structure also relies on the paper at the top and bottom of the tube being folded back on itself – without that fold, the tube would collapse by unrolling. This technique of reinforcing an edge to gain strength is another mechanical engineering principle that has been used for thousands of years.

Figure 12.10 Bridge D, a paper tube with reinforced edges at the top and bottom to retain the shape required

The circular hollow cross-section shape created here is theoretically the most efficient shape to carry a load like this because it is symmetrical in all directions, which means that a load applied at the top will (theoretically) be transferred through the whole structure to the base. Any minor movements in the load at the top will distribute evenly across the circular cross-section shape and vertically to the base.

You looked at cross-sections in Chapter 10.

The word 'theoretically' was used in the previous paragraph because if you look closely at Figure 12.10 you will actually see creases, folds and bumps appearing in the surface of the paper. Theoretically it may be perfect, but in reality this piece of paper was rolled imperfectly. When a load is applied, these imperfections are often the points at which failure starts, which then propagates to the rest of the system.

You can see an example of this structure scaled up in Figure 12.11. In this example it is not only vertical weight that is being supported – this structure is also being affected by the wind, which applies a horizontal force. The chimney is now acting like a vertical beam, and it will bend when it gets windy.

Figure 12.11   A typical example of a brick tower chimney illustrating a structure with a hollow circular cross-section and reinforced edge at the top

If you added to the load on each of these paper bridges until they collapsed, your prototyping would reveal a range of different results. In order to choose a single solution, you would need a bit more information than what was given in the original brief. For example, if aesthetics and a distributed load were most important, then you might think that Bridge C offers the best solution. If a wider span and stiffer structure were required, then Bridge B might be the solution. Regardless of which bridge 'wins', the others are failures. But they are failures that took minutes to create; they have provided a lot of information about paper structures, and they have provided the project with questions that need to be answered before you can move to the next stage. As IDEO says: 'Fail early and often to succeed sooner'.

12.1.3   Strength by design

Before moving on, it is useful to explore some of the main points that came out of prototyping the paper support. They are good examples of design engineering because they involve both the engineering (the structure or material itself) and the appearance (the shape). Good design engineering is about how both these aspects can be made to work together to provide the most efficient and effective way of solving a problem. Manipulating the effective depth of a material is one example of this approach to design engineering. It is simply demonstrated by taking a ruler and trying to bend it in two different directions, as shown in Figure 12.12. The ruler will bend much more easily in one direction than in the other – it is the same ruler, so what is different?

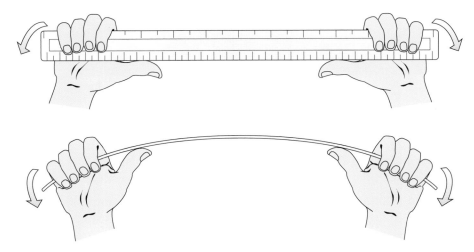

Figure 12.12   A plastic ruler with force applied in two different directions

Activity 12.2

Try to put into words what is happening in Figure 12.12. In each case, consider the forces being applied to the ruler by the hands and what is happening in the ruler. What are the differences between the two situations shown? Think about these things in your answer:

- the size and direction of any forces, and how they are distributed
- the shape of the ruler and how it changes under the force
- the properties of the material the ruler is made of – use words like strong, weak, stiff, tough, etc.
- the effective depth of the ruler.

Use this as practice in applying the engineering terms you have learned.

Flat materials can work like this because of the way the forces are distributed across the shape of the structure. Both the material properties and the shape of the structure determine how this happens, and this is something that the designer can influence directly. Figure 12.13 shows this principle applied to improve the strength of a bicycle frame. What is required here is a stiff, strong structure that is as light as possible. The diamond frame (Figure 12.13(a)) consists essentially of a pair of triangles. Open triangular structures like this can be stiff and strong, but the small amount of material required keeps the weight low. In the monocoque design (Figure 12.13(b)), the load is supported by the external skin of the structure, and the shape is designed to distribute the load across the skin. So with a suitable choice of material the frame can be kept thin and light, while retaining stiffness and strength.

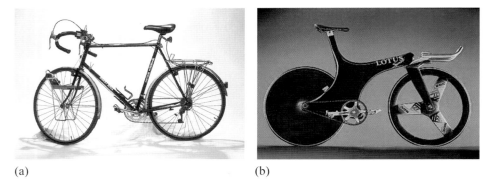

(a)   (b)

Figure 12.13   Two examples of shape being used to increase effective depth in structures: (a) a diamond-frame bicycle; (b) a monocoque racing bicycle with carbon fibre frame

The paper bridge structures also provided examples of how manipulating shape can change the overall performance of the structure. In that case, as with the ruler in Figure 12.12, a shape of structure that provides greater stiffness is what is needed.

You saw another example of this with the bookshelves in Chapter 4, Figure 4.1, where the stiffness of the shelf in one direction (vertically) matters most. In that example, increasing the physical depth of the shelf itself solved the problem because this increased the amount of material that could share the load.

But the shelf example is not a particularly efficient use of the material. As you will see in this chapter, there are other ways to achieve the same result without simply using additional material. The ability to work with materials to get the most out of them is one of the most valuable aspects of design engineering. To do this well, the designer has to balance efficiency and effectiveness of the overall structural design.

These methods of applying design engineering to a structure can be seen in the paper bridges shown previously:

- **Making best use of the material properties**: Bridge A makes use of this principle by allowing the thin and flat paper shape to move in the way it does. The flexibility and tensile strength of the paper is used to support the weight easily.

- **Creating effective depth**: Bridge B uses this principle by creating a scallop-shaped cross-section, increasing the effective depth from the thickness of the paper, a fraction of a millimetre, to a structural shape that is many millimetres thick.

- **Using curvature**: Bridge C uses curvature, albeit as a series of straight lines that combine to make a curve. Each triangle contributes to the overall structural capability of the shape.

- **Edge strengthening**: Bridge D uses this method where the material and shape is poorest at 'sharing' the load. By strengthening the edges, the overall structure can be made significantly stronger.

Once you know some of these structural design shape methods, you will start to see them in many different places. You can find them used in packaging, product casings, and the structure of buildings. Try to spot examples of these over the rest of this week and keep a note of them in your sketchbook.

Optimising the shape of something can often contribute to incremental innovation by making a small improvement to an existing product. For instance, you may be able to change the shape of a plastic bottle so that it holds the same amount of liquid, but requires less material to make and produces less waste. Even a small change can have a dramatic effect when applied to a product produced in the millions.

There are more examples in the online study resources to illustrate how small, incremental changes, combined with some creative and analytical thinking, can make an impact.

12.2   Developing concepts into detailed design

As with turning ideas into concepts, taking a concept and finalising a design project requires a series of further steps. Even with a well-developed concept, a designer might still be uncertain about how it will work or whether it will meet the requirements of the original design problem.

Sometimes these unknown elements are deliberate – it might be impractical to know any more until further investigation has been carried out. Similarly, it is usually impractical to develop each and every design concept in detail. Even a relatively simple concept might take days of analysis to work out fully. So the design engineer needs to be able to efficiently evaluate design concepts – to avoid waiting too long to know something, but also prevent moving too fast and wasting time with too many options.

12.2.1   Design evaluation

As a designer works with an idea, they are attempting to understand more about it, to answer questions and to progress the design project. At the concept design stage, the designer might still be relatively uncertain about what the solution might be. As with problem framing in Chapter 11, this process is an iterative one – it can be repeated many times. With each repetition, something is changed until a certain point is reached.

But what point needs to be reached, and how does a designer know they have reached it?

The answer to this depends on the project and the design process itself. For example, any of the following situations might apply at the concept stage:

- A single, excellent potential solution is created that needs to be explored in greater detail to move forward.
- Several good, possible solutions are created that need to be either evaluated further or reduced in number.
- Gaps in the problem framing are identified or further research is needed to create possible solutions.

This list is not exhaustive, and in many ways it is part of the design process to determine when a project can proceed to the next stage – i.e. the requirements needed for the project might progress.

In some design processes these requirements might be clear – in fact they might be the conditions, constraints and considerations identified at the start of the project (see Chapter 10). In this case, simply checking against these might be the best way to proceed. But a designer never relies on these requirements alone because the process of design can change the needs of the project itself, meaning that the original requirements may also change.

At all key stages in the design process it is worth being as objective as possible and carrying out a general evaluation. The simplest way to do this is to ask the question 'does it work?' but then ask further questions about the quality of it working. The machine in Figure 12.14 certainly works, but is it really a practical solution to the problem? Never underestimate the effectiveness of common sense when it comes to checking a design!

Figure 12.14 Rube Goldberg's self-operating napkin – one of his many over-complex cartoon machines. Just asking 'does it work?' is usually not enough to verify a design solution.

Beyond these simple checks, when you ask 'does it work?', you are usually asking a much more complex question, such as 'does it meet the conditions outlined?' or 'does it consider the needs of user Y?'. These specific questions are essential in design engineering, and together with the conditions, constraints and considerations, they form a **specification** for a project.

In the early stages of a project, the specification might be quite vague and open-ended (it might not even exist!), but as the project develops, detailed specifications will be developed to ensure that what is required is provided in the final outcome. Very often the creation of the specification is itself part of the design project.

- A **technical specification** is a detailed description of how something *should be*, usually in terms of its physical, material and technical (or operational) properties. This is often a series of quantitative properties that can be measured.

- A **performance specification** is a detailed description of how something *should perform*, usually in terms of its value, usefulness, efficiency and effectiveness. This is often a qualitative property that has to be judged.

There are really crucial differences between these two types of specification, and both have important roles in any design project. Examples of the differences between these two types of specification are given in Table 12.1, using the example of a coffee cup.

Table 12.1   Example of possible performance and technical specifications for a cup

Basic conditions	Performance specification	Technical specification
It needs to hold someone's coffee.	It has to be able to contain enough coffee for one person.	It will have a volume sufficient to hold 200 ml to 300 ml of liquid.
It needs to be picked up by hand.	The entire system has to be lifted easily by one person using one hand and without injury or discomfort.	A handle will be attached to the side of the cup measuring 35 mm × 90 mm as set out in Drawing X.
It needs to be stable on a flat surface.	It should be able to be placed on a table easily without it becoming unstable.	The base will have a contact area that provides a flat, stable interface with a flat, level surface.
It needs to provide some way of drinking the coffee.	It needs to have an opening to drink through.	An opening of not less than 180 mm^2 will be provided to allow the transfer of fluid from product to mouth without loss of fluid to the external environment.

Activity 12.3

Come up with two further basic conditions for the cup, and for each one create a performance specification and a technical specification. These can be specific to your own preferences or they can be general to all cups. The technical specification does not need to be accurate – just give a rough idea suitable for a non-expert.

You may think that the example given in Table 12.1 is simple and such a detailed specification would never be required in real life. But describing *precisely* what something should be in order to design, manufacture or use it is actually quite a difficult thing. The problem is similar to that identified in Chapter 9 – people! Different people will view the same instructions differently, and this can lead to problems in any design engineering project.

One way to avoid this difficulty is to ensure very clear communication, which is something you will look at in the next chapter. At the evaluation stage it is vital that the designer and the design team are all aware of what it is that has to be evaluated and how that evaluation is to take place.

In the absence of an agreed means of evaluation, a basic framework can be created by using these starting questions:

- Does it address the problem?

  (e.g. the problem statement)

- Does it meet the necessary conditions?

  (e.g. safety, industry standards, legal issues, etc.)

- Does it achieve the above within the constraints?

  (e.g. cost, time, resources, etc.)

- What considerations were relevant, and does it meet these?

  (e.g. considerations that arose during research or problem framing)

For each of these basic questions, more detailed sub-questions can be asked to help answer the main question. You might then use the matrix tool introduced in Chapter 10 and use it to capture the responses to these questions.

You might immediately realise that there are a lot of questions that can be asked in an evaluation, and it is not always appropriate or efficient to ask every single one. At the concept design stage the project's main focus might only be to select two or three feasible solutions to a problem – and that problem might have one particularly relevant criterion for success.

For example, in the desk height problem in Chapter 9 you looked at several specific problems – ranging from solving an individual height problem to creating a desk suitable for a person of any height. Evaluating any concept design will depend on which problem you are trying to solve, and you might answer these questions differently for different problems.

How you answer these questions also matters as part of this process. Some evaluations are easy to check, while others are a bit more complex. The desk height problem is easy to evaluate for the single user but much harder to test for lots of different users. In the latter case, the design process must also include a method of evaluation – perhaps some user testing with a product prototype.

In design engineering a lot of evaluation can be carried out through modelling. You first came across mathematical modelling in Chapter 3, and when this is combined with prototyping, a whole set of criteria can be evaluated using **analytical methods**. For example, the desk height problem could be modelled by spotting a relationship between people's height and the appropriate desk height. This might then allow a simple model to be created, which could then specify the range of heights the solution would have to achieve.

Another more involved example is the prototype model for Bridge B (Figure 12.6), which provides a clue as to how you can proceed to the next design stage. For this prototype, the number of folds and the distance between them makes a significant difference to its overall strength. If this solution were to be taken forward to detailed design, this aspect could be modelled mathematically to optimise the number, spacing and depth of folds. But, importantly, you have a very good indication from the prototype that developing this idea further will yield an effective result. You also have a good indication that you can then optimise this result to make it even more efficient. That's a good sign for the next stage of the design process.

Arguably, the core of design engineering can be summed up as follows: taking an idea, evaluating it and making it work using creative and analytical thinking. Sometimes all of this happens at the same time, or it may loop backwards and forwards. The design engineer should be aware of this iteration and always have their attention focused on the overall progress of the project – at some point, someone has to get the project finished.

12.2.2   Working out the details – a case study

A key transition in engineering design is taking the design from an idea or concept to a detailed prototype. This can be a long and iterative process where new ideas are introduced continually to improve the design details or to make manufacture easier.

This iteration and incremental development continues throughout the entire design process. It is arguably most important in the detailed design stage, where the concept is worked out in much more detail to meet the conditions of design evaluation.

You will now consider a case study of a design where the details of a concept are fleshed out as part of the overall design process. The basic question 'will it work?' is addressed mainly by asking other questions, such as 'what do we need to do to make this work?'. As you go through this case study, try to also see where iteration occurs, where failure led to a better design, and how sketching helped in moving the project forward.

The design driver and problem statement

This case study is about a product called Res-Q-Rail, a device that is used to transport equipment to and casualties from the site of a railway accident. A particular challenge is that many railways pass through remote areas, with no alternative means of overland access. Fire and ambulance emergency services called to the scene of an accident may be able to gain access to the track only within a few miles of the accident. This design started life as a problem identified by the emergency services in Northumberland, where the railway line to Scotland is inaccessible for long distances. This was the design driver for this project – a user-identified problem and need.

Figure 12.15 Carrying a stretcher beside a railway track in a simulated training accident

Figure 12.15 illustrates the design problem: an emergency rescue team carrying a stretcher alongside a track in a simulated training accident. Note that six people are needed – four to carry the stretcher and two to attend to the casualty – and progress can be hazardous.

The emergency services require a lightweight, portable and compact trolley to take breathing apparatus and cutting equipment to the scene. Moreover, they identified that the track itself could be used by any prospective design solution. Casualties on stretchers then need to be transported using the rails to waiting ambulances. These basic statements form the fundamental *design conditions* and *constraints* for this project. Any final design idea, concept or final product has to fulfil these basic needs.

The concept design for Res-Q-Rail is shown in Figure 12.16. This is a diagram of the concept and it shows the specific features proposed for the final design. The annotations explain the reasons for the features introduced when developing the concept. These all respond to the conditions and constraints which (ultimately) aim to meet the original design problem.

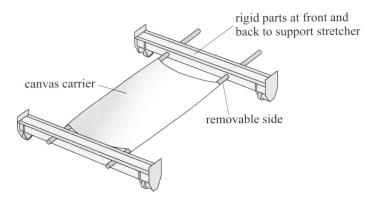

Figure 12.16 Stretcher carrier concept diagram showing main features

Concept and detail development

The concept was then developed to a detailed prototype by the design engineer Rob Davidson. It is patented and in production under the name 'Res-Q-Rail'. For this a far greater level of detail was required, some of which you can see in Figure 12.17. Some of these detailed points are technical specifications and others are performance specifications.

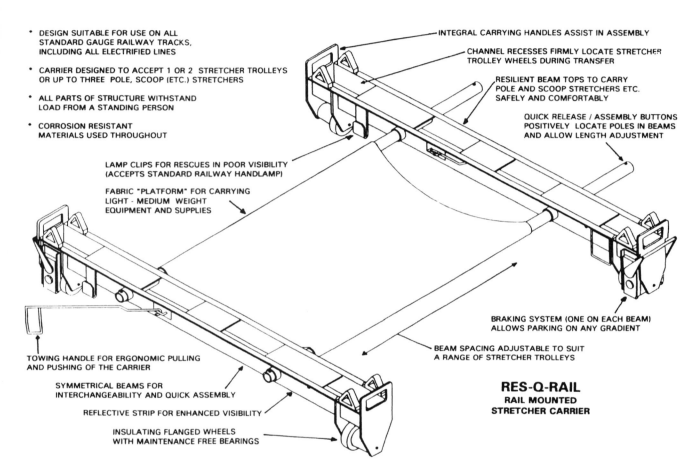

Figure 12.17 Stretcher carrier – the concept developed to detailed design stage

Note the difference in detail between this and Figure 12.16. Looking at one aspect of the design can illustrate the level of detail considered.

The design of the front and back support beams uses an aluminium structure fabricated by bending a thick sheet. This must fulfil its basic function (to support the rest of the structure) but it also has to be very light to be carried manually by the rescue services personnel. This sort of design problem, where two needs must be met, is very common, as you saw in Chapter 10.

To address this requirement and choose aluminium, the designer will have used design and analytical techniques, and divided particular problems into smaller problems or questions, such as:

- How heavy the structure can be and still be carried easily by a certain number of people.
- How much weight the structure needs to support.
- How that weight can be supported (the poles in Figure 12.17 suggest the load is transferred in particular places).
- How all this weight is transferred to the rails (the junctions, joints and other elements that are needed to do this).

For each of these problems, a suitable answer has to be found in order to satisfy the basic performance need for that element. Some of these questions require only basic research (such as finding how much weight a person can carry), but some of them require further analysis using structural or material modelling. At this stage it is very likely that several ideas and iterations will have been made. For example, the designer might have considered using steel instead of aluminium and quickly calculated the weight difference to see if it could be carried easily.

In this case, the designer relied heavily on his own experience and previous knowledge that aluminium can gain significant strength when it is formed in particular ways. As you saw in the previous section, shape can affect mechanical properties. In this case the designer specified aluminium, with a cross-section designed to provide rigidity, effective depth and strength.

If you look closely at Figure 12.17, you will see several other features that are also incorporated into the design of the support beams:

- They are also used to store the stretcher poles (this saves space, weight and makes carrying easier).
- They are symmetrical, to allow them to be installed any way round (this saves time in an emergency).
- Aluminium is resistant to corrosion, even when the surface is damaged.

This represents a general design engineering principle – that of making strong things cheaply, from simple materials. Good engineering is effective (it does what it needs to) and efficient (it does this with the minimum of resources). Good design provides a solution that does more than originally required.

The aluminium beam support is only one of many elements identified in Figure 12.17. There was most likely a stage in the design process where all of these ideas were in the designer's head at the same time, but as the design progressed, each one would have been evaluated, taken away, or kept and developed further, to make progress with the project.

'Failing to succeed'

After the detailed design stage, the product was manufactured in small volumes and tested by emergency crews (Figure 12.18). However, as with many designs, this was not the end of product development. In testing, a number of new requirements emerged. One was that it was important to keep the carrier stationary, so users requested a brake be added.

Figure 12.18   Tests of the final production stretcher carrier carrying stretchers and people

Brake concepts were examined by the designer, who decided on a lever design operating by friction of a pad against the track. Notice that the project went right back to concept design again just for one component of the Res-Q-Rail. This is necessary in order to creatively solve the problem presented.

The key requirement was to transform the vertical motion of a lever (like a car handbrake) to the sides of the carrier and then onto the track. The wheels are plastic for lightness and corrosion resistance, so they might deform if the brake were applied directly to them. The overall concept of the brake is outlined in Figure 12.19. The 'natural' position of the brake handle is 'on'. Positive action (pulling the brake handle up against a spring) is required to pull the brake pads away from contact with the rails. Thus the brake is conceived quite differently from a car handbrake, which requires effort to apply the brake. In this case the effort is needed to release the brake.

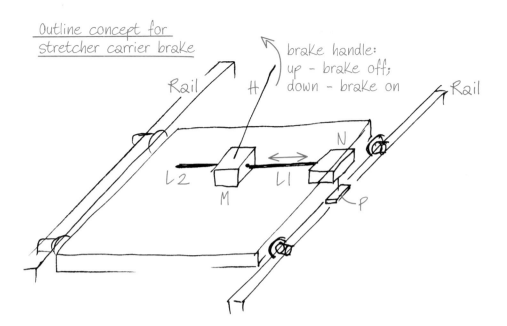

Outline concept for
stretcher carrier brake

brake handle:
up – brake off;
down – brake on

Rail

H

Rail

N

L2

L1

M

P

Figure 12.19 Concept for stretcher carrier brake. H is the handle. Pulling up H raises brake pad P against a spring. Releasing H causes P to spring down against the rail. Mechanism M converts up/down motion of H into side-to-side movement of link rods L1 and L2. Mechanism N converts motion of link rods L1 and L2 into up/down motion of pad P.

A detail (in detail)

Now look a bit more closely at one part of this brake design, namely the mechanism M for converting up/down motion of the brake handle into side-to-side movements of link rods L1 and L2. The spring loading of the brake will be incorporated in the mechanism N. Focusing only on the brake handle mechanism M, the question is how to realise this in detail for the concept shown in Figure 12.19.

Figure 12.20 shows a sequence of developments for the mechanism M using sketches made by the designer while in the process of designing. The designer considered several possible operating principles for M, including using gears: this is the one that was adopted.

brake handles

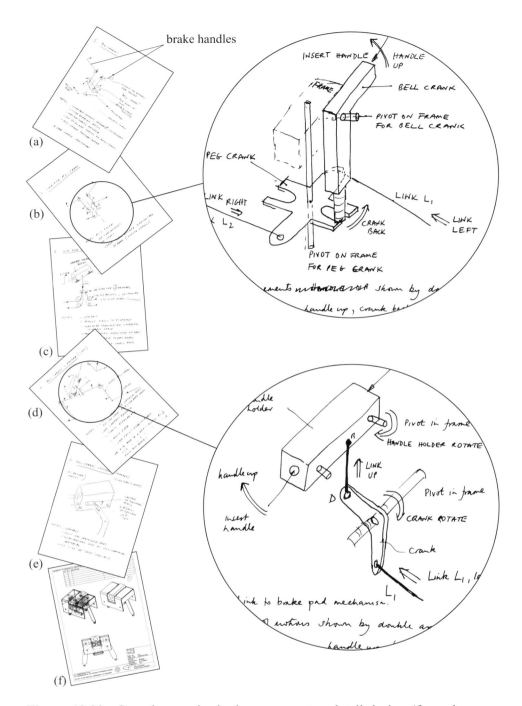

Figure 12.20   Stretcher carrier brake – concept to detail design (from the designer's sketches)

Six stages are shown down the left of Figure 12.20 as a sequence of sketches and drawings made during the design. The first five stages are rough sketches made by the designer, and the final drawings representing the detailed design are the last stage. On the right of Figure 12.20 are two further sketches relating to the design sequence on the left: these are not actually enlargements, but refinements of the design. Notes are included in each stage.

Don't be concerned if these notes are hard to decipher – they are transcribed directly from the designer to show the design 'in progress'. As these are the designer's sketches and notes, there are many things that are not being explained. This series of sketches has been included to show you something about the process used, rather than for you to achieve a detailed understanding of how the brake works. There are several engineering 'judgements' made about tolerances and how materials could deform that are also needed to make a design like this work.

The brake handle is designed so that it can point either forwards or backwards. Someone may need to operate the brake from on the carrier (when transferring equipment and people to the accident scene) or from a position off the carrier (when transporting casualties away from the scene). The handle is detachable, so it can be inserted into mechanism M in either the forward or the backward position.

The second sketch in the sequence (Figure 12.20(b)), and the drawing and annotations that go with it, is a first idea for the mechanism M. A 'bell crank' is attached to the handle. This crank is pivoted on the cross members of the stretcher carrier frame. The other end of the bell crank moves backwards or forwards in slots in a rotating 'peg crank'. The rotation then pulls the rods that operate the brake on the track. The designer simplified the final brake connection in the sketch in Figure 12.20(d), which is getting close to the final design. All the essential elements are present, and you'll notice that it is quite different from the initial sketch. Designers draw on their experience, knowledge and creativity to explore possibilities and converge on a solution. The final design (Figure 12.20(f)) is not a sketch. It is an accurate computer-generated picture.

The sequence in Figure 12.20 follows a design logic – changes to the design do not occur randomly. At each stage the designer considers the current design and looks for opportunities to develop it, perhaps by changing a shape, combining separate components into one, or adding a new feature to meet user requirements. However, the designer is always constrained. The design must be easily manufactured and must be very robust (the design will be treated roughly by people in a hurry in difficult conditions). This is a typical design problem in the engineering industry where many constraints are present. The Res-Q-Rail is an example of a designer being creative in meeting one main need but also a wide range of others at the same time. It is not a straightforward problem, and it needs creativity, thought, logic and intelligence to bring such a product to market.

This account of how parts of the Res-Q-Rail were designed gives you a glimpse of the middle of the design process. Unfortunately, hindsight tends to present the design process as a smooth and 'logical' progression from need to concept and then detail. In reality the process is often messy and creative as designers try to come to terms with a problem, its constraints, and possible ways to solve it. Designing is full of guesses, blind alleys, failures and successes.

Above all, it's a lot of hard work. That's what makes design engineering fun.

12.2.3   The process so far

You may have noticed that the Res-Q-Rail case study has summarised many of the things you have come across so far in Chapters 9 to 12:

- It started with a problem (poor access to remote rail locations in an emergency).
- This became a design driver (an identified need by the emergency services).
- This was explored as a design problem and generated a problem statement (in this case a design brief, setting out the conditions, constraints and considerations) which ultimately became the project specification.
- The designer came up with creative 'solutions' to the problem statement.
- These were developed into design concepts by using sketches and prototypes.
- These were all evaluated and the 'best' one chosen.
- This was then designed in detail, using analysis and modelling to work out further problems and ensure the original specification was met.
- The detailed design was tested and additional features specified, designed and developed.
- This final product was tested and then put into operation and use.

Of course, it was not a simple, linear process as set out above. Some of the steps listed merged into others, and at one point the well-developed product had to have an additional element designed and added to make it meet the users' needs.

But overall, the project moved in a general direction and flow. It is this direction that is more important than the particular steps in the process. A good design project may feel as if it's going nowhere when individual steps are considered (such as a design idea that doesn't work). But when you look at the overall direction of the project, the individual steps all contribute to the overall progress.

12.3   Introduction to vectors

You have seen that the development of a concept takes more than simply continuing to think about things – you need to actively analyse, test and assess the feasibility of your ideas in order to develop them further. The folded paper structure used in Section 12.1 is a good example of how you can make and then test a prototype to quickly test an idea.

But what if you now wish to scale this up? What if you want to make a real bridge? How can you be sure it will be safe?

To carry out more detailed analysis, you need to use more than just trial and error. You will study analysis in more detail in Chapters 15 and 16, but for now you will focus on one of the most useful mathematical tools for analysis – vectors. You have already encountered the idea of vector quantities in previous chapters; this section will remind you what they are, and begin to introduce the tools you need in order to work with them mathematically.

12.3.1   What are vectors?

Some quantities in engineering cannot be specified by stating their size alone – they also require a direction in order to be meaningful. For example, displacement is defined as distance from a point in a particular direction. This means displacement is composed of two measures: distance and direction.

These sorts of quantities can be represented by **vectors**, mathematical quantities that have both **magnitude** (size) and direction. For example, if you stand up from your chair and walk across the room to the door, you could describe this movement as a vector displacement. To do this you would imagine an arrow along the path taken – this arrow would then tell you two things: how far and in which direction you travelled from your starting point (Figure 12.21). This vector is an abstract way of showing your movement.

Figure 12.21   An example of a displacement vector

An example of displacement vectors in use comes from the motions required to operate smartphones and tablets (Figure 12.22). On these devices, both distance and direction matter in terms of how the software responds – a vertical short swipe is different from a horizontal long swipe.

Figure 12.22   Vectors in use on a smartphone

Other examples of vector quantities you have come across previously are velocity, acceleration and – particularly useful for analysing structures – force.

In contrast to vectors, quantities that have size but no direction are called **scalars**, or **scalar quantities**. Examples of scalar quantities are distance, speed, time, temperature, area, volume, energy and power.

Representing vectors

There are different ways of representing vectors, used to suit different situations. A vector can be represented as the line between two points, with the points written as capital letters and the order of these letters specifying the direction. For example, for the vector in Figure 12.21 you could call the starting point, the chair, point A, and the endpoint, the door, point B. This means the displacement vector is the imaginary line between A and B, which you can write as $\overrightarrow{AB}$. The arrow above the letters indicates the direction (from A to B). Another way to write a vector is as a bold letter, such as $\mathbf{a}$, or as an underlined letter, $\underline{a}$ (underlining is used when writing vectors by hand). The magnitude of the vector (in this case the distance from A to B) is represented by the length of the line and is written as $\left|\overrightarrow{AB}\right|$, $|\mathbf{a}|$ or $|\underline{a}|$. For vector $\mathbf{a}$, this is read as 'the magnitude of a'.

Even though vectors are represented by imaginary lines, they represent real information. Figure 12.23 shows the displacement from York (Y) to Glasgow (G), as if you were flying directly between these two places. On the right-hand side of the figure you can see three ways to show the displacement vector, which you can write as $\overrightarrow{YG}$, $\mathbf{b}$ or $\underline{b}$.

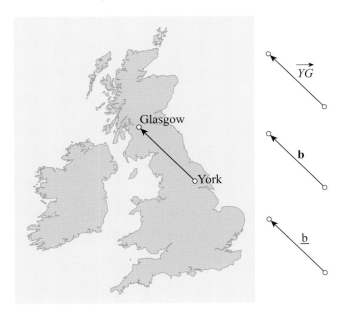

Figure 12.23   The displacement from York to Glasgow shown on a map and as displacement vectors $\overrightarrow{YG}$, $\mathbf{b}$ or $\underline{b}$

It may seem odd to take the vector 'out of' the map in Figure 12.23, but doing this allows you to represent key information in a much simpler diagram. Vectors are geometrical objects (lines), so they can be scaled, added, subtracted, and manipulated visually and mathematically. This makes them a very powerful tool for all sorts of engineering. For now, the focus will stay on displacement and movement vectors to show how you can work with them. In the next chapter, their use will be extended to forces.

Representing vectors

A vector consists of two elements, both of which are measurable quantities: magnitude and direction.

A vector can be represented by an arrow, and written in the form $\overrightarrow{AB}$, **a** or <u>a</u> (when handwritten).

The magnitude of a vector is represented by the length of the line and is written as $\left|\overrightarrow{AB}\right|$, $|\mathbf{a}|$ or $|\underline{a}|$.

The direction of a vector is represented by the direction of the arrow and relates to the geometry of the situation being considered.

Activity 12.4

(a) Draw a vector to represent a horizontal displacement of 25 mm, moving from left to right.
(b) Choose a single letter to represent the vector, and add this to your drawing.
(c) Write down the magnitude of the vector using symbols.

Direction and magnitude in displacement vectors

How you describe the direction of a vector depends on the context you are considering and how you want to use the vector. For example, to give the direction of the vector in Figure 12.23 you might use compass directions, and this would be appropriate for the context. Figure 12.24 shows the principal compass points north (N), south (S), east (E) and west (W), and the secondary points north-east (NE), north-west (NW), south-east (SE) and south-west (SW).

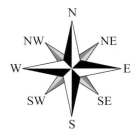

Figure 12.24   The primary (north, south, east, west) and secondary (NE, NW, SE, SW) bearing points on a compass

Applying this to the vector in Figure 12.23, you can see that the direction (from York to Glasgow) is north-west (NW). Note that the direction depends on where you start – Glasgow is north-west of York, but York is south-east of Glasgow. The magnitude of the displacement vector is the distance along its length. For Figure 12.23 this is about 290 km, measured in a straight line between York and Glasgow. In symbols you can write $\left|\overrightarrow{YG}\right| = 290$ km. You can put these two quantities together and say that the displacement vector of someone travelling directly from York to Glasgow is 290 km in a NW direction.

Activity 12.5

(a) Write the displacement vector for travelling from Glasgow to York using the letters G and Y.

(b) What is the magnitude of this vector?

(c) Add in the direction to give the total displacement vector.

In that example, you knew both points and could easily draw a line between them. But vectors are particularly useful when you know only the starting point and the displacement vector. To specify the position of a point P on a map from some starting point O, you can specify this relationship as a displacement vector by saying that point P is a certain distance in a certain direction from O. For example, in Figure 12.25, to describe the position of a mobile phone mast in relation to the base station, you would specify point P as being 5 km south-east of O.

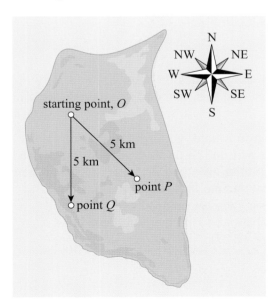

Figure 12.25 Positions of mobile phone masts specified as displacement vectors from the base station

Activity 12.6

(a) Write down in words the location of the mast at point Q in Figure 12.25 as a displacement vector in terms of distance and direction.

(b) Draw the vector on its own, and label it with a letter.

(c) Write down the magnitude of the vector using symbols.

For both $\overrightarrow{OP}$ and $\overrightarrow{OQ}$ the magnitude is 5 km, but they describe different things because their direction is different.

For a more accurate measure of direction, a **full compass bearing** can be specified. A **full compass bearing** is an angle between 0° and 360°, measured clockwise in degrees from north to the direction of interest (Figure 12.26).

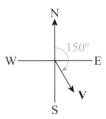

Figure 12.26   An example displacement vector **V** with a bearing of 150°

Activity 12.7

Write down the bearings of $\overrightarrow{OP}$ and $\overrightarrow{OQ}$ in Figure 12.25.

Using a full compass bearing (in degrees) provides the most accurate way of locating objects in relation one another, and this method is commonly used in engineering applications.

For example, to set out a new building in a field, you need to create new points to mark out where the building will go. To do this, you can use a fixed point (a tree, the corner of another building, or a peg in the ground) and then use displacement vectors to specify new points in terms of distance and direction. This is precisely how modern sites are mapped and set out – although the traditional magnetic compass and tape measure have been replaced by electronic versions (Figure 12.27).

(a)   (b)

Figure 12.27   (a) An electronic theodolite (for measuring angles) and distance measuring machine; (b) a laser scanner

The technology has advanced but the method is the same – from a single point, the distance and direction are set as vectors.

Special vectors and other vector properties

Here are two more mathematical terms you may come across:

Special vectors

- **Equal vectors**: as you'd expect, two vectors are equal if they have the same magnitude *and* the same direction.
- **Zero vector**: the zero vector, **0** (bold zero) or handwritten as $\underline{0}$, is the vector with a magnitude of zero. It has no direction.

Equal and zero vectors are particularly important in mechanics where they are used to consider forces working in a system. You will have the chance to work with these vectors in Chapter 13.

Activity 12.8

The following diagram shows several displacement vectors. You may find it helpful to use a ruler to answer these questions.

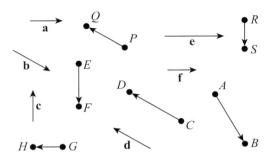

(a) Which vector is equal to the vector **a**?

(b) Which vector is equal to the vector **d**?

The vectors used here have all been two-dimensional vectors. They can be specified using two pieces of information (e.g. two coordinates, or distance and bearing). It is also possible to have vectors in three (or even more) dimensions – all you need are three (or more) pieces of information. This module will only use two-dimensional vectors.

12.3.2   Adding and subtracting vectors

Following the displacement vector shown in Figure 12.23 is possible only if you travel *directly* from York to Glasgow. More typically such a journey is carried out via a less direct route. Such a journey can still be described using vectors, which can be added together. An example is shown in Figure 12.28.

Figure 12.28 The journey from York to Glasgow via Newcastle. Two displacement vectors can be added together to give an overall displacement vector (shown as an orange dashed line).

Both journeys start and end in the same place, so the original vector and these two new vectors are the same in terms of overall displacement.

This method can be generalised and used to add any two vectors and is known as the **triangle law for vector addition**. It is more convenient to use the single-letter notation for vectors to represent this.

Triangle law for vector addition

To find the sum of two vectors **a** and **b**, place the tail of **b** at the tip of **a**. Then **a** + **b** is the vector from the tail of **a** to the tip of **b**.

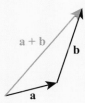

Figure 12.29 Triangle law

The sum of two vectors is also called their **resultant** or **resultant vector**.

You can add two vectors in any order, and you get the same result either way. This is illustrated in Figure 12.30. Diagrams (a) and (b) show how the vectors **a** + **b** and **b** + **a** are found using the triangle law for vector addition. When you place these two diagrams together, as shown in diagram (c), the two resultant vectors coincide, because they lie along the diagonal of the parallelogram formed by the two copies of **a** and **b**.

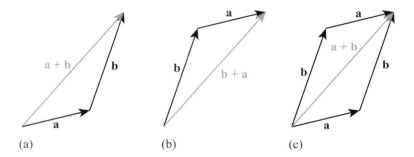

(a)   (b)   (c)

Figure 12.30   The vectors a + b and b + a are equal

You can add more than two vectors at once. To add several vectors, you place them all tip to tail, one after another; then their sum is the vector from the tail of the first vector to the tip of the last vector. For example, Figure 12.31 illustrates how three vectors **a**, **b** and **c** are added.

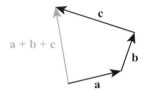

Figure 12.31   The sum of three vectors **a**, **b** and **c**

The order in which you add the vectors doesn't matter – you always get the same resultant vector.

As you'd expect, adding the zero vector to any vector leaves it unchanged. So for any vector **a**,

  a + **0** = **a**.

Activity 12.9

Add the following vectors by drawing them in your sketchbook. For each one, draw the resultant vector in a different colour or line style.

Don't worry about getting them perfect, but try to make the directions and magnitudes as accurate as you can.

(Remember to underline vector letters when you are writing them by hand.)

(a) Add the vectors **a** + **b**.

(b) Add the vectors **f** + **g** + **h**.

Note that you can't add a vector to a scalar because these are two very different entities – remember, a vector represents magnitude *and* direction; a scalar represents only magnitude.

The negative of a vector is a vector with the same magnitude but going in the opposite direction. In other words, a vector **W** has a negative vector −**W**, so that **W** + (−**W**) = **0** (Figure 12.32). For example, if you journey from York to Newcastle and then back again, the resulting displacement is **0** (you're in exactly the same place as when you started).

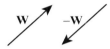

Figure 12.32 The vector **W** and its negative, −**W**

Activity 12.10

Look back at the figure in Activity 12.8 and answer the following questions.

(a) What is the negative vector of **c**?
(b) What is the negative vector of **d**?

Vector subtraction works in the same way as working with negative numbers – subtracting a number is the same as adding the negative of that number.

Vector subtraction

To subtract **b** from **a**, add −**b** to **a**. That is,

   a − **b** = **a** + (−**b**).

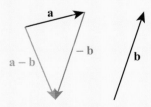

Figure 12.33 Vector subtraction

Activity 12.11

Using the vectors shown in Activity 12.9:

(a) subtract **b** from **a**

(b) subtract both **g** and **h** from **f**.

(Hint: to subtract more than one vector, just add each negative vector in turn.)

Hopefully you can see that working with vectors gives you a powerful, alternative way of visualising numbers and how they relate to properties in the world. In this chapter you have used vectors visually and manually – by moving or drawing lines that represent values. In the next chapter you will explore how to do this mathematically and still retain the usefulness of having a vector diagram. You will also find out how vectors can be used to represent and work with other properties, such as forces.

Solutions to activities in Chapter 12

Solution to Activity 12.2

There are a number of ways to respond to this but you should have come up with items such as the following:

- In both situations a force is being applied to the ruler by the hands holding it.
- It is probably reasonable to assume that the force applied is roughly the same in both situations, and that the force applied by each hand is roughly the same.
- You could assume that the force is distributed symmetrically across the ruler in each situation.
- The ruler reacts to these forces in an equal and opposite direction (or does so until it fails!).
- The main difference is the location and direction of the force applied to the ruler.
- The material is quite tough, because the ruler doesn't break easily.
- In one situation (the bottom one) the ruler deflects, or bends, a lot, and in the other it deflects only a small amount.
- You can say that the stiffness of this structure is greater in one direction compared to the other (i.e. the top image is stiffer than the bottom image).
- You could also say that the effective depth of the structure is greater in the top image, which would explain the point above.

Solution to Activity 12.3

There are lots of ways you could have completed this.

For example, you might want the cup to keep the coffee hot for a long time, in which case you would need to include some extra insulation in the design, and you would need to specify using a material with low thermal conductivity. You might want a cup that won't break if you drop it on a hard surface, which would affect the choice of material. In this case you would be looking for a tough material, perhaps a metal or a polymer rather than a ceramic. You might want the cup to be a particular colour, or to be printed with an image on a particular theme. Think of your own favourite cup, and what is specific about the design that makes you like it.

Solution to Activity 12.4

(a) A horizontal arrow (an example is below), 25 mm long.

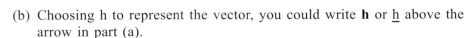

(b) Choosing h to represent the vector, you could write **h** or <u>h</u> above the arrow in part (a).

(c) The magnitude can be written either as $|\mathbf{h}| = 25\,\text{mm}$, or as $|\underline{h}| = 25\,\text{mm}$.

Solution to Activity 12.5

(a) This can be written as $\overrightarrow{GY}$.

(b) The magnitude of this vector is the same as $\left|\overrightarrow{YG}\right|$, which is

$$\left|\overrightarrow{GY}\right| = 290\,\text{km}.$$

(c) The displacement vector of someone travelling directly from Glasgow to York is 290 km in a SE direction

Solution to Activity 12.6

(a) The mast at point Q is located 5 km south of the base station at O.

(b) You could have chosen any letter to represent the vector; here **q** is used.

(c) $|\mathbf{q}| = 5\,\text{km}$ (you may also have written $|\overrightarrow{OQ}|$ or $|\underline{q}|$).

Solution to Activity 12.7

For $\overrightarrow{OP}$, point P is on a bearing of 135° (= 90° + 45°).

For $\overrightarrow{OQ}$, point Q is on a bearing of 180°.

Solution to Activity 12.8

(a) The vector **f** is equal to the vector **a**.

(b) The vector **d** is equal to the vector $\overrightarrow{PQ}$.

Solution to Activity 12.9

(a) and (b) are shown below.

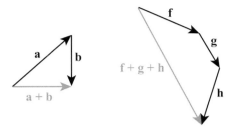

You may have added the vectors in a different order (e.g. **h** + **g** + **f**), but the resultant vector should be the same.

Solution to Activity 12.10

(a) The negative vector of **c** is $\overrightarrow{RS}$.

(b) The negative vector of **d** is **b**.

Solution to Activity 12.11

(a) and (b) are shown below.

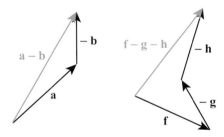

Part 2: Chapter 13   Design communication

Introduction

Much of the daily business of design is about communication, whether this is communication to explore ideas and concepts, or providing information to manufacture and assemble an actual product. Being a design engineer, therefore, requires a basic understanding of the needs and methods of communication in order to work effectively.

There is a phrase in project and design management that is relevant here that suggests the success of a project depends on:

> The right information, to the right people, in the right place, at the right time.

Of course, this adage doesn't tell you what is 'right', but there are certain basic aspects of communication that are simply good to know in design engineering. These will help you go on to develop good practice and (especially) good habits as a practising professional.

13.1   The need for communication

Different design disciplines can use very different methods of communication. Some of these have arisen through tradition and practice; some because they are simply the most effective way of achieving communication. For example, the way some aspects of buildings and structures are communicated has changed relatively little for hundreds of years – the types of representations shown in Figure 13.1 are still used today.

Figure 13.1   A watercolour reproduction of a bridge design by Italian architect Andrea Palladio (1508–1580)

Conversely, engineering a new digital software and hardware system will not have many precedents from Renaissance Italy, and may require digital prototypes and other newer modes of communication.

What have not changed, however, are the *needs* for communication in design engineering. As noted previously, a great design idea in someone's head is of very little value if it stays there and cannot be brought out. Extending this further, the development of ideas with other specialists, users and clients requires effective communication in order to share an understanding of a design.

The following three needs and reasons for communication are commonly occurring examples, which will be discussed in turn:

- create and develop ideas
- develop and analyse concepts
- record and confirm proposals.

13.1.1   Create and develop ideas

Sketching and prototyping can be considered a form of personal communication and this is something that many design theorists and writers discuss. By treating the process of developing ideas as conversation, you can begin to see the individual elements (sketches, scribbles, notes, etc.) as part of the process of design, where each part is working towards the overall outcome.

In Chapter 11 you used a sketchbook to extend your thinking and in doing so you may have noticed a kind of dialogue taking place as you developed ideas. For example, you might have drawn an idea, realised something important and then immediately drawn another version of it, as in Figure 13.2. This process of repetition to improve the result, known as iteration, can be considered a type of dialogue – a kind of talking to yourself that is useful in a wider design process.

You have already seen the value of being able to quickly sketch and generate a number of ideas, including building on previous ideas. The efficiency of this process is exceptionally valuable so keep using that sketchbook!

Good sketchbook habits and tips

- Date your ideas or number your pages – just because they're open ideas doesn't mean they can't have an index!
- Review your sketchbook regularly and add things to older ideas (even better, use a different coloured pen/pencil to do this).
- Where you can, set out an idea using a recognisable method to save time, for example a drawing type (plan, section, elevation), an analysis sheet, or an ordered list.
- Get into the habit of using a sketchbook regularly – you get better at sketching by doing it.
- Remember, sketching is not about being good at drawing – it's about being good at expressing ideas.

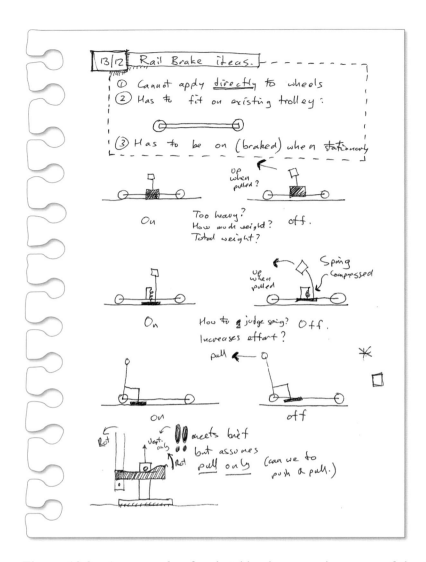

Figure 13.2   An example of a sketchbook page using some of the tips outlined in the text

Activity 13.1

Look back through your sketchbook and try to find an example of an idea you *developed* using sketches.

Spend 5 minutes developing these ideas further and coming up with even more options.

(Note: there is no feedback for this activity, but Figure 13.2 shows an example.)

You may not have generated as many options and ideas as shown in Figure 13.2, but you may have changed or drawn over the top of an existing sketch. Get into the habit of using, and going back to, a sketchbook like this in order to develop your own ideas as well as your ability to articulate and communicate them.

13.1.2 Develop and analyse concepts

At some point a design idea has to be shared in order to develop it further. No design engineering projects happen without a team of people – even if it is only the relationship between client and design engineer.

Developing effective communication methods as a professional in a wider team is essential. The roles people play in such teams rely on communication and the ability to articulate ideas to others and work with the ideas of others. As you develop your own skills as a design engineer you will develop confidence in such communication. So take any and every opportunity you can to observe how other professionals communicate – and start to think about your own contributions too.

As new digital modes of working emerge and become common, this ability to communicate professionally still applies. In fact it is even more important when physical communication is replaced by digital communications. Figure 13.3 shows a building information model (BIM) of a building – a digital prototype of the proposed building created using software.

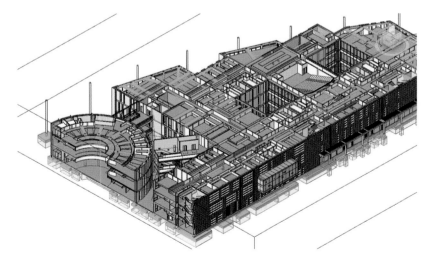

Figure 13.3 A building information model (BIM) showing all the elements in a digital prototype for a building

What you might not appreciate from this image is the number of people who can work on this model. This is a collaborative digital model and the architects, technicians and engineers working in it are all doing so at the same time. Individual professionals contribute particular aspects of the design (Figure 13.4). This allows them to make team decisions and to develop a single version of the representation – something that significantly improves the effectiveness of communication when it comes to manufacturing and construction.

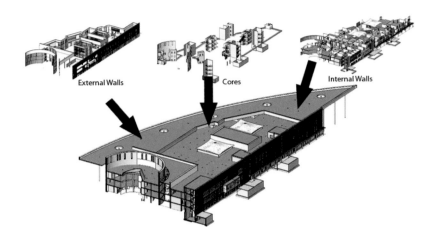

External Walls   Cores   Internal Walls

Figure 13.4   The BIM showing the individual parts that make up the whole model. Each part may be the responsibility of a different project team member.

As a quick (but important) aside – the sketching mentioned in the previous subsection and this digital model might seem to be extreme examples that bear no relation to one another. In fact, research in design and engineering practices shows that being able to sketch quickly to develop ideas and then going straight to digital prototyping is one of the most efficient and effective methods of design for complex projects.

But most importantly, it is the ability of the individual to communicate effectively and efficiently with the wider team that makes a successful project. For this, you have to be able to know your own strengths and weaknesses in communication.

Activity 13.2

Go back to one of the sketches in your sketchbook from Chapter 11. See if you can understand (or remember) what you meant by what you drew.

Try to re-describe using a few sentences the idea you were trying to draw.

Now note down what you communicated well and what you think you could have been clearer about.

13.1.3 Record and confirm proposals

Not all of the people involved in a design engineering project will be in the design team, and some communication is (necessarily) less collaborative than in the previous examples. In Chapter 10, methods for making decisions were introduced, and the points at which these decisions take place are often very important in a design process.

For example, perhaps a decision has been made with a client to choose one option out of several design ideas. Recording precisely what was decided at that stage then gives the project a key point from which it may move on to another stage – perhaps from design to product manufacture.

Similarly, the analysis done for a project is very likely to be kept and recorded in case it's required at some future date – perhaps for checking or updating.

Other examples of when you might produce records include:

- planning permission for a structure
- a patent application
- visuals for client approval
- images for the press or marketing
- drawings for manufacture.

Each of these needs might have very different methods of communication and representation. You can see examples of two of these in Figure 13.5.

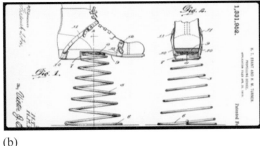

(a)   (b)

Figure 13.5 (a) A 3D rendering of a building for planning permission; (b) a 2D drawing (elevation) for a patent application record

Some of the needs listed above are also conditions or constraints of some projects. For example, any building or large structure in the UK requires planning permission, and representations are used as a form of legal document to ensure that what was granted permission is what was built.

The purpose of this communication can be as much to persuade as to record what was agreed. The needs outlined here can therefore overlap, and the artefacts used to communicate might serve multiple purposes.

Activity 13.3

Imagine you are working on a new alternative energy project, such as a wind or solar farm, or a new hydroelectric installation.

List two or three people or groups of people who might be involved in such a project, as end users or stakeholders. Beside each one, list examples of information they might need (or want) as part of developing the project.

For example, local residents and potential workers near such an installation might want to know about the safety implications of some aspect of the design.

The lesson from this last activity is important – one of the most effective ways of considering communication is to look at it from different points of view. As with the design process itself, being able to imagine situations from other perspectives generates new ideas and thinking.

13.2 Communication methods

Just as different design and engineering domains can use very different methods of communication, different stages of a design project will also use methods best suited to those stages. But many design engineering projects use similar forms of communication because they have proven useful and effective previously.

This section considers some examples and techniques.

13.2.1 Common methods of design communication

These are a few common methods of design communication that you are likely to meet in your work.

Drawings, graphics and images

You have already seen many examples of visual communication in this module. The effectiveness of this method of communication means that it is found in almost all domains of design engineering. For example, a great deal of information can be conveyed in a plan, or elevation, of a building. An **elevation** is a view taken as if the viewer were looking directly at the object (usually from the front, rear or sides): Figure 13.6 shows a front elevation of a house.

PLOT 1A - FRONT ELEVATION

Figure 13.6 A drawing (elevation) of a building drawn 'to scale' and showing materials, sizes and shadows

This image may appear to be a simple picture of a house but it actually conveys a lot more information than you might immediately recognise: it is drawn 'to scale' (meaning you could take measurements from it); it shows materials (meaning it's a form of specification); and it is also presented in a way that most people would recognise and be able to imagine in reality (meaning it can be used to communicate and record what is to be built).

Drawings like this, such as plans, sections, layouts, etc., are common throughout all design engineering domains since they all share these same useful attributes – they represent a lot of information in a very efficient way.

Physical models, prototypes and mock-ups

You came across the prototype as a physical sketch in Chapters 9 and 12, where it was presented as a very quick way of testing whether some aspect of a design 'works'. Developing a number of cost-effective sketch models quickly allows a designer to check existing assumptions and ideas about a design but also to learn new information that would not be possible to find out using other methods.

For example, the folding mechanisms shown in Figure 13.7(a) can be exceptionally complex but they can be modelled very quickly using cheap materials. Similarly, a large-scale, expensive project can still be visualised very effectively using a physical model (Figure 13.7(b)). This allows design decisions to be made in a much more effective and efficient way.

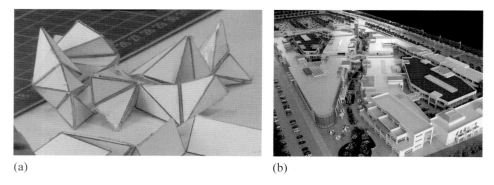

(a)   (b)

Figure 13.7 Images showing two prototypes: (a) sketch model of a folding structure; (b) scale model of an architectural scheme

Digital models, visualisations and presentations

Digital models were mentioned in the previous section and their use is becoming very common in all domains of design engineering. As with sketching and drawing, the efficiency and effectiveness they can bring to the design process is significant, allowing the designer to consider far more options and ideas without having to go through the expensive process of prototyping. For example, being able to quickly simulate aspects of an environment, such as variations in daylight, can provide a designer with useful information that would not otherwise be available without significant time and effort using other methods (Figure 13.8).

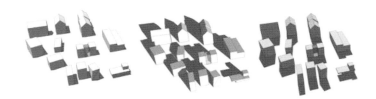

Figure 13.8 Images showing the shadows of buildings at three times in the same day, allowing the designers to 'see' the light distribution at different times

Documents and writing

Designers use a surprising amount of words and text to describe their designs, whether these are verbal or written. Earlier in the module you came across list making as a method for sorting ideas, and you have also been encouraged to add text to your sketches and other ideas. Essentially, design engineers are pragmatists – if it's easier to use words, they use words!

For example, creating specifications for the properties of a design requires a lot of intricate detail that can be set out in enough detail only using words, and very often quite specialised words with precise meanings. Similarly, a contract to build or manufacture a complex product, system or service will also be a specialised form of written communication. Patents and standards (Chapters 3 and 9) are other examples (Figure 13.9).

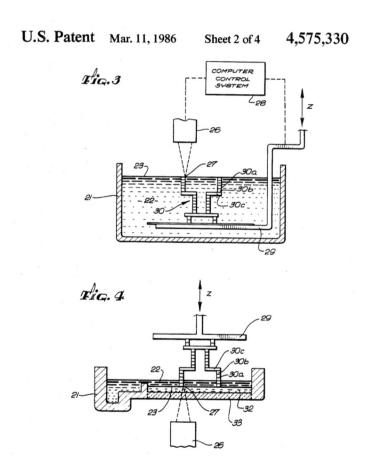

U.S. Patent   Mar. 11, 1986   Sheet 2 of 4   4,575,330

Figure 13.9   Extract from a US patent application for 'Apparatus for production of three-dimensional objects by stereolithography' – an early form of 3D printing

Existing objects and precedents

Using existing objects can be a really effective shortcut to express a design idea or concept. Conveying the concept of a product feel, sound, mood or even colour can be difficult, so having a reference object, sometimes known as a precedent, can be very useful. In design engineering, being able to refer to an existing product is a very good way of explaining an entire technical feature set quickly. For example, explaining the 'wing' doors of the McLaren MP4-12C with reference to the Mercedes-Benz SLR McLaren car is a lot easier than starting from scratch (Figure 13.10).

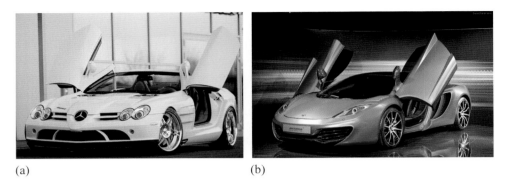

(a)   (b)

Figure 13.10   Using the 'wing' doors of the Mercedes-Benz SLR McLaren (a) to communicate how the doors of the McLaren MP4-12C will look (b)

13.2.2   Common techniques in graphic communication

You may have noticed some common features in many of the representations in the previous sections.

Scale and projection

Representations of something are not usually created at the full size of the object itself. Figure 13.11 shows four objects at different scales. The pictures have similar proportions but represent objects that are not really that size. Being able to draw objects that are very small or large at a scale that is practical to use can benefit the design process.

Figure 13.11   Image from *101 Things I Learned in Architecture School* showing four objects that are not the same size in real life but have similar ratios and are *represented* at the same size for the diagram

The images in Figure 13.11 are examples of elevations. The elevations of the house, door and door handle are all useful views at different scales showing different information. The elevations of the whole house and the door handle will be useful to different people.

A **plan representation** (often known as just a 'plan') is a view taken as if the viewer were looking down on the object shown. This type of view is useful in a wide range of domains, from the smallest scales (such as microchips) to the largest (such as geographical maps).

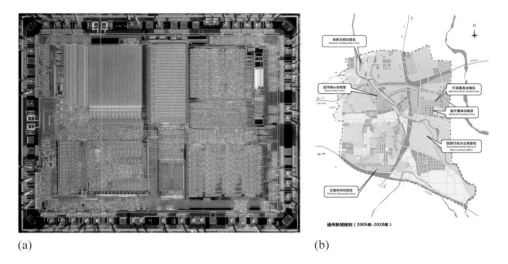

(a)   (b)

Figure 13.12   Different scales of plans: (a) plan of a microchip; (b) plan of Tongzhou city, China

Both plans and elevations have another feature in common: they are represented as if the viewer is looking straight on to the object (they are at 90° to it). In real life you don't usually see the world this way. This form of representation can be used to measure and relate elements in the drawing. For example, if you take a ruler and measure the objects shown in Figure 13.11 you will find they are all approximately 10 mm wide. The actual sizes are much larger and are given in Table 13.1.

Table 13.1   Sizes of objects in Figure 13.11

	Representation size	Actual size	Scale
Part of town	10 mm	20.0 m	1:2000
Part of house	10 mm	2.0 m	1:200
Door	10 mm	1.0 m	
Door handle	10 mm	100 mm	

Using these two sizes you can work out the scale at which each element is represented by using the formula

scale = representation size ÷ actual size.

This scale is usually given as a ratio rather than a fraction. For instance, the part of the town shown is about 20.0 m wide, meaning that the scale is

scale = 10 mm ÷ 20.0 m.

First, you need to convert the units: scale = 10 mm ÷ 20 000 mm.

Simplify and write as a ratio: scale = 1 ÷ 2000 = 1:2000.

So the scale of the part of the town is about 1:2000 – in other words, each millimetre in the representation is equal to 2000 mm (or 2.0 m) in the actual object.

Activity 13.4

Complete Table 13.1 by calculating the scales of the door and the door handle.

Symbols

Sometimes it is not appropriate to draw elements to scale simply because it would be hard to communicate effectively. For example, when designing and setting out electrical services it is common to work with plan layouts that can show many elements at once. A single plug socket is a relatively small object, and if it were drawn to scale on plan, it would be difficult to see. So for practical purposes, objects can be represented as symbols – non-scaled graphic objects that communicate something quite specific.

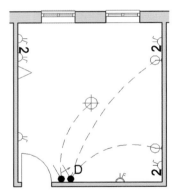

Figure 13.13   A plan showing some examples of electrical equipment symbols drawn for clarity, not to scale

Figure 13.13 shows a few examples of symbols for electrical fixtures and fittings. These are simply a few examples of thousands of symbols across a wide variety of sub-domains in engineering. Standards for this type of communication are commonly agreed to avoid misinterpretation. For example, the electrical symbols shown are specified in BS 3939.

Multiple representations

Different plans may have different purposes and therefore show different aspects of a situation or use different graphic elements to meet their purpose. A map, for example, is a plan representation that can show a range of things, such as physical or political features. You may have come across this if you have used an online mapping service (Figure 13.14).

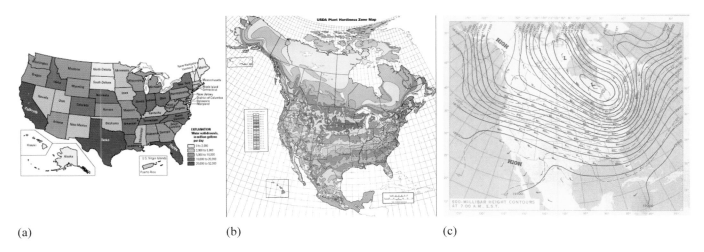

(a)   (b)   (c)

Figure 13.14 Different map types showing the same location (USA) but different information using different graphical techniques: (a) water withdrawal on a state-by-state basis; (b) plant hardiness zones across the whole country; (c) weather information at a specific time

Put these different elements together and you realise just how useful plan representations can be. One plan view can communicate a huge range of information and then be used to layer many different types of other information (Figure 13.15).

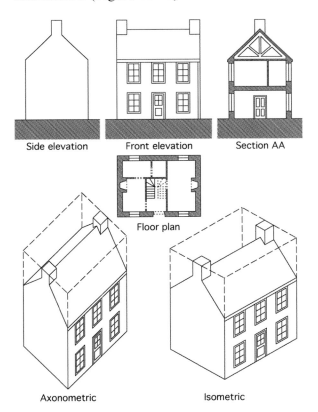

Figure 13.15 Common view types used in design representations

13.2.3   Failure to communicate

Most failures in projects occur because of poor communication. One example is when NASA lost the Mars Climate Orbiter, mentioned in Chapter 1, where the difference between imperial and metric units led to failure of the project. You might find it incredible that no one thought to check such a basic thing, but it is all too common in complex projects – what was thought to be a simple problem (transfer of data) turned out to be a complex human one (the understanding of the data being transferred). There are two important points to learn from this.

First, what is being communicated is usually very complex. This complexity arises for many of the reasons already discussed in the module, including:

- the amount of information required, such as the hundreds of drawings that may be required for even a relatively simple civil engineering project
- the different types of information, such as drawings, spreadsheets, calculations, specifications, etc.
- the range of audiences the same information is intended for, such as a set of concept drawings for client, design team, members of the public, etc.
- the reason for the information, such as for approval, legal purposes, records, etc.

Second, a central problem with communicating ideas is the assumptions made about what the recipient knows. The challenge here is that when there is a problem, people are rarely aware of it until it's too late (hence the NASA/ESA problem). Here are a few examples of different ways in which communication can be affected:

- One party assumes something that is not communicated to the other.
- Omissions in communication: one party forgets to communicate something to the other.
- One party communicates something badly.
- One party misinterprets a communication.

Activity 13.5

Think about experiences of miscommunication you have been involved in (e.g. workplace instructions, misunderstanding between friends, misinterpretation of a written document – there will be many of these when you think about it!).

Now choose one of the following tasks:

- Describe one example briefly as a series of steps in the communication. Then try to assign some of the ways communication can be affected to these steps.
- Start with the list of ways communication can be affected and explore which of these may have occurred in each of your examples.

When you start to list the things that go wrong with communication, it may seem incredible that some of the huge projects you have come across in this module so far have been successfully achieved.

Be under no illusion – all of these projects will have had failures of communication at some point. Much of the actual activity of designers and engineers around the world is dealing with the results of failures of communication. Design and engineering are both very complex activities that require a lot of very complex information. As with design process risks, minimising the chances for such errors is vital.

13.3   Communicating analysis

The previous section introduced a range of useful representation methods in the design process. These representations are not only useful for the visual aspects they show – they can also be useful analytically. In the previous chapter you saw that vectors can be used to visually represent quantities, and you looked at a number of examples using vectors representing displacement. This makes vectors particularly useful in computer-aided design (CAD) software.

CAD software allows design engineers to represent and analyse their designs. Modern CAD packages can carry out some very advanced analyses but almost all rely on vectors to run such modelling. As a simple example, vector-based and procedural drawing packages will provide information about the geometry being created in a way that makes the process of drawing much easier.

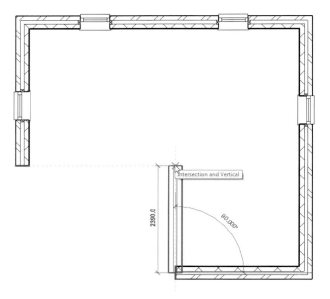

Figure 13.16   BIM software showing simple real-time analysis of geometry informing the designer as they place elements

Figure 13.16 shows a wall being drawn to represent a small building. In this example the length, angle and endpoints of the wall are all presented to the designer and updated in real-time. These vector-based calculations allow the designer to make decisions immediately as they design – in many ways, the designer is effectively using vectors to design.

But vectors can be used to represent more than just distance. In particular, representing the individual forces acting on a structure in a vector diagram allows the designer to calculate the resultant force and assess the consequences of that (i.e. change in movement, or stability).

13.3.1   Using trigonometry with vectors

In Section 12.3 you saw how displacement vectors can be used to represent distance in a particular direction, and how they can be added or subtracted to find the overall result of several successive displacements. Other vector quantities you have already come across are velocity (a speed in a particular direction) and acceleration (a change of velocity in a particular direction).

Vectors are also very useful for representing forces, which you have encountered several times before in this module. A vector can be drawn where the magnitude represents the amount of force being applied and the direction is the direction of the force itself. Figure 13.17 shows a few examples of using a vector to represent a force.

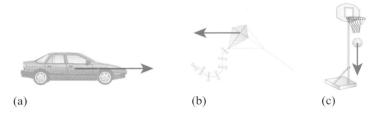

(a)   (b)   (c)

Figure 13.17   Examples of force vectors, showing only one of the forces acting on: (a) a car; (b) a kite; (c) a basketball

Although the visual methods used for working with vectors in Section 12.3 are useful (and sufficient for some purposes), most engineering applications require a greater level of accuracy. You may have noticed that the shapes formed when adding and subtracting vectors lend themselves to the geometrical methods you learned in Section 11.3. In particular, when you add or subtract two vectors, you will often end up with a third vector. These three vectors make a triangle, and you can use the rules that you have already learned to 'solve' triangles. You will look at the special case of vectors adding to 0 later in the chapter. As before, it is helpful to start by considering displacement vectors as these are easier to visualise, before moving on to apply the same methods to the analysis of forces.

Here is an example of adding two displacement vectors involving a right-angled triangle. The trigonometric ratios and other properties of triangles are included in the *Handbook* if you need a reminder.

Example 13.1   Adding two perpendicular vectors

In her journey from home to work, a student travels 3 km due east and then 4 km due north. What is the actual distance from home to work, and in what direction?

(a) Find the answer by drawing a scale diagram (you will need a ruler and a protractor to measure the distance and the angle).

(b) Calculate the total vector using trigonometry.

Solution

Represent the first part of the journey by the vector **a**, and the second part by the vector **b**. Then the resultant displacement is **a** + **b**.

Draw a diagram showing **a**, **b** and **a** + **b**. Since **a** and **b** are perpendicular, you obtain a right-angled triangle. The angle between **a** and **a** + **b** has been marked θ.

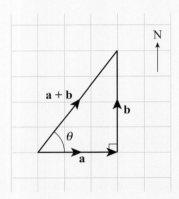

(a) On the diagram, 1 square represents 1 km. Measuring the resultant vector gives a measurement corresponding to a length of approximately 5 units, which represents 5 km. The measured value of θ is about 53°. The bearing of the resultant vector is the angle between north and the vector **a** + **b**, which is 90° − 53° = 37°.

(b) The exact distance can be calculated using Pythagoras' theorem. Since $|\mathbf{a}| = 3$ km, $|\mathbf{b}| = 4$ km and the triangle is right-angled. Omitting units from the calculation for clarity,

$$|\mathbf{a} + \mathbf{b}| = \sqrt{|\mathbf{a}|^2 + |\mathbf{b}|^2} = \sqrt{3^2 + 4^2} = \sqrt{25} = 5 \text{ km.}$$

This agrees with the result obtained by measurement. The direction of the resultant vector can be found using trigonometry to find the value of the angle θ. From the diagram, where **b** is opp and **a** is adj:

$$\tan \theta = \frac{|\mathbf{b}|}{|\mathbf{a}|} = \frac{4}{3},$$

so $\tan^{-1}\left(\frac{4}{3}\right) = 53°$ (to the nearest degree). The calculated value could have been given to more significant figures, but this is probably not justified as the distances are given only to the nearest kilometre. So again, this agrees with the measured value. As before, this can be expressed as a bearing of 37°. So the actual distance from home to work is 5 km, at a bearing of 37°.

Try this yourself in the next activity. There are more practice examples in the online study resources.

Activity 13.6

A yacht sails on a bearing of 60° for 5.3 km, then turns through 90° and sails on a bearing of 150° for a further 2.1 km.

Find the magnitude and bearing of the yacht's resultant displacement. Draw a rough sketch, then find the values by calculation.

Give the magnitude of the displacement in km to 2 s.f., and the bearing to the nearest degree.

For solving vector problems involving non-right-angled triangles, you can use the sine and cosine rules that were introduced in Section 11.3, which are also in the *Handbook*. But in engineering, right-angled triangles are particularly useful. It is often helpful to take a vector and to express it as the sum of two different vectors that are at right angles, or perpendicular, to each other (the reverse of the process in the examples above). This process is called taking **components** of a vector, or **resolving** a vector into components.

13.3.2   Taking components of a vector

You have seen that two vectors, when added together, can be replaced by a single vector, the overall effect of which is the same. This is known as the resultant vector.

Conversely, a single vector can be replaced by two vectors that have the same overall effect. Calculations can often be simplified by splitting a vector into two equivalent vectors at right angles to each other. In other words, a single vector can be resolved into two perpendicular components.

For example, imagine a powered boat crossing a river, as illustrated in Figure 13.19. In this case it is the velocity of the boat that is being considered.

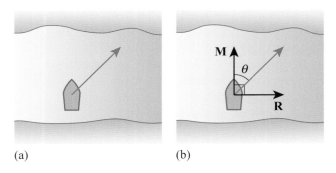

(a)   (b)

Figure 13.19   A powered boat on a river showing: (a) the resultant velocity vector; (b) the component vectors **M** caused by the boat's motor and **R** due to the current in the river

In this example, the final velocity of the boat is shown as a vector in Figure 13.19(a). But this final velocity vector can be usefully split into two component vectors to represent the motion arising from the two main forces acting on the boat, as shown in Figure 13.19(b). The boat's motor causes the boat to move across the river at a certain velocity, while the current in the river causes the boat to move down the river at a different velocity. As a result, the boat moves across the river at an angle θ, as shown. If you know any two of these values, you can calculate any of the others. For example, if you know the velocity produced by the motor and the angle that the boat actually moves at, you can calculate the velocity at which the water in the river is flowing.

When taking components of vectors you need to decide which directions you are referring to. For a displacement vector you might use a bearing, so you could for instance replace a journey of 5 km, at a bearing of 37°, by components of 3 km due east added to 4 km due north – the reverse of Example 13.1.

Figure 13.20 shows a more general example, where vector **A** is shown in relation to an *x*-axis and a *y*-axis. You can define the *x* and *y* directions in whatever way best suits the problem you are dealing with, provided that they are at 90° to each other. Using horizontal and vertical directions for *x* and *y* is often most useful for problems involving forces.

Splitting a vector into components

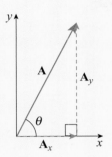

Figure 13.20   Splitting a vector into components

Figure 13.20 shows that the vector **A** (at θ degrees to the x-axis) can be replaced by two vectors $\mathbf{A}_x$ (in the x direction) and $\mathbf{A}_y$ (in the y direction), such that $\mathbf{A}_x + \mathbf{A}_y = \mathbf{A}$.

The components are often shown as dashed lines, as in the diagram, as a reminder that they are a replacement for a single vector. Alternatively, you could use a different colour for the component and resultant vectors.

$\mathbf{A}$, $\mathbf{A}_x$ and $\mathbf{A}_y$ form a right-angled triangle, so you can use trigonometric ratios to express $|\mathbf{A}_x|$ and $|\mathbf{A}_y|$ in terms of $|\mathbf{A}|$ and θ:

$$\cos \theta = \frac{|\mathbf{A}_x|}{|\mathbf{A}|}$$
$$|\mathbf{A}_x| = |\mathbf{A}| \cos \theta$$

and

$$\sin \theta = \frac{|\mathbf{A}_y|}{|\mathbf{A}|}$$
$$|\mathbf{A}_y| = |\mathbf{A}| \sin \theta.$$

Example 13.2 Finding components of a vector

A person pulls a trolley along a flat road with a force of 400 N at 35° to the plane of the road. This force can be split into two components. The most obvious direction to choose for the first component is a direction parallel to the road, which is the horizontal direction in this case. The second component will then be at right angles, or perpendicular, to the road.

Figure 13.21 Pulling a trolley

Calculate the components of the force parallel and perpendicular to the road. Give your answer to the nearest 0.1 N.

Solution

First draw a vector diagram to illustrate the situation.

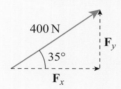

Now use the trigonometric identities $|\mathbf{A}_x| = \mathbf{A}\cos\theta$ and $|\mathbf{A}_y| = \mathbf{A}\sin\theta$ to calculate the forces:

$$|\mathbf{F}_x| = 400\text{ N} \times \cos 35° = 327.7\text{ N}$$
$$|\mathbf{F}_y| = 400\text{ N} \times \sin 35° = 229.4\text{ N}.$$

The magnitude of the component of the force parallel to the road is 327.7 N.
The magnitude of the component of the force perpendicular to the road is 229.4 N.

Activity 13.7

(a) A boat moves at a velocity of 18.0 m s^{-1} at a bearing of 25°. At what speed is it travelling north? Give your answer to the nearest 0.1 m s^{-1}.

(Hint: think about which angle to use in your calculation – a diagram will help.)

(b) A horse pulls a barge along a canal. The rope makes an angle of 20° to the direction of motion of the barge. If the horse applies a force of 204 N, what is the resultant force in the forward direction? Give your answer to the nearest N.

As illustrated in the answer to the first part of the previous activity, there is always more than one possible way to do calculations like these (although sometimes one approach may be more straightforward than another). It doesn't matter which you use, provided that you make it clear what you are doing. The activity revealed a general relationship that applies to all right-angled triangles, and there are a few others that you may find useful.

Trigonometric identities

Figure 13.22 shows a general right-angled triangle. Since its two acute angles add up to 90°, one is marked θ and the other is marked 90°− θ.

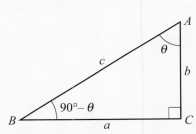

Figure 13.22   General right-angled triangle

The following relationships apply:

$$\cos \theta = \sin (90° - \theta)$$
$$\sin \theta = \cos (90° - \theta)$$

and, provided that $\cos \theta \neq 0$,

$$\tan \theta = \frac{\sin \theta}{\cos \theta}.$$

Activity 13.8

The figure below shows a pendulum, at a point in its swing when it makes an angle of 45° with the vertical. Vectors representing the forces acting on the pendulum bob have been added to the diagram. The string exerts a tensile force of 8.5 N in the direction of the string, and the weight of the bob is 6.0 N acting vertically downwards.

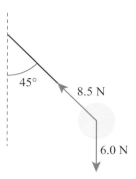

(a) Resolve the tensile force into two components, $\mathbf{T}_V$ acting vertically upwards and $\mathbf{T}_H$ acting in a horizontal direction from right to left. Give your answers to the nearest 0.1 N.

(b) What do you notice about the values of the two components?

(c) How do the components of the tension relate to the weight of the pendulum bob?

This activity illustrates a situation where one component of a force balances another force, but another component is unbalanced. The next subsection explores the significance of this.

13.3.3   Analysing forces: free body diagrams

The ability to work with forces as vectors is essential when analysing any mechanical or structural system. There are some very useful features of forces arising from Newton's laws (Part 1, Chapter 3, Section 3.2) that make vector analysis particularly powerful.

Newton's first law tells you that a system won't change unless an unbalanced external force acts on it. Intuitively, that means:

* if all forces are balanced in a system, then nothing changes
* if all forces are not balanced in a system, then something does change.

Remember those two sentences and you have the basis of all mechanics!

Static systems

A balanced system where nothing is moving is described as a **static system**. A book lying at rest on a table (Figure 13.23) is one example.

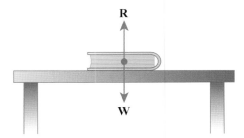

Figure 13.23   The static system of a book on a table

In Figure 13.23 the forces must balance since nothing is moving. The first force that is working is that of gravity on the mass of the book. This gives us a force vector with a magnitude that is the weight of the book and a direction that is directly down (the direction of gravity). This is shown as the vector **W**.

The weight of the book pulls it down towards the Earth, but the table prevents it moving. As a result, the force **W** acts downwards on the surface of the table. Newton's third law states that there must be an equal and opposite reaction, and this is the table resisting the fall of the book (it's actually the material of the table resisting the weight – the table is bending slightly). This is a force vector with the same magnitude as the weight but in the opposite direction. This force is called a reaction force and is shown as the vector **R**. Reaction forces act at right angles to the surface. The term **normal** is sometimes used to describe a line at right angles to a given line or surface, so you will also see reaction forces referred to as *normal forces*, and shown using **N**. Similarly, you may come across other letters used for common forces in other books or material.

If you were to add these two vectors, you would get

   W + **R** = **0**.

You can also think of this using the geometry of the vectors themselves as shown in Figure 13.24, where the size and direction of the vector arrows cancel one another out to give the **0** vector.

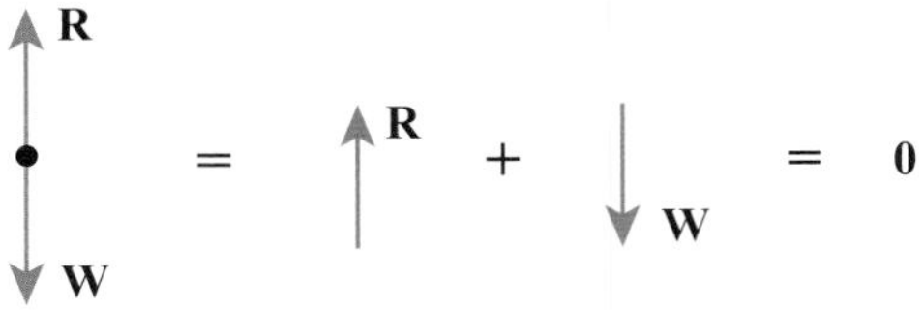

$$\text{R} \,\Big\updownarrow\, \text{W} \quad = \quad \text{R}\uparrow \quad + \quad \downarrow \text{W} \quad = \quad 0$$

Figure 13.24   The vectors from a static system where the magnitude and direction of **R** and **W** cancel one another out, resulting in the **0** vector.

If you knew the weight of the book (magnitude of **W**), you could calculate the force of the reaction (magnitude of **R**).

Example 13.3   Static forces on a book

Calculate the magnitude and direction of **W** and **R** if the mass of the book is 0.5 kg.

Solution

The magnitude of **W** is the weight of the book.

This can be calculated using the formula **W** = m**g**, where m is the mass and **g** is the acceleration due to gravity (9.8 m s^{-2}). Notice that **g** is also a vector quantity.

This gives:

$$|\mathbf{W}| = 0.5 \text{ kg} \times 9.8 \text{ m s}^{-2}$$
$$= 4.9 \text{ kg m s}^{-2}$$

So the magnitude of **W** is 4.9 N (remember that 1 N = 1 kg m s^{-2}).

You know that the direction of **R** is the opposite of **W**, directly upwards. The magnitude of **R** must be exactly the same as that of **W** because nothing is moving – the system is static so the forces must be balanced.

Activity 13.9

A car is parked on a flat road and has a mass of 670 kg.

(a) What is the force it exerts on the road?

(b) What is the reaction of the road on the car?

State the direction and magnitude of these forces.

Take the acceleration due to gravity, **g**, to be 9.8 m s^{-2}. Give your answer to 2 s.f.

A diagram that shows all the forces acting on a single object is called a **free body diagram**. The two forces shown in Figure 13.23 would provide an example of a free body diagram, showing the forces acting on the book.

This method of vectors adding up to **0** can be applied to any static system. In fact, the general result is exactly the same no matter how many forces are used:

$$\mathbf{F}_1 + \mathbf{F}_2 + \ldots + \mathbf{F}_n = \mathbf{0}.$$

As before, you can think of this general formula using the geometry of the vectors themselves. As long as the head of the final vector meets the tail of the first, the resulting vector has to be **0** (Figure 13.25)

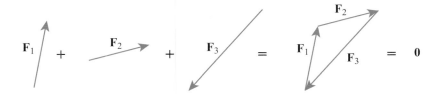

Figure 13.25 Addition using vector arrows and showing vectors adding to **0**

The previous example and activity were quite straightforward, because the forces were all acting in a vertical direction, so their magnitudes could be added or subtracted numerically. By using the technique of splitting vectors into components, you can turn any number of forces into a set of vectors acting in one direction, and a set of vectors acting in a direction at right angles to the first – then the maths becomes much more manageable.

Figure 13.26 shows an example of a box resting on a slope. A gravitational force equal to the weight of the box acts vertically downwards; this is labelled **W**. There is a reaction force from the slope, which acts in a direction normal (at 90°) to the slope; this is labelled **R**. The box doesn't move because of friction between the box and the slope. There is a frictional force opposing the motion: this is marked **F**, and it acts in a direction parallel to the slope, as shown. Figure 13.26(a) illustrates the situation; Figure 13.26(b) is the corresponding free body diagram with the box approximated to a point.

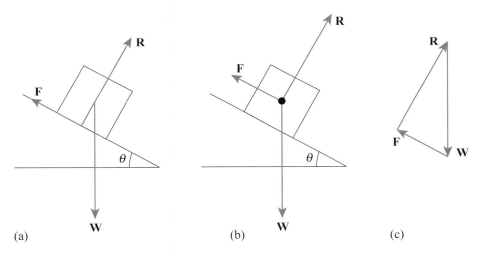

Figure 13.26 A box on a slope: (a) illustration of forces; (b) free body diagram; (c) vector diagram

Since the box is not moving, the three vectors **W**, **R** and **F** must add up to **0**. One way to check this is to draw a vector diagram, as shown in Figure 13.26(c). If the sum of a set of vectors is **0**, then the end of the final vector will coincide with the beginning of the first, to form a closed shape – a triangle in this case.

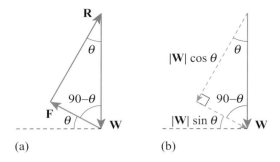

(a)   (b)

Figure 13.27   (a) The vectors representing the three forces acting on the box add up to **0**; (b) the vector **W** can be split into two components, parallel to **F** and **R**

Calculations will be easier if you use components. Figure 13.27 shows the three forces again, with angles added. Two of these vectors, **F** and **R**, are already at right angles to each other, so these can be taken as the reference directions. The third vector can be split into two components. The component $|\mathbf{W}| \sin \theta$ is parallel (but in the opposite direction) to **F**, and the component $|\mathbf{W}| \cos \theta$ is parallel (but in the opposite direction) to **R**, as shown in Figure 13.27(b). So you can write two equations:

$\mathbf{F} = -|\mathbf{W}| \sin \theta$

$\mathbf{R} = -|\mathbf{W}| \cos \theta.$

If you know the weight of the box and the angle of the slope you would be able to find the value of the other two forces (you are not expected to do that here).

Activity 13.10

The figure illustrates another example of a static system: a stationary ring supported by two strings, from which a weight is hanging. Three forces act on the ring, as shown in the diagram.

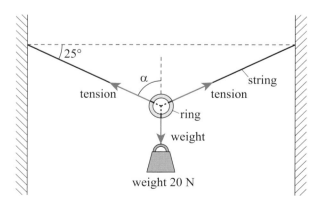

(a) Sketch a free body diagram to show the forces acting on the ring.

(b) Sketch a vector diagram to show how the three forces, added together, add up to **0**. Start with a rough sketch, then if you can, draw an accurate scale diagram.

(c) Draw a diagram (similar to Figure 13.27(b)) illustrating how each of the tension vectors could be split into horizontal and vertical components, and write down two equations that must be satisfied for the ring to be stationary.

Dynamic systems

You will end this chapter by having a quick look at a couple of systems where motion is involved: these are called **dynamic** systems. These will be covered in greater detail in later modules, but the basic principle of using vectors to represent forces still applies.

Remember Newton's second law, force = mass × acceleration or, using vector notation, $\mathbf{F} = m\mathbf{a}$. This tells you that an unbalanced force will cause an object to accelerate. If an object is moving at a constant velocity (so the acceleration is zero), then the forces acting on it must add up to $\mathbf{0}$, just as for a static system.

But if the force vectors do not add up to $\mathbf{0}$, then there is a resultant vector that will cause the object to move (if it is stationary) or to change its speed (if it is already moving). If you drew the force vectors end to end they would not form a closed shape, and the components would not balance in every direction.

As before, this can be generalised and you can write this using vector notation as follows:

$$\mathbf{F}_1 + \mathbf{F}_2 + \dots + \mathbf{F}_n = \mathbf{V}_R$$

where $\mathbf{V}_R$ is the resultant vector.

Again, you can also visualise this using the vector geometry as shown in Figure 13.28. Here, the head of the final vector and the tail of the first do not meet. The vector created between these two gives you the resultant vector.

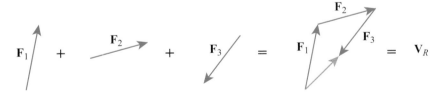

Figure 13.28 Addition using vector arrows and showing vectors adding to a resultant vector $\mathbf{V}_R$

Figures 13.29 and 13.30 show examples of vector diagrams of dynamic systems. Note that the vectors here are used as symbols to illustrate the general principle – the magnitudes are not intended to correspond to specific values.

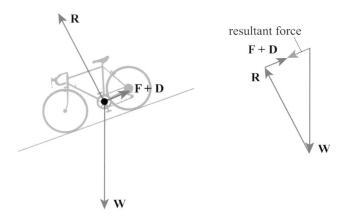

Figure 13.29   Forces acting on a bicycle free-wheeling down a slope

In Figure 13.29 you can see a bike free-wheeling down a slope. The main forces acting on it are:

- **W**, the weight of the bike, acting in the direction of the Earth's gravitational field
- **R**, the reaction of the slope surface to the bike, acting at 90° to the surface of the slope
- **F**, the friction between the bike wheels and the slope surface acting in the opposite direction to the direction of motion.
- **D**, the drag caused by air resistance acting in the opposite direction to the direction of motion.

The resultant force shown in orange (Figure 13.29) will produce an acceleration down the slope.

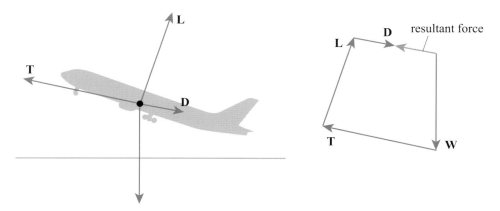

Figure 13.30   Forces acting on an aeroplane

Figure 13.30 shows a plane taking off. The main forces acting on it are:

- **W**, the weight of the plane, acting in the direction of the Earth's gravitational field
- **L**, the lift generated by the difference in airflow across the plane's wings
- **T**, the thrust generated by the plane's engines acting in the direction of the engine's outlets

- **D**, the drag caused by air resistance acting in the opposite direction to the direction of motion.

The resultant force shown in orange (Figure 13.30) will produce an acceleration in the direction of the thrust.

Applications of vectors

The key difference between the forces acting on static and dynamic systems is summarised below.

Forces acting in static and dynamic systems

Static	Dynamic
The vectors representing the forces acting on the system *add to zero*.	The vectors representing the forces acting on the system *do not add to zero*.
$F_1 + F_2 + F_3 \ldots F_n = 0$	$F_1 + F_2 + F_3 \ldots F_n = V_R$
The tail of the first vector meets the head of the last vector.	The tail of the first vector does not meet the head of the last vector. There is a resultant vector V_R.

Remember that vectors can represent any quantity spatially, such as magnetic fields, fluid flows, traffic patterns, or even system processes. Regardless of what quantities vectors are used to represent, basic analysis using vectors can be approached by sketching them out and applying geometry and trigonometry.

Even if you are engineering a system or service, you can still use vectors in this way. For example, a traffic control system has values that relate to one another spatially: traffic can be at a location and moving at a certain speed. In the next chapter you will see examples of software that visualises vectors for designers to use directly.

No matter how complicated the model, basic vector methods still apply and are exactly the same. Vectors are one of the most powerful ways of working analytically with the physical world.

With this in mind, put vectors in your mathematical toolkit and practise using them. Don't worry if you don't get it perfect first time – working with vectors is a skill to develop, not a series of exercises to get right. You will also have a chance to practise working with force vectors in the online module resources.

Solutions to activities in Chapter 13

Solution to Activity 13.2

You could provide many different ideas for this but you may recognise some of the following general points:

- Some ideas may immediately be obvious and make you remember exactly what it was you were thinking.
- Some ideas you might not even recognise and you might struggle to think back to what they were trying to resolve.
- You may struggle to read some of your notes or sketches.
- You may think there is little order to some of your pages, or the pages around your sketch might have helped you remember something.
- You may look back and think there are too few ideas (or too many!).

Solution to Activity 13.3

Here are a few examples. You may have come up with others but if your list is very different, try to think about why that is.

A good way to tackle this is to come up with a list of people who may be involved as users or as individuals affected by the project:

- local residents
- planning officials
- local businesses
- interest groups
- politicians
- electricity suppliers.

Then for each of these, think about what you would want to know if you were in their position.

- Local residents: What will it look like? Will it be noisy? Will it operate all night? Will it make what I do now different?
- Planning officials: Does it comply with relevant legislation? What will the local reaction to it be? Will it be visually suitable/can it be improved? How will I consult with the right people to make sure it gets a fair hearing?
- Local businesses: Will it have an impact on my business? Are there other opportunities I might find from it? Will there be local jobs from this?
- Interest groups (e.g. sustainable energy advocates): How can we support the proposal and help convince local people? How can we obtain a wider recognition of the benefits it will bring? Are there better ways to obtain a similar outcome?

- Politicians: How many people in the constituency are for or against it? Does it fit with party policy? Will it affect the way people vote?
- Electricity suppliers: How much power might be generated? Would it be a steady supply?

Solution to Activity 13.4

Door is

10 mm ÷ 1000 mm

1:100.

Door handle is

10 mm ÷ 100 mm

1:10.

Solution to Activity 13.5

Here is one example answer:

A member of OU staff was organising a day school in connection with a project module and had asked the module chair to attend to provide an introduction to the module. She told him the date, time and general location of the session, but assumed he would look up the event on the OU system to get travel directions.

The module chair assumed that the event would be held in the local OU centre because that was the norm in the location where he worked. In fact, the event was being held at a local college. The module chair went to the wrong venue and, by the time the mistake had been recognised and corrected, arrived half an hour late.

This is an example of a situation where there is an omission in communication, made worse by one party assuming something that has not been communicated to the other. In this case it only caused minor inconvenience, and provided a useful teaching point! But in other circumstances it could have had much more serious consequences.

Solution to Activity 13.6

Represent the first part of the motion by the vector **a**, and the second part by the vector **b**. Then the resultant displacement is **a** + **b**.

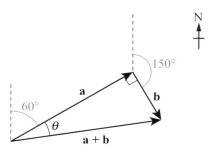

Since **a** and **b** are perpendicular, they form a right-angled triangle, where $|\mathbf{a}| = 5.3$ km and $|\mathbf{b}| = 2.1$ km. Omitting units from the calculation for clarity,

$$
\begin{aligned}
|\mathbf{a} + \mathbf{b}| &= \sqrt{|\mathbf{a}|^2 + |\mathbf{b}|^2} \\
&= \sqrt{5.3^2 + 2.1^2} = \sqrt{32.5} \\
&= 5.70\ldots \text{ km}
\end{aligned}
$$

The angle marked θ is given by

$$
\tan \theta = \frac{|\mathbf{b}|}{|\mathbf{a}|} = \frac{2.1}{5.3}
$$

so

$$
\theta = \tan^{-1}\left(\frac{2.1}{5.3}\right) = 22° \text{ (to the nearest degree).}
$$

So the bearing of **a** + **b** is $60° + 22° = 82°$ (to the nearest degree).

The resultant displacement of the yacht has magnitude 5.7 km (to 2 s.f.) and bearing 82° (to the nearest degree).

Solution to Activity 13.7

(a) You need to find the component of the velocity in the direction of north, shown as $\mathbf{V}_N$ in the diagram below. Your diagram might look like the red lines below, or the purple lines – both are equally correct. You have been told that the bearing is 25°, so you can easily work out the value of the other angle shown ($90° - 25° = 65°$), which has been added to the diagram.

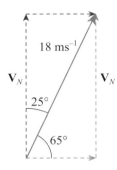

Using the triangle made by the red lines,

$$|\mathbf{V}_N| = 18.0\,\text{ms}^{-1} \times \cos 25° = 16.3\,\text{ms}^{-1}$$

(*Check*: does this seem reasonable? It's clear from the diagram that the vector representing $\mathbf{V}_N$ is slightly shorter than the one representing $18.0\,\text{ms}^{-1}$, so this seems a reasonable answer.)

Or, using the triangle made by the purple lines,

$$|\mathbf{V}_N| = 18.0\,\text{ms}^{-1} \times \sin 65° = 16.3\,\text{ms}^{-1}.$$

(b) Force in the forward direction $= 204\,\text{N} \times \cos 20° = 192\,\text{N}$

Solution to Activity 13.8

(a)

$$|\mathbf{T}_V| = 8.5\,\text{N}\,\cos 45° = 6.0\,\text{N}$$
$$|\mathbf{T}_H| = 8.5\,\text{N}\,\sin 45° = 6.0\,\text{N}$$

(b) In this case, the values of the components are the same, because $\cos 45° = \sin 45°$.

(c) The vertical component of the tension acts in the opposite direction to the weight and has the same value, so these forces are balanced. The resultant force in the vertical direction is zero. The horizontal component is at 90° to the weight. This is an unbalanced force.

Solution to Activity 13.9

(a) The force exerted is the force vector weight; call this **W**. So

$$|\mathbf{W}| = 670 \text{ kg} \times 9.8 \text{ m s}^{-2}$$
$$= 6566 \text{ kg m s}^{-2}$$
$$= 6.566 \text{ kN}.$$

The force exerted on the road is 6.6 kN (2 s.f.) directly downwards (in the direction of the force due to gravity).

(b) The reaction force has the same magnitude, 6.6 kN, but in the opposite direction – directly upwards.

Solution to Activity 13.10

(a) Each string is at 25° to the horizontal direction, so the angle each string makes with the vertical is 90° − 25° = 65°. Since the ring is small, the three forces can be treated as if they are all acting at the same point. Using $|\mathbf{T}_1|$ and $|\mathbf{T}_2|$ to represent the tensions in the strings, and **W** to represent the weight, the free body diagram looks like this:

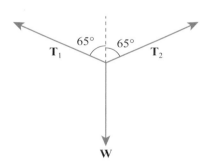

(b) Because the ring is stationary, the three vectors must add up to **0**. If they are drawn end to end, they will form a closed triangle like this:

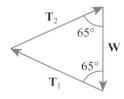

Since you know that $\mathbf{W} = 20\,\text{N}$, you could draw a scale diagram by starting with $\mathbf{W}$ (choosing a suitable scale) and drawing two lines at $65°$ to $\mathbf{W}$, as above. The point where the lines cross will be the end points of $\mathbf{T}_1$ and $\mathbf{T}_2$. (From this you would find out that $|\mathbf{T}_1| = |\mathbf{T}_2|$, and both are equal to approximately 24 N.)

(c) Your diagrams should look something like this:

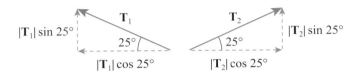

For the ring to be stationary, the horizontal components of the tension forces must balance, so

$|\mathbf{T}_1| \cos 25° = |\mathbf{T}_2| \cos 25°$

$|\mathbf{T}_1| = |\mathbf{T}_2|$.

The vertical components of the tension forces must balance the weight, so

$|\mathbf{T}_1| \sin 25° + |\mathbf{T}_2| \sin 25° = \mathbf{W}$.

Or, since you now know that $|\mathbf{T}_1| = |\mathbf{T}_2|$ and $\mathbf{W} = 20$ N,

$2|\mathbf{T}_1| \sin 25° = 20$ N

You weren't asked to solve the equation, but you could use this to calculate the values of $\mathbf{T}_1$ and $\mathbf{T}_2$:

$$|\mathbf{T}_1| = \left|\mathbf{T}_2\right| = \frac{20\,\text{N}}{2 \sin 25°} = 23.66... \,\text{N}$$

So the tension in each string is 24 N, to the nearest N.

Part 2: Chapter 14 Design processes

Introduction

Each chapter in Part 2 has introduced a step in the process of design engineering projects. So far, however, these steps have not been formally considered in terms of how they relate to the wider project processes referred to throughout Part 2.

This chapter will look at this relationship and how the design process can be managed, and even designed itself, to suit the project. You will see that being able to manage and organise a design process is absolutely vital in order to get the most out of that process. A few approaches to achieving this will be introduced, but as with everything in design engineering, it is more important that these are used appropriately, rather than blindly following a formula.

Being able to balance the iterative and open-ended nature of creative design with the need to manage and direct an overall design project is, therefore, essential. How to enable such a balance is the focus of this chapter.

Section 14.1 focuses on how different design processes contribute to design phases, which themselves build into an overall design project, and introduces some useful approaches to describing and representing the individual stages and the relationships between them. Section 14.2 looks at some practical examples of design process management. Section 14.3 considers some more mathematical examples of iterative processes.

14.1   Basic design processes

If you were to watch any creative design process, you would probably see what appears to be a simple process. For example, you might only see a designer coming up with solutions and ideas but miss all the little steps and actions that have contributed to the overall outcome.

This is an inherent difficulty in researching and understanding the design process – so much of it happens in the designer's head, and that is something that is hard to observe! But it is still possible to make useful observations about the activities seen in these processes, and this can, in turn, allow generalisations that might be useful (or not) in any design process. So as you go through this section, remember that last point – *think* about the ideas presented and ask 'does this seem useful?'

14.1.1   The iterative design process

To start to piece together a design process, consider the creative problem-solving process you came across in Chapter 11. There, you saw ways to frame problems differently in order to come up with different ideas. Figure 11.3 showed that the process of design is a repetitive one in which the designer repeats certain steps in a process that steadily develops an overall idea. This, then, is a **basic creative design cycle** (Figure 14.1).

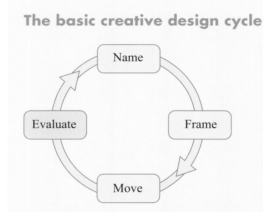

Figure 14.1   A basic creative design cycle

Name: Start from some point (a need, problem or driver) and state what needs to be achieved.

Frame: Consider the context of that starting point and decide how it is going to be considered and approached.

Move: Generate ideas and concepts to address the framed starting point.

Evaluate: Evaluate or check what has been done and consider whether it is satisfactory.

This process is fundamentally different from a simple problem-solving process in two ways. First, it is not linear and recognises that design problems are not simple problems with single solutions. Second, it can look at the problem itself in order to reframe the problem and then creatively consider ideas and solutions.

For the basic creative design cycle to work, it has to be repeated a number of times. In each cycle, the design is improved or made worse, and for either outcome a bit more information is known about the design problem and solution at the same time. Because this cycle repeats until some outcome is satisfactory, it is not possible to be sure how much iteration is required or how long the whole procedure might last. This uncertainty is an inherent part of the creative design process.

But uncertainty is also part of an attitude the designer has to adopt in order to be creative – if a design project is approached without uncertainty, then the possibilities of that project tend not to be questioned or explored. As has been mentioned before, this does not mean a designer has no idea what is going on – it simply means they are balancing the most useful aspects of creative and analytical thinking in order to come up with the best solution.

As Frederick states in *101 Things I Learned in Architecture School*: 'Being genuinely creative means that you don't know where you are going, even though you are responsible for shepherding the process' (Frederick, 2007, p. 81).

Activity 14.1

For both of the characteristics of the design process outlined (i.e. iteration and uncertainty), explore the risks by completing these two sentences:

(a) The design process is iterative, and if this iteration goes on too long, the project …

(b) The design process can feel uncertain, and this …

There is a tension in the basic creative design process – it involves an uncertain process where completely controlling it is impossible. But at the same time that process has to be guided in some way.

One way to start to deal with this is to realise that the *individual* design process is part of a wider *project* design process.

14.1.2   Project design phases

From your own experience of design, you may already have noticed that the basic creative design cycle is not precisely what happens. For example, it is quite possible that you have used iteration inside this design cycle. You may have had a problem frame that you really wanted to explore, and may then have gone between the 'move' and 'evaluate' stages many times. Sometimes, you may have even changed your mind or completed a cycle halfway through a pencil stroke!

In fact, you may have noticed that you go through many cycles – and even cycles of cycles. For example, you may experiment with an idea inside another creative cycle: you could perhaps imagine this as circles within circles. Or you might also be working on several parts of an idea at the same time: parallel circles. Or you may even imagine these circles as spirals, where the design continues to develop and expand after each iteration (Figure 14.2).

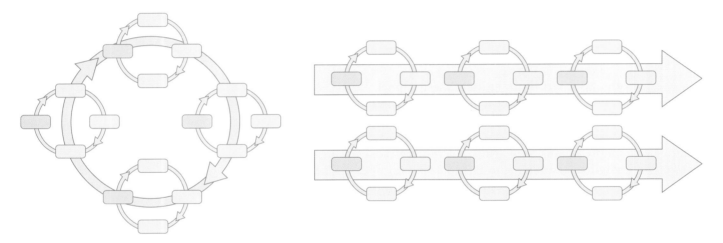

Figure 14.2   Alternative shapes as ways of visualising the design process

Activity 14.2

Think back to one of the creative design processes you have been through in one of the activities so far (for example, the desk height problem design from the start of Part 2).

Consider the cycles and iterations you went through, and try to sketch out a diagram to show the process.

Generally, these individual activities are contributing to a larger design process. This is generally true of all design engineering – as you progress through a series of smaller design cycles, you are also contributing to a wider project process. As with the basic design process iteration, you can visualise this as a series of iterations within the wider 'direction of travel' of the project itself (Figure 14.3).

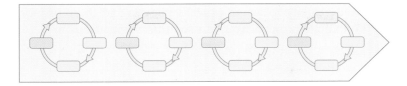

Figure 14.3   Basic design process iterations within a wider design project phase

In this wider design process, the project is clearly going in some direction or has some purpose or constraint, such as an endpoint goal or maybe simply a time limit. It may be a phase to create a series of design options or even a formal phase to approve a fully detailed design prior to manufacture. The exact purpose and nature of the phase will depend on the project itself and, sometimes, how the design process is proceeding. This is called a **design process phase**.

As a quick example, you could view the paper bridge building activity in Chapter 12 as a series of options to meet the same brief. You might then have given your own condition for this phase being complete.

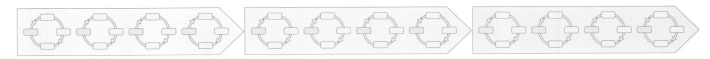

Figure 14.4   Design process phases as part of a larger, linear process

As with individual design iterations, these phases can be joined together to form a linear series of processes (Figure 14.4). For example, moving from ideas to concepts and then evaluating those concepts for approval might represent three phases in a linear process. In this example, each phase depends on the previous one in order to progress the overall project.

14.1.3   Types of design process phase

Different design projects demonstrate certain patterns that commonly appear, as with the basic design process itself. Consider one you have already come across – each chapter so far in Part 2 has actually been going through phases in a wider design process:

- In Chapter 9 you considered starting points for a design project: needs and problems.

- In Chapter 10 you looked at the conditions, constraints and considerations that might apply.

- In Chapter 11 the basic process of creative design was presented, generating ideas after framing a design problem.

- In Chapter 12 you saw how design ideas can be converted to design concepts and then evaluated to make design decisions.

- In Chapter 13 you considered the communication of design concepts and how these matter in the wider project context.

This was summed up in Chapter 12 when it was noted that the individual steps, activities and processes all contributed to the wider project. These smaller activities contribute to larger design process phases, and these phases in turn contribute to the overall project. You can see this mapped out in Figure 14.5.

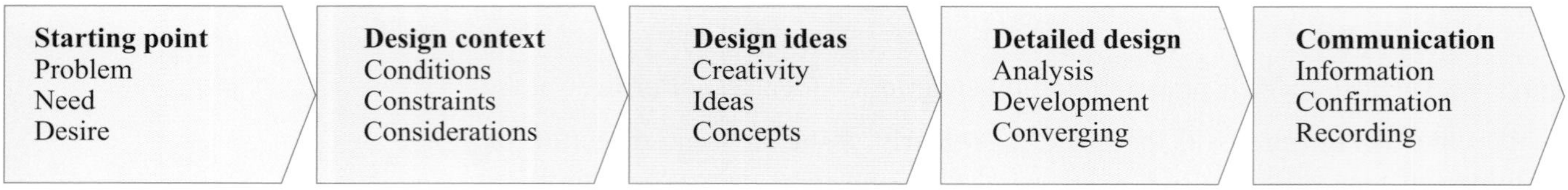

Starting point	Design context	Design ideas	Detailed design	Communication
Problem Need Desire	Conditions Constraints Considerations	Creativity Ideas Concepts	Analysis Development Converging	Information Confirmation Recording

Figure 14.5 Design process phases introduced in Part 2

These are relatively generic phases, often seen in creative design projects. From some starting point the project team considers the context, then generates ideas that are turned into concepts and then detailed designs, which are finally communicated for some purpose. This process diagram misses out many other possible phases (such as manufacturing or decommissioning) and it is independent of any single project type or design engineering discipline.

In fact, there are as many design process models as there are people who use these diagrams. Some of them are useful and some of them can actually harm a project. It all depends on how they are used as part of the design process itself.

In this module, you will mainly use the five phases outlined above. However, being aware of some of the other common types of phase in any design project can be useful because it gives the designer an overview of a design project 'ecology'. What you can perhaps see emerging from the above discussion are common phases that could be useful to consider when managing any design project.

Common phases in a design project

- **Starting point** – some problem, need, demand, desire, market push or pull.
- **Preparation** – researching the starting point and finding out the conditions, constraints and considerations around it.
- **Exploration** – taking the starting point and preparation, and framing it for further consideration.
- **Idea creation** – coming up with ideas and creative solutions.
- **Concept development** – developing ideas into useful or testable concepts.
- **Detailed design** – developing concepts into working information that demonstrates how the design operates.
- **Specifying and procurement** – developing the detailed design into specification information that allows the making of the design.
- **Making and production** – taking the specification and detailed design to make, produce or see it realised.

- **Use and operation** – using the design produced in its intended context.
- **Maintenance and upkeep** – continuing the use of the design by maintaining it.
- **Repurposing and reusing** – adapting and updating the design to extend its life or improve it during use.
- **Decommissioning** – dealing with the design at its end of life.

This list has been presented very much as if one stage depends on the previous one, and this is generally the case. But some projects may involve these phases overlapping or being applied quickly out of sequence. For example, a quick idea creation phase might be run to check some of the research in a preparation phase. Or, as you saw with the Res-Q-Rail, even at the use and operation stage, a project might have to return to previous phases in order to complete the overall project.

You may have started this module thinking that design is really involved only in the idea creation phase and, traditionally, this has certainly been the case. But increasingly companies and design practices are realising that greater value can be extracted from the design process if it is extended into other phases. You will look at a famous example of this later in the chapter.

14.1.4 Checkpoints: stage gates versus soft landings

All of the project process diagrams shown above contain an assumption: that in each phase there is some means by which the project can move on to the next phase. This is similar to the reflection or evaluation step in the basic design process – there must be a check that the process has achieved what is needed before moving on.

In many design process diagrams you may find that an evaluation or checking stage is included as an independent phase in the process itself. Throughout this chapter it has been assumed that evaluation and checking are an integral part of each iterative design cycle as well as in each design phase. Checking, evaluation and reflection should always be necessary parts of any design process at all times.

There are occasions when a more formal approach to evaluation is required. You saw this in Chapter 12, where simply checking against the design conditions was given as an example. This might be considered quite a simple check – the design may either meet the conditions or not meet them. This is known as a 'hard checkpoint'. Similarly, you came across methods of checking that involve less definite approaches, such as using a decision matrix to 'score' ideas, a technique used in Chapter 10. This is important when developing design solutions that do not have single 'right' answers and is known as a 'soft checkpoint'.

These 'hard' and 'soft' checkpoints have both disadvantages and advantages. Once again, it is how they are used in the process that makes them useful (or not) when placed at the appropriate points in a design process.

The **stage-gate process model** is one approach that uses hard checkpoints, where there are clearly defined points at which something must be confirmed. For example, a company might be developing a physical product that has to go through certain business, design and development stages to meet that company's business model.

Figure 14.6 Example of a stage-gate process model

Figure 14.6 shows such a stage-gate model where each phase has to meet some specific criteria before the project can proceed to the next phase (the analogy here is that it has to pass through a gate). For example, the product development cannot begin until the business case has met some target, perhaps demonstrating that the product manufacture will meet a particular financial target.

Conversely, the **soft landings process model** for procuring public buildings in the UK replaces 'hard' stage-gates with a longer process of approval and checking that is actually part of the beginning and end of each phase (Figure 14.7).

Figure 14.7 The basic soft landings process model

The intention behind this model is to recognise that for large and complex projects there may be many different types of approval required. Some of these might be easy to achieve (checking against conditions) but some of them might be very difficult (satisfying stakeholders' and users' considerations).

Activity 14.3

Note down some advantages and disadvantages for both the stage-gate and soft landings models.

If you find it easier, try to apply these models to a specific design project, such as one you have already come across in the text.

As with many of the other concepts you have come across in this module, there is no right or wrong design process. Being too rigid with a design process means ideas can be missed and opportunities ignored. Being too open with a design process means a project might take too long to develop. It is how the design process is applied that matters more, and being a design process manager is very often just as creative and difficult as being a product designer.

14.2 Design process management

You have seen that the iterative nature of design is necessarily uncertain and that this can be a risk to the wider project process unless it is carefully managed. You also saw that different design projects go through different project phases and that there are no specific rules about how to utilise and manage the phases in a design project.

In order to assist with these uncertainties it is possible to generalise and make the following observations, for all design projects:

1   In general, the entire design project has to move forward to make progress.
2   In order to do this, at some point it has to go through different phases, such as the ones you have come across so far.
3   Sometimes the process itself has to adapt and change, just as the individual design cycles also have to adapt and change, depending on how the overall process is going.

Using these general principles to think about and manage the design process can make a significant difference even though they are quite general statements. They allow a designer to adapt the design process to suit the needs of the project itself. You will now look at a few examples of how this is achieved by a few world-famous design engineering companies.

14.2.1 Incremental innovation

One of the main ways of managing the risks in the design process is to simply repeat a previous (successful) process, or to develop a successful product in some additional way (which you may recall is known as incremental innovation). Much of design engineering takes place in this way and it can lead to significant efficiencies if managed well. However, the danger of simply repeating mistakes or reusing a poor process is always present with this approach.

To show how this can be managed carefully but still achieve innovative product development, you will examine how Rolls-Royce achieves it when producing a complex product like a turbofan jet engine, the type of jet engine that is currently used on all major passenger aircraft (Figure 14.8).

Figure 14.8 Turbofan engine on an aircraft wing

Designing a jet engine from scratch does not make financial sense – the costs are simply too great. Doing just that nearly caused the collapse of Rolls-Royce in 1971, when the cost of developing the RB211 more than doubled to £170 million (equivalent to about £2.3 billion in 2016). The manufacturing industry in the UK might have looked very different today if the company had not been rescued. This means that other ways to balance available resource, but still remain innovative, have to be found.

Consider the development of the blades inside a turbofan engine (Figure 14.9). These blades have to operate in very high temperatures because a high combustion temperature increases the efficiency of a jet engine. This, however, requires very careful consideration of both the materials and the design of the blades.

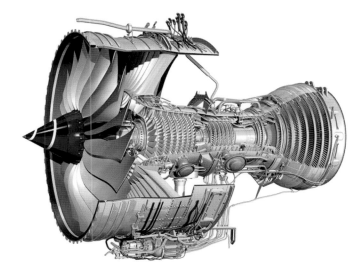

Figure 14.9 Cutaway view of a turbofan jet engine showing the turbine blades

In Rolls-Royce there is a distinction between the 'research and development' (R&D) and product development processes. Usually R&D is concerned with the development of new technologies, and it is often carried out at or in collaboration with universities or research centres, which are remote from the day-to-day business of the company. For example, Rolls-Royce is continuously trying to develop new materials to suit performance criteria set for its engines. This includes research on materials able to withstand very high temperatures.

Product development processes, by contrast, are concerned with the development of a specific engine for a specific aircraft to a given timescale and budget. Concepts that have been tried and tested in R&D are deployed when required in product development projects. The jet engine design process starts with a small team developing a concept. They interact with the aircraft makers and find out the specific requirements for the type of aircraft and the intended use; engines built for long-haul routes, such as London to Los Angeles, will have different requirements from engines built for short flights within Europe, for instance.

By separating these two streams (R&D and product development), innovation can still take place within a managed context – the product development team can creatively use developments from the R&D stream. This team will be aware of R&D as well as recent engines developed within the company. They will know which technologies the company is working on – including those that are ready to be deployed on a new engine within the required timescale, and those that are still in too early a stage of development to be safely employed.

It is how these two streams are brought together that allows successfully innovative design to take place in Rolls-Royce and other organisations. For the turbine blades, a material being worked on for a particular temperature range will still have uncertainties about manufacturing and operation in terms of the shapes and surface finishes required. Turbine blades have cooling channels, but these may have to be designed specially or a new technology deployed for the particular temperatures desired in the new engine.

The blades have to withstand temperatures in the order of 1400 °C and must work totally reliably and safely for tens of thousands of flight hours. To achieve this, materials with special-purpose coatings as well as interior cooling channels are used (Figure 14.10). These turbine blades are cooled, using cool air coming in at the bottom and hot air coming out at the top, as shown in image (a); hot air is also vented from the small cooling holes along the passage of the cooling channel (image (b)); and the profile of the cooling channels is shown in image (c). The exact shape of the cooling channels and position of the cooling holes requires significant design effort and very detailed evaluation.

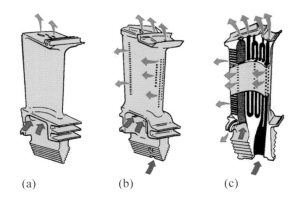

(a) (b) (c)

Figure 14.10 Turbine blades and cooling channels: (a) the airflow through the cooling channels; (b) the small cooling holes that connect with the cooling channels; (c) the profile of the cooling channels.

To ensure that the design will work under all the given operating conditions, computer analysis and simulation are carried out to model variables within the engine such as stresses, heat and air flow. The results of these analyses are used to modify the components until the designers are confident enough to build and test a physical prototype. In order to complete such analyses, both streams of development have to work together to pool knowledge and contribute to the overall project.

This would not be possible if the teams were starting completely from scratch – there simply would not be enough time. By focusing on adaptation, change and development of this particular component, Rolls-Royce knows that the project will benefit. This is often referred to as incremental innovation: the steady development of some particular aspect of a design.

This certainly does not mean that the process is any quicker or easier. The design work can take several months. Designing a jet engine requires people with very different specialisms to work together, combining their expertise in areas such as:

- aerodynamics to understand how the air flows through the engine
- materials science and engineering to develop or select appropriate materials
- mechanical engineering to design and analyse static and moving parts
- control engineering to ensure correct operation of the engine.

To design and make jet engines requires numerous staff to support the engineers and designers. Everyone makes a coordinated contribution that requires them all to have a level of understanding of how their activities and skills fit into the bigger picture in the design of a jet engine.

Above all it requires close and detailed management of all activities to complete the project on time. Design process models are the basis for constructing these plans but they are no replacement for management that is responsive to what the design project requires to succeed.

14.2.2   Design for manufacture

One benefit from extending the design process is in manufacturing – especially when it comes to mass manufactured products and processes. This is called **design for manufacture** and it relies on designing the product with manufacturing in mind from the start. In doing so the designers have a particular focus, and alternative ideas will address that specific focus.

The design of the new Mini provides an example of exactly this approach to project innovation. Without the design team framing the challenge using manufacturing materials, methods and processes, this product would not have achieved the innovative success it has. In fact, the entire product relies on the manufacturing process, providing a unique product to each customer. But these techniques can also be shared across *different* products related in particular ways.

In the mass market automotive industry, prices are kept down by sharing components across a number of products. These are structured in so-called **product platforms**. For example the Volkswagen group shares components, such as those shown in Figure 14.11, across its Volkswagen, Skoda and Audi brands. This would typically include key functional components, such as the chassis, the axles, the suspension and the powertrain. The platforms also include options for some components: for example, there is a choice of engines for each car size across the group.

Figure 14.11   Some of the components that were used to build a Volkswagen Golf

The use of existing designs to create new ones is one way to reduce the risk involved in creating a new design. The reference design is known as a **design precedent**, and this can be an entire product or technology, or simply an idea that is used to inform a future design. In some companies these design precedents are used regularly and may even form platforms to develop entire projects.

These product platforms can then be used to create **product families**, where more than individual components are shared – an entire system of components might be shared. For example, in domestic appliance product design, some products share so much that only the outer shell is actually any different. Have a careful look at the toasters the next time you are in a shop that sells them.

In fact, BMW has taken this parts and systems interchangeability right through to the manufacturing stages with the new Mini, allowing a process of **just-in-time manufacture** to take place. Each car produced is made to order using careful control of the logistics of manufacture, supply and assembly. To achieve this, the entire process from inception through to delivery has to be designed – not just the part you might normally associate with the word 'design'.

This is known as an agile process and it can also be used as a design technique, called **agile design**. The principle in both is the same: the end result is carefully managed throughout to ensure that it serves only the very specific needs of that end result. It would certainly not be possible if one phase in the project ignored all the other phases. The overall effect is that the entire business operation is also designed, from the buying of components (and how many) right through to the delivery operations using specifically designed car transporters.

As a counter-example to this, the McLaren MP4-12C super car is a unique design solution in many respects. It does not share parts with other cars, but it does share technologies with McLaren F1 racing cars, and design features such as the wing doors with the Mercedes-Benz SLR McLaren (shown in Figure 13.10). From a design engineering perspective it is very atypical, because it is not based on an existing car and therefore does not share common components with other cars. One such feature is the tub, a single material shape that forms the main structure of the car. Figure 14.12 shows some parts in a McLaren car with the tub as the central part.

Figure 14.12 Parts in a bespoke McLaren car design. None of these are readily transferable to other cars.

Activity 14.4

Think of a product in your home that comes from a product family or product platform.

Look for products that you have replaced a few times in the past few years. These are most likely to have the same components on the inside, but they may look very different on the outside.

Alternatively, consider products that include replaceable components, or connections to other devices.

Once you have chosen your product, try to identify parts of it that you think might be common to other similar products, or that might be part of a product family.

It's worth noting that design for manufacture does not only relate to mass manufacture – even large-scale, bespoke projects often have to consider the manufacturing project phase. For example, the new Forth Road Bridge requires very careful consideration of the methods and process of construction – it is being built over quite a deep body of water, so simply ignoring this is not an option (Figure 14.13). How it is built has to be a major aspect of the design process itself. In construction and civil engineering this is referred to as **buildability**.

Figure 14.13 An extract from Figure 10.19 in Chapter 10 showing several temporary structures used during the construction of the new Forth Road Bridge

As with manufacturing design, careful consideration of the making phase of a project means that significant savings and improvements can be achieved, making it well worth the effort involved in design for manufacture.

14.2.3 Design for service

Going beyond traditional design phases allows new products and markets to be expanded and developed. Designing for the service of jet engines is now considered an essential 'product' for airline clients and end users – it is not only the technical operation of the engine that matters but also how good its performance is. For example, fuel is a key cost in operation for an airline and consequently a major factor in determining ticket prices. How an engine uses fuel is not only to do with how much power it can put out, but also how effectively this power can be applied over the service life of the engine.

Hence, it will be no surprise that relating these two criteria is important for aircraft designers. Being able to design a product and say that it can deliver a specific service, not simply some performance criteria, allows a company to market and promote their products in a completely different way.

You will now look at some calculations to evaluate how an engineered product performs in service. The fuel consumption of the A380 aeroplane provides an example. These calculations involve finding out how much fuel is used in total during a flight but also, more importantly for an airline deciding on a competitive ticket price, how much fuel is used per passenger.

Start with a simplified calculation by assuming that an A380 uses its entire fuel capacity over its maximum range – a rather unlikely scenario, but all mathematical modelling has to start somewhere. Take a look at the data in Table 14.1, which is derived from the Airbus published figures on the A380. There appears to be a lot of information here so go through it carefully. There are four columns, from left to right, detailing performance, (passenger) capacity and dimensions, with the fourth column including pictures of the engine options and aircraft profiles.

Look at the performance column and note that the A380 has a maximum operating speed of 1090 km h^{-1}, which is equivalent to Mach 0.89. The Mach number is named after the famous nineteenth-century scientist Ernst Mach (1838–1916) who made many advances in the fields of mechanics, sound and vision. It represents the ratio of the relative speed of an object in a fluid (air in this case – remember that a fluid can be either a liquid or a gas) to the speed of sound in the same fluid. However, this is not a piece of data that is required in our fuel consumption calculations.

The next two entries in the performance column are the maximum take-off and landing weights. You will notice that Table 14.1 refers to aircraft weight in tonnes, which is actually a unit of mass (1 tonne = 1000 kg). This data has been taken directly from the tables of published data by Airbus (2013) so their exact terminology has been retained, including their reference to 'weight' when they actually mean mass. This is a very common practice, and one to beware of if you are using data like this in calculations.

Notice that maximum take-off and landing weights are significantly different. If an A380 takes off with fuel for a long-haul flight and with a full complement of passengers, it is likely to be somewhere near this maximum take-off weight. For example, let's suppose it was 500 tonnes, which is 500 000 kg. Before it can land, its weight must be less than 386 tonnes. This means that it must use or jettison at least 114 tonnes of fuel before it can land.

The next performance figure gives the fuel capacity as 320 000 litres (the litre, l, is a commonly used non-SI unit of volume, equivalent to 1000 cm^3). This represents the volume capacity of the fuel tanks in the wings and tail. But the mass of the fuel is also important to know.

Table 14.1 Manufacturer's information for the Airbus A380

PERFORMANCE		CAPACITY		DIMENSIONS		ENGINES AND PROFILES
Speed (MMO) Max Mach Operating Speed	1090 km hr^{-1}	Typical seating	525 (3-class)	Cabin length	Main deck 49.90 m Upper deck 44.93 m	
		Max seating	853	Max cabin width	Main deck 6.54 m Upper deck 5.80 m	
Max take-off weight	560 tonnes					
Max landing weight	386 tonnes					
Max fuel capacity	320 000 litres			Wing span (geometric)	79.75 m	
Range	15 700 km			Height	24.09 m	
				Overall length	72.72 m	

(Source: Airbus figures at: http://www.airbus.com/aircraftfamilies/ passengeraircraft/a380family/a380-800/specifications/)

Activity 14.5

If the density of jet engine fuel is $0.8\,kg\,l^{-1}$ what is the mass of a full load of fuel on an A380?

What percentage of the 'maximum take-off weight' (i.e. mass) does a full tank of fuel represent?

Now think about how far an A380 might be capable of travelling with full fuel tanks at take-off. The next entry in the performance column gives a range of 15 700 km. (Of course, in practice a flight would be somewhat less than this.) The next activity asks you to calculate fuel consumption on a flight of maximum range in terms of the number of litres of fuel used per 100 km.

Activity 14.6

If an A380 takes a flight for a maximum range (15 700 km) starting with full tanks (320 000 litres), what is the fuel consumption in litres per 100 km for this flight assuming that the A380 uses all its fuel? Give your answer to 3 s.f.

Using the maximum range in a calculation of fuel consumption is not very realistic. The aircraft may make several stopovers, which will increase fuel consumption significantly. However, the figure of 2040 litres per 100 km does give a minimum figure for fuel consumption which can be used as a benchmark for comparison.

When an airline operates the A380, revenue depends to some extent on the number of passengers carried. Look at the second column, headed 'capacity', in Table 14.1. Two ways of configuring seats in the available space are listed. First a typical seating plan with three classes (for example, Economy, Business and First) allows the aircraft to take 525 passengers. Another configuration with all seats as Economy allows 853 passengers. This latter figure is a highly unlikely configuration, as this long-haul aircraft is designed for a mixed mode operation and advertised as providing space and comfort.

Using the data on fuel capacity together with this data on passenger capacity, it is possible to calculate how much fuel might be consumed per 100 km for each passenger. This is a more useful measure of fuel consumption than the 2040 litres per 100 km you calculated in Activity 14.6 as it allows comparison between the fuel consumptions of the A380 and of other aircraft which have different passenger and fuel capacities. It also allows comparison with other modes of transport, on road and rail for example, as you will see shortly. Finally, note that fuel consumption is also one measure of the environmental impact of air travel. Of course, this impact could be allocated to each flight but it might also be useful to focus on individual passengers' environmental impact.

Example 14.1   Calculating fuel consumption per passenger

Consider an A380 with a maximum seating capacity of 853 passengers which is full, on a flight over its maximum range (15 700 km) with full fuel tanks (320 000 litres). Calculate the fuel consumption per passenger per 100 km.

Solution

In Activity 14.6 you calculated the fuel consumption for the A380 at 2040 l per 100 km. With 853 passengers, the average fuel consumption per passenger is therefore $\frac{2040}{853} = 2.39$ litres per passenger per 100 km.

This gives an estimate of the *minimum* fuel consumption for the A380 per passenger per 100 km, since the calculation assumed a maximum flight distance and maximum number of passengers. It did not include allowance for take-off and landing at stopovers which might use significant amounts of fuel. You will now calculate a more realistic figure for fuel consumption based on typical seating of passengers configured in three classes.

Activity 14.7

For a typical seating capacity of passengers on an A380, calculate the average fuel consumption in litres per passenger per 100 km. As before, assume that the aircraft has a full complement of passengers, and takes a flight for its maximum range (15 700 km) with full fuel tanks (320 000 litres).

To obtain more realistic estimates of fuel consumption, it would be necessary to have detailed data on the fuel consumed during different phases of flight such as take-off, landing and cruising. This is precisely the type of data that is essential for an airline customer when making decisions on buying or leasing an aircraft to use on its routes.

Activity 14.8

Identify two factors that a designer should take into account when estimating the likely fuel consumption of the A380 for a long-haul flight of 15 000 km with two stopovers.

For an airline making decisions on which aircraft to use on particular routes, data on factors such as refuelling and passenger occupancy will be essential. Relevant data might include fuel consumed at take-off under different take-off weights, and average occupancy of seats for different routes.

With fuel as a major cost, accurate calculations are vital for airlines making decisions on which aircraft to buy or lease. This accuracy can then be used by airlines to consider their own models of operation, for example, how busy they might expect a particular flight to be.

Activity 14.9

Assuming that the occupancy for an A380 is 70% of the typical seating configuration, what will the minimum fuel consumption be per passenger per 100 km?

This subsection on design for service has concentrated on fuel consumption as an example. It has indicated the types of in-service calculations designers might undertake on products. These characteristics are key to the performance of a product or design in service and as such are particularly relevant for potential customers. Designers will, as they conceive and develop new products, assess their designs carefully against such service measures. Calculations of this type are a vital element of designing.

14.2.4   Limitations

Design process models are useful but they represent *idealised* design processes that are rarely seen in reality. Do not take these models literally and expect them to work perfectly. In fact, the real value of these models is to present a generalised process, not specific actions and activities. Care is required not to confuse these two aspects of design – individual actions in a part of a process do not necessarily lead to success at the project level. There are no simple design process recipes that can be followed for predictable results every time.

Many people make this mistake and invest significantly in process models that allow very little creativity or adaption to suit the needs of a project. Good design management is about being aware of this and having the ability to adapt and change the process as and when it is necessary to do so, but to also realise when it would be inappropriate.

The main lesson to take from this is that there is no substitute for some common sense and a bit of critical and creative thinking when it comes to managing any complex design project.

14.3   Analytical and design processes

In Chapter 3 you were introduced to a cycle for creating a mathematical model. In this chapter you have seen the basic creative design cycle. Both processes are examples of iterative procedures that repeat until some condition is met (Figure 14.14).

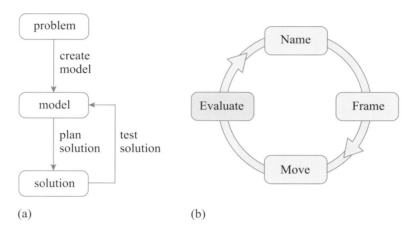

(a)   (b)

Figure 14.14   (a) The mathematical model creation cycle; (b) the basic problem-based design process

However, there is a critical difference between these two processes. Recall that one of the key aspects of the creative design cycle was that it can consider the context of the problem itself, not just the problem in isolation. This is what makes it valuable to the design process. It is precisely the opposite that is valuable with the mathematical modelling cycle. In that process a very specific problem is considered and either solved or not solved. Success is either achieved or not achieved.

This does not mean that problem solving and creative processes can't go together – in fact they complement one another well precisely because of how they each work. For example, a creative cycle might use a problem cycle to confirm solutions. Similarly, a problem cycle might fail to derive a suitable solution and have to expand within a creative cycle.

This is a vital conceptual link to make in your mind because it links two critical design engineering processes, meaning you can interchange and mix them as part of the wider design process. These can also be used in two ways:

- as iterations of the process itself
- as a means to check that one phase can move into another.

In fact, this is one of the foundations of the best design engineering – the most appropriate methods are employed at the right times to make progress in the project. This section and the remainder of Part 2 look at examples of how mathematical methods are applied to design, starting with iteration itself as a mathematical process.

14.3.1   Dots instead of lines

You saw briefly in the previous chapter how vectors can be used in computer-aided design (CAD) software to assist the designer, and some examples were given of applying this to geometry. Most modern design software can perform even more complex analyses to assist the designer with other aspects of the project. Figure 14.15 shows software illustrating the stresses in a component being designed, where the different colours represent different ranges of stress. Now, instead of changing only the surface of the model, the designer can 'see' the properties of the design and manipulate the model to suit those.

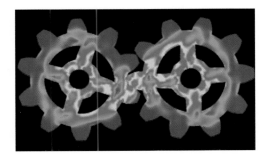

Figure 14.15   Finite element model of a component – in this case, a pair of gears. The colours indicate the stress at different points.

If you were to model these kinds of systems manually, it would take many hours of calculation. But the basic model underlying the computer analysis is very simple and relies on a process of repeated calculation, which is another form of iteration.

For the gears in Figure 14.15 the virtual object is divided into smaller pieces, or elements. Each element is then modelled by taking a starting point, seeing how it changes in response to a change in conditions, and then feeding that change back in to start the process again. Doing this repeatedly with lots of elements produces the complex and useful representation shown, which can inform valuable design decisions.

This basic process of iteration is represented in Figure 14.16. You start with a number (e.g. the stress of a part of a cog at the start); apply some rule to that number (e.g. to change the stress); recalculate the new number (e.g. the new stress); then use that new number to repeat the process.

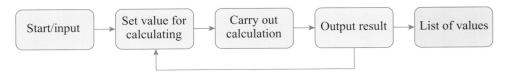

Figure 14.16   The basic process of mathematical iteration to calculate repeated changes

The useful feature of this process is that it uses a very simple set of rules that can be calculated quickly using a computer. When the calculations for all the small elements are put together, the overall results can be used in other ways to perform different analyses. This allows the design engineer to 'see' the effects of an aspect of a more complex system.

For example, a fire simulation can be used to work out how wide a corridor or stairwell needs to be for safety. In such a case, you are not interested in how *one* person behaves, but you need to know how *many* people are likely to travel in that direction in different periods of time. Being able to visualise the results of complex, iterative calculations allows you to do precisely that. Figure 14.17 shows two such mathematical models and their representations – one representation is a graph of results, and the other is a 3D representation of people moving.

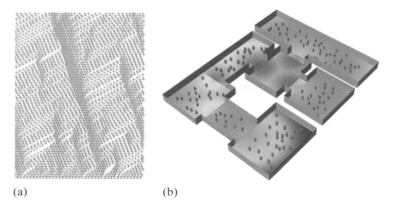

(a)   (b)

Figure 14.17 'Particle' simulations of: (a) cars speeding up and slowing down on a road (the *x*-axis shows the position of cars and the *y*-axis shows the successive time intervals); (b) people evacuating from a simulated fire in a building

These methods of analysis are useful in terms of saving time as well as providing the design engineer with different ways to view and think about their ideas. Mixing these techniques with the creative prototyping and decision-making techniques you have seen previously means that better decisions can be made earlier (and cost-effectively) in the design process. Being able to change a virtual building is far more practical, safer and cheaper than having to change the real thing.

14.3.2   Iteration using numbers

You will see further examples of how digital tools can assist the design engineer in the final chapters. Before that, it's worth exploring the mathematics behind iteration and adding that to your maths toolkit. Iteration is particularly suited to practical and applied situations – here are some examples.

Interesting iteration …

Interest calculations for banks and investments are based on an iterative calculation. A sum of money you put in is used to calculate the interest you should receive. This interest is now your money, in addition to the original amount. So in the following year, the next calculation will be based on the new (larger) amount.

As with any problem of this nature, setting it out clearly can help you to think about it. You could try using some of the methods from Chapter 10 and the online study materials.

You might start with a list to set out the process.

1   Start with a number (say £100.00). This is now the INPUT.
2   Take the INPUT and:

- ○   work out what interest on the INPUT will be
- ○   add that to the INPUT to get the OUTPUT.

3   Write down the OUTPUT.
4   Use the OUPUT to be the INPUT in the next iteration.
5   Go back to step 2 and iterate.

(Stop when you get too tired or run out of paper.)

Or you might use a diagram:

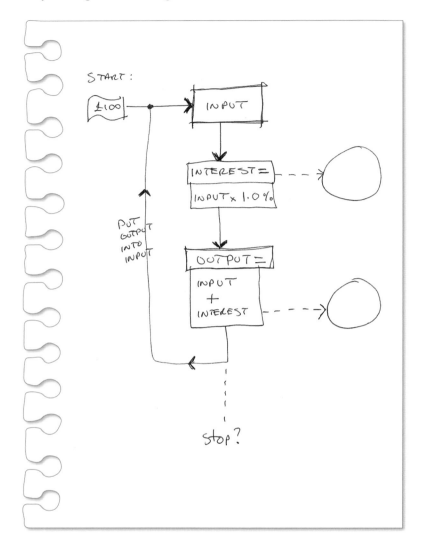

Figure 14.18   Diagram of an iterative process for calculating interest

Or you might use a table:

Table 14.2 Using a table to calculate interest iteratively

Iteration number	Input (£)	Calculate interest	Add interest to input	Output (£)
START	100.00			
1	100.00	100.00 × 1% = 1.00	100.00 + 1.00	101.00
2	101.00	101.00 × 1% = 1.01	101.00 + 1.01	102.01
3	102.01	102.01 × 1% = 1.02	102.01 + 1.02	103.03
4	103.03	103.03 × 1% = 1.03	103.03 + 1.03	104.06
5	104.06			
6				
7				
8				

Activity 14.10

Complete Table 14.2 by continuing the calculations.

How much money would you have at the end of Year 8?

(Note: if you see a pattern forming in this table, pause to note down some thoughts – this is discussed later in this chapter.)

If you felt frustrated by having to complete Table 14.2 manually, then spare a thought for the people who had to do this sort of calculation before computers became available – and they had to get it right!

Creepy iteration ...

Consider the following specific engineering example of iteration in practice. In materials and mechanical engineering, the properties of a material can change over time simply because the material is being used. One example of this is a material property called **creep**, which is the tendency of a solid material to deform slowly or permanently when subjected to repeated mechanical stress.

For example, an elastic band doesn't stretch and contract at exactly the same rates. If you hang a weight from elastic, it can take a few seconds to fully stretch to the extended position but will return to the original length more quickly.

In addition, the band will lose its elasticity over time because when it is stretched, its material properties are changed very slightly – each time it's stretched, it never quite recovers to exactly the same position.

So this is a system with an element that changes over time in three ways:

1 It behaves in an elastic manner and seems to bounce back to its original shape over short periods of time.
2 It doesn't stretch out as quickly as it springs back.
3 It also changes over very long periods of time depending on how many times it has been stretched.

From the design engineer's point of view, all of these behaviours are important.

1 The basic property of elastic to return (mostly!) to its original shape is very useful as a spring or shock absorber.
2 The fact that it is slower to stretch means that if the mechanical event is timed correctly, the elastic can also absorb energy and not act entirely like a spring (some of the energy will be converted to other forms; for instance, there may be a small rise in temperature).
3 The long-term performance needs to be known because it will eventually degrade and no longer operate as intended.

In many ways it is the 'unknown' or less obvious behaviours of this material that are important here. You can use common sense to see that elastic springs back, but your senses might not realise the second and third properties at all. This problem of 'knowing' is significant.

If you are designing a product with a lifespan of 10 years, the long-term effects and properties of a material that is subject to creep need to be considered. You need to know that all the components can achieve that same specification (or to consider the design of the maintenance to take account of such limitations).

Even for such a complex model, iteration can be used to explore the medium- and long-term behaviour. You can explore further how this might be approached mathematically in the online study resources.

14.3.3 Iteration versus solving

What iteration as a method cannot do is give a *complete* solution to the original problem. Using the method above to calculate interest, you would have to perform ten iterations to get to the tenth, say. For the creep example, as a design engineer you would ideally want to know what the extent of creep will be after thousands (maybe millions) of iterations, not one or two.

But you may have noticed a pattern emerging in the values coming from the interest example above. If you look carefully at the *difference* between the interest calculations, you will see that this varies by the same amount each time: the interest added is £1.00 in year 1, £1.01 in year two, £1.02 in year 3, etc. That means that you only need to know how many times you want to repeat the calculation and then do some multiplication to work out the correct amount.

So there is another way of finding a solution without having to go through many iterations and calculations to get there. In other words, there is an

analytical solution – one that can be worked out to give all possible solutions.

In fact, the formula for the compound interest A is

$A = D(1+r)^n$.

where

    A is the total amount, including interest

    D is the amount of money you started with

    r is the interest rate

    n is the number of years you want to calculate to.

So, for the interest example, you can substitute the numbers (starting amount $D = £100$ and interest rate $r = 0.01$) to give the formula

$A = 100(1.01)^n$.

To calculate how much money you have after 6 years, substitute

    $n = 6$

giving

    $A = £100 \times (1.01)^6$

    $A = £100 \times 1.0615$

    $A = £106.15$.

Activity 14.11

Use the formula to check your answers in Activity 14.10, to practise substituting numbers for symbols in an equation.

Calculate how much money you would have after 50, 100 and 150 years.

For some types of mathematical model, iteration might be a good start, but an analytical solution is much quicker. For others, there might not be an analytical solution so iteration is one of a few methods that can be used to find something out about possible solutions.

The real benefit of iteration in computing comes when dealing with very complex models that have no simple solutions. It is then necessary to rely entirely on iterative methods to find out anything. For example, the fire evacuation shown in Figure 14.17 is a very complex model that does not have simple solutions. In fact, it is a purely iterative model, where the rules of how particles interact depends on where the particles are at each step in the process. You can see this type of calculation operating in the intriguing mathematical simulation Conway's Game of Life (Figure 14.19).

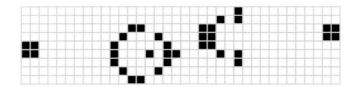

Figure 14.19 Image from Conway's Game of Life, where each cell either 'lives' or 'dies' depending on how many other cells are around it

For most complex, iterative methods, you can 'solve' the problem for one given starting point, but if you were to run the simulation again with a different starting point, you would get a very different answer.

As with design engineering itself, the process of using mathematics to create, test and use an analytical model is an iterative process requiring both creative and analytical thinking to get the most out of it.

Solutions to activities in Chapter 14

Solution to Activity 14.1

You may have written something like this:

(a) The design process is iterative, and if this iteration goes on too long, the project may run out of time and not meet a deadline (e.g. to present a design concept to the client or to go to manufacture).

(b) The design process can feel uncertain, and this might make people with no experience of the process nervous or unsure (e.g. a client might not understand why everyone isn't panicking!).

Solution to Activity 14.2

There is no right answer to this question, and you may have generated a very simple or very complex diagram. Both are absolutely fine, but consider the following points in relation to your answer:

- If your diagram was very simple, then you may have been thinking about the process overall. If so, can you think of specific actions you took within that wider process? For instance, you may have had a problem and come up with solutions – but how did you do that? Sketches? Thinking of ideas? Talking to someone? Writing down ideas?

- If your diagram was very complex, then you might have been thinking about the detail of the process – perhaps what you did at each step. If so, can you group together individual activities and elements to make large ones? For example, you may have come up with lots of ideas using a number of different methods – could these be grouped together into one creative phase? Or perhaps you had two distinct creative phases – if so, what was different about them?

Solution to Activity 14.3

The following are a few examples of pros and cons. You may have come up with very different ones, especially if you chose to use a specific project. Try to see whether your points were generally similar.

Stage-gate process

Pros	Cons
• Quick decision making is possible • Good certainty between phases	• If the wrong criteria are used, a poor design might get through a gate • The time of checking a design is limited by the gate

Soft landings process

Pros	Cons
• Approval is by a broader consensus, meaning more people will have been involved and therefore are satisfied	• Approval is likely to take a lot longer, possibly delaying a phase if not controlled
• The time for checking is extended, meaning problems are more likely to be identified	• Non-approval could have an effect on two phases, not just one

Solution to Activity 14.4

Here a few examples you may have chosen:

- **Product family:** kettle, toaster, coffee machine, DVD player, fridge or cooker.

  For example, your kettle probably has almost exactly the same functional parts as many other kettles – they all have to have a heating element, a thermostat, a switch, etc. So there is a good chance this is from a product family.

- **Product platform:** desktop computer

  For example, many desktop computers have standard arrangements and systems inside to allow the swapping or replacement of components. They also have some standard connections on the outside.

Solution to Activity 14.5

A full load of fuel will have a mass of

$$320\,000 \times 0.8 \, \text{kg} = 256\,000 \, \text{kg} = 256 \, \text{tonnes}.$$

The 'maximum take-off weight' is 560 tonnes, and the full fuel load is 256 tonnes, so the percentage of the total due to the fuel is

$$\frac{256}{560} \times 100\% = 45.7\% \text{ to 1 dp.}$$

Solution to Activity 14.6

Fuel consumption in $1 \, \text{km}^{-1}$ is

$$\frac{320\,000 \, \text{litres}}{15\,700 \, \text{km}} = 20.4 \, \text{l km}^{-1}.$$

So the consumption in litres per 100 km is

$$20.4 \, \text{l km}^{-1} \times 100 = 2040 \, \text{litres per 100 km}.$$

Solution to Activity 14.7

The fuel consumption for the A380 was previously calculated to be 2040 litres per 100 km. With 525 passengers, the average per passenger is:

$$\frac{2040}{525} = 3.89 \text{ litres per passenger per 100 km.}$$

Solution to Activity 14.8

With two stopovers (requiring three take-offs) refuelling is likely to be necessary, as it's already close to the maximum range of 15 700 km. Therefore refuelling below full capacity may be possible at each stopover. A first factor to take into account is to reduce the amount of fuel carried at take-off. As this reduces total aircraft weight at take-off, it will also reduce overall fuel consumption. But there will be associated costs in refuelling, including time.

A second factor is that the aircraft is unlikely to be full to capacity. This will mean a reduced payload, with less fuel used at take-off.

Solution to Activity 14.9

The consumption per passenger per 100 km operating at typical seating capacity (525 passengers) was calculated previously as 3.89 litres per passenger per 100 km. At 70% occupancy, the fuel consumption increases to

$$3.89 \times \frac{100}{70} = 5.56 \text{ litres per passenger per 100 km.}$$

(This is 5.55 litres per passenger per 100 km if you used the more accurate, unrounded, figure from the previous calculation.)

Solution to Activity 14.10

Table 14.2 (solution)

Iteration number	Input (£)	Calculate interest	Add interest to input	Output (£)
START	100.00			
1	100.00	1.00	100.00 + 1.00	101.00
2	101.00	1.01	101.00 + 1.01	102.01
3	102.01	1.02	102.01 + 1.02	103.03
4	103.03	1.03	103.03 + 1.03	104.06
5	104.06	1.04	104.06 + 1.04	105.10
6	105.10	1.05	105.10 + 1.05	106.15
7	106.15	1.06	106.15 + 1.06	107.21
8	107.21	1.07	107.21 + 1.07	108.28

Solution to Activity 14.11

For 50 years:

$$A = £100 \times (1.01)^{50}$$
$$A = £100 \times 1.6446$$
$$A = £164.46.$$

For 100 years:

$$A = £100 \times (1.01)^{100}$$
$$A = £100 \times 2.7048$$
$$A = £270.48.$$

For 150 years:

$$A = £100 \times (1.01)^{150}$$
$$A = £100 \times 4.4484$$
$$A = £444.84.$$

Part 2: Chapter 15   Design
materials

Introduction

In previous chapters you have seen the importance of being able to translate aspects of design projects into forms that can be analysed. Here you will look in more detail at how some of these analytical models can be used in practice.

To do this you first have to know a bit about knowing! How is it you can say that a cable is strong enough? What does strong actually mean? What does it mean that a component can last so many repeated movements? Or that a rechargeable battery will perform so many charging cycles?

To make these claims, each of which is vital in design engineering, you need to know how good the knowledge you have actually is. In this chapter you will look at three ways of knowing something about materials in engineering. Each of these ways of knowing is a valid and useful way of understanding something in a design engineering context. But, as always, it is using these methods in the most appropriate way that makes them valuable in the process. Later, you will see how useful graphs can be in representing, analysing and modelling material properties.

15.1   Material characteristics

The history of design engineering is filled with people who experimented with what they knew (or thought they knew). Generally this knowledge was sufficient and was developed by incremental innovation, allowing change to take place slowly and safely. Where this change was much faster, or the knowledge was being explored and pushed to its limits, there were failures, such as Beauvais Cathedral, mentioned in Chapter 10.

A notable exception in that same chapter is Brunel's Clifton Suspension Bridge, where practical and experiential understandings of the structure came together to create a successful outcome. It was the bringing together of different types of knowledge that allowed Brunel to innovate so successfully. Combining knowledge from experience, testing and systematic experiment that allows theories to be developed is something that is central to modern design engineering.

15.1.1   Knowing through experience

The first method of knowing considered here is making use of your own senses, memory and knowledge, and how you apply that to a particular situation. Typically, you do this practically, using your senses to provide information about what is happening. Early engineering relied on this to a large extent, such as the dependence on the individual knowledge of blacksmiths to produce reliable products (Figure 15.1).

Figure 15.1   Early engineering depended on experiential and practical knowledge

Imagine you need to design and build a shelf. You might use a material that feels strong enough and would find this out by testing it directly – perhaps trying to bend it manually. You might then test it by placing it between two supports and applying a mass to it, a form of design prototyping. The immediate knowledge you gain from this is **experiential knowledge**, which can be a useful starting point for any design engineering process. This knowledge is probably also based on your memory and knowledge of the material or even a specific prior activity.

The shelf may seem quite a trivial problem to solve – but the process that leads to the solution *is* important because it can be scaled up to any structure. For example, you could think of the shelf as a beam supporting the floor of a building, or the arm of a hard disk drive, or the structure inside an aircraft wing. For each of these situations, what you need to do is understand how the structure might fail and then make sure it is designed to never meet those failure conditions.

These are the main steps you might go through, but remember that they are idealised steps in a process – very often you might not even be aware of doing this explicitly.

1   Think of ways the shelf will be used, the conditions under which it will have to operate, and how that will affect the system.
2   Think of ways the system could fail from these uses and conditions.
3   Design a solution that will never get close to the failure modes identified in step 2.

Go through that process to see how it works in a bit more detail, starting with step 1. The same kind of shelf that you saw in Chapter 4 will be used as an example, as in Figure 15.2. Focus on the shelf itself – a simply supported slab of material – not the fixings.

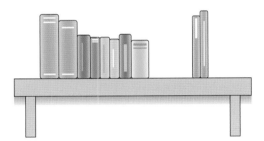

Figure 15.2   The shelf from Chapter 4 – an unfixed, simply supported slab of material

Activity 15.1

Think about several ways in which the shelf might be used, and try to describe these.

It's good to get the basic uses down first, but don't just think about the normal condition of the shelf (when it's loaded).

Think about the activity of loading and unloading it. Think about reasonably normal activities that might cause extreme effects on the system.

A discussion of this activity will follow in the main text – but don't read on until you have considered this problem.

When considering how something will be used, it is not just the simple or 'normal' uses that you need to think about. The shelf being considered is intended to store or support objects, so you can expect that it will need to support a particular mass. You could even have a guess at how much that would be.

A mass placed on a shelf will exert a force on the shelf, equal to its weight. This is another example of a situation where the terms 'mass' and 'weight' tend to be used interchangeably in everyday life. You probably have a more instinctive feel for the mass of an object – for example, a standard paperback book has a mass of about 0.3 kg. But if you want to know what the force on the shelf is, it's the weight you need, which (assuming your shelf is on the Earth) will be about 3 N. Try to be clear in your own head of the difference between the two, even though you will be surrounded by examples of misuse!

So what sort of loads will the shelf need to support?

For example, for a pile of books you might estimate how many books might be stored and assume that the shelf will have to support them over a long period of time. This type of load is unlikely to change for long periods of time and is known as a **static load**. It is also likely to be spread across the length of the shelf, and this is known as a **distributed load**.

But the shelf could also be used to store other things – perhaps even heavier objects, or ones that place their weight in one area (not distributed as the books are). This is known as a **point load**.

Finally, moving loads have to be considered, such as when things are placed on the shelf. If an object is dropped on the shelf, the initial force applied will be greater because the object is moving, and needs to decelerate to zero. This moving or changeable load can be described as a **dynamic load**.

What you are doing when thinking through these situations is considering the structural and mechanical conditions under which the shelf will have to operate. In fact, you are considering the loading conditions of the shelf. For the shelf, the general examples shown in Table 15.1 will be used.

Table 15.1 Types of loads that can be applied to a shelf

Name of load	Description	Example
Distributed static load	The shelf will have to support a distributed force due to weights acting on it for long periods of time.	Books stored on the shelf for a year.
Point load	The shelf will have to support a localised force for long periods of time.	A heavy ornament object sitting on the shelf.
Dynamic load	The shelf will have to support some distributed and localised force in excess of normal for short periods of time.	A person pressing down on the shelf while adding or removing an object.

In reality it is very unlikely you would go to such trouble for a shelf! (However, a company that builds and sells shelves might do so, because they probably have to specify maximum loads for health and safety purposes.) Treat this as an example that lets you think about something using your own experience. The principles you are about to use apply to much larger structures too.

The main point is that experience is used to think about what properties the shelf will have to exhibit in order to avoid failing. To take it beyond simple experience, the ways in which it might fail have to be considered in greater detail.

Activity 15.2

List different ways the shelf might fail.

To help with this, consider each use condition outlined above and how these might lead to failures.

Remember, the focus is only on the ways the shelf itself could fail – not the connections or supports.

A discussion of this activity will follow in the main text – but don't read on until you have considered this problem.

Most failures will be due to weight (i.e. a force) being applied to the shelf. This weight might be applied too quickly or normally, or it might have an effect over a long period of time. The main causes of failure will be:

- The shelf breaks at some point along its length.
- The shelf cracks but does not break.
- The shelf bends but does not crack.
- The shelf bends but does so over a long period of time.

This provides several ways in which the shelf could fail so the next concern is ensuring that any design avoids each of these failure methods. Applying experience to the design at this stage would probably lead to a focus on how the shelf bends as weight is added to it. This bending is called **deflection** and it is measured by how much an element moves from its resting position. It is essentially a convenient way to think about **deformation** in a particular direction.

Some materials, under some conditions, are able to deflect (bend, twist, stretch, etc.) but then return to their original shape after the force causing the deformation has been removed. This is known as **elastic deformation**; you came across this property in Chapter 4. The opposite of this is **plastic deformation**, where the material does not return to its original shape after the force is removed. Many materials exhibit both types of behaviour, depending on how much they are deformed. Plastic deformation is more likely for higher values of load. You can try this for yourself by deforming a food or drink can – if you apply a little force it deforms but returns to its original shape when you let go, but apply greater force and it is permanently deformed (Figure 15.3).

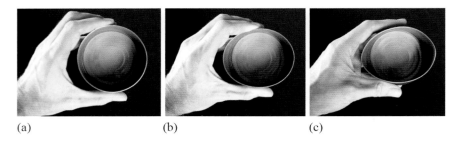

(a)   (b)   (c)

Figure 15.3   Elastic and plastic deformation of a food can: (a) original shape; (b) elastic deformation – can returns to original shape after force is removed; (c) plastic deformation – can remains in this shape even after the force is removed

For the design of a shelf it is usually desirable to have it undergo only elastic deformation, and even then only a moderate amount of this deformation. Because experience is being used, the deformation could be further estimated by adding weight to the shelf and watching it bend. You might even test this by 'adding' weight with your hands – perhaps to see how much movement is generated when you press down on the shelf. If the shelf deflects too much, the shelf design needs to be reconsidered – it is judged to be unstable, or not strong enough.

This has now become an iterative process where observations are used to determine whether a design is satisfactory. In other words, you are looking for a shelf design that avoids failure completely – that doesn't even come close to it. This process might be repeated for other failure criteria until a set of criteria for failure or success is generated.

Bending bridges

How a structure deflects, and how that deflection affects the material of the structure, is a vital consideration in engineering. All structures are designed to deal with deflection in some way since all objects are subject to changing forces when they are put to use. An extreme example is the suspension bridge. In 2015, the Forth Road Bridge was closed because of concern over the connections between the bridge deck and main vertical supports. The bridge was designed for a fraction of the traffic load and frequency it now experiences.

Figure 15.4   The Forth Road Bridge – unloaded and loaded

In order to see how the problem was developing, engineers used the process discussed here – they simply kept adding weight to the bridge to see what would happen. Figure 15.4 shows the unloaded and loaded bridge. The amount of deflection is most obvious if you look between the two main supports on the right-hand side of the picture. Engineers needed to add weight to the bridge in order to put stress into the joints that were the main problem. These loaded joints could then be measured in a variety of ways and compared to their unstressed condition. This comparison gives an idea of how well they are coping with continual and dynamic loads.

Can you suggest ways in which the engineers were able to load the bridge with 518 tonnes?

This method of experiential engineering is usually fine for shelves but there is a major problem associated with it. Different people will have very different experiences of what is strong. Different people also have very different attitudes and approaches to safety – some people might design a shelf that is only just stable, while others might design a shelf that could support a weight far in excess of that required (Figure 15.5).

Figure 15.5   Different perceptions of safety in design engineering

In engineering design you should aim to avoid these extremes. Experiential knowledge is a good starting point and it can tell you a lot, but in order to avoid extremes of design you need another way of 'knowing'.

15.1.2   Knowing through testing

To go beyond the limitations of relying on your own experience and beliefs, you need to be able to think a bit more systematically. One way to do this is to observe some measurable aspect of a situation and then use those measurements to infer something.

For example, for the shelf you could add known mass and observe what happens to the shelf each time. You could continue to do this until the shelf breaks, and then 'know' how many books the shelf will support before failure. This test can be repeated to confirm the first findings, thus providing more confidence about what is 'known'.

This approach does have to be quite carefully managed – for example, care is required to ensure specific, known mass is added each time until failure. Similarly, you would also want to test more than one shelf. The experiential method gave you information about only one shelf – with a testing method you want to say something about all shelves made using this material.

Consider the following simple experiment run to test a particular shelf material: corrugated cardboard. Five shelves were made and then tested to failure by applying loads to them as shown in Figure 15.6.

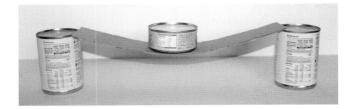

Figure 15.6 The cardboard shelf test setup, showing one can as a load

A few other conditions were applied to make the test consistent:

- The shelf was simply supported – i.e. it was not fixed at either end.
- Mass was added in 200 g (0.2 kg) increments using small food cans.
- 1 minute was allowed to elapse between placing the mass and deciding whether the shelf remained stable.
- Only the number of cans at the point of catastrophic failure is relevant, and this failure happens when the shelf folds or collapses. This is the failure load.

You may wish to try this experiment yourself using a similar setup and cans or some other standard mass. You might want to improve the experiment; for instance, smaller masses would give a more accurate result. If you do this, feel free to use your own data in the activity below

Using this setup, the data shown in Table 15.2 was obtained.

Table 15.2 Mass applied to generate a catastrophic failure in cardboard test shelves

Test number	Failure load (number of cans)	Notes
1	2	Failed as soon as the second can was placed.
2	2	Took about 20 seconds to fail.
3	3	Failed very quickly indeed – as soon as the third can was placed.
4	1	Took nearly a minute to fail.
5	2	Took about 10 seconds to fail.

This data now needs to be analysed to see what can be learned from it.

Activity 15.3

(a) Calculate the median and average (mean) of the failure load, measured in cans.

(b) Calculate the mass added to the shelf at the point of failure (the 'failure mass') in kg (recall that 1 can has mass 200 g).

(c) Convert your failure mass to a failure load, measured in N. (Use $g = 10 \, \text{m} \, \text{s}^{-2}$. For such a rough experiment, this value is good enough, and makes the calculations much easier.)

(d) Based on this information, what value would you give for the failure load of these cardboard shelves?

(e) What problems do you think there are with this answer, for example its accuracy?

Making a claim about the mass a shelf can hold safely is actually quite difficult, and it is not only about the results obtained above. If this were a bridge, you would probably feel a bit nervous about setting the failure load at 4 N because you know that one test did fail at 2 N. If you went with the average, then about as many shelves will fail as will remain safe. But if you go with the minimum failure load, 2 N, how can you be sure that even this is safe, as you know that at least one shelf has failed at this load? How can you say that something is safe?

In reality, some margin of safety would be applied to these values, but how that is determined is beyond the scope of this module. For now, you may have already realised that another failure occurs long before the shelf collapses.

So far, the only failure considered has been an unrecoverable one: the shelf collapses as a result of the cardboard folding – a plastic deformation. This means the shelf will never be the same again and is known as a **catastrophic failure** for this particular structure (Figure 15.7).

Figure 15.7 Photograph showing catastrophic failure of the test shelf material

But you learned from the experiential method that the shelf should not bend too much either. That is, its deflection should not be so great that it does not perform well as a shelf – a straight, flat surface onto which items can be placed. Deflection that precludes this is another kind of failure – it's not about the design 'breaking', it's about the design not performing well enough for it to be used as it should be. If you look back at Figure 15.6, you can probably imagine that a shelf that deflects by this amount is not going to hold books properly.

This type of failure is a **performance failure**, and in structural design it is very often this mode of failure that matters more than any other. The London Millennium Footbridge mentioned in Chapter 10 was not a complete structural failure; it was really a performance failure. In other words, the bridge would not have collapsed (catastrophic failure), but people do not like walking on a bridge that sways too much (performance failure).

In many ways this takes us back to the very start of Part 2 – what conditions, constraints and considerations must be taken into account in order to judge a project a success? If these have been set out well and applied correctly, then everything should be fine, and very often the design engineer can rely on standards to help with this for normal situations. But sometimes a design engineer has to define the parameters under which such conditions, constraints and considerations can be judged.

15.1.3 Knowing through experiment

From the previous test, you now have some knowledge from testing a few cardboard shelves and you probably have a good idea that a single sheet of cardboard is not going to be enough to fulfil its function. From the structural principles introduced in Chapter 12, you will know that it is probably sensible to concentrate on different *thicknesses* of shelf.

Consider a second experiment that simulates varying thickness by using multiple sheets of cardboard stacked (but not glued) on top of one another. This time, the thickness is changed and then tested to failure only once using as many cans as are required (Figure 15.8).

Figure 15.8 Experiment showing four layers of cardboard partway through testing

Similar conditions were applied to make the test consistent:

- The shelf was simply supported – i.e not fixed at either end.
- Mass was added in 200 g increments using the same type of can.
- 1 minute was allowed to elapse between placing the mass and deciding whether the shelf had remained stable.
- Only the failure load is relevant, as before.

From this experimental setup the following data was obtained.

Table 15.3   Table showing data from testing thicknesses of cardboard shelf

Sheets of cardboard	Card thickness (mm)	Failure load (number of cans)	Failure mass (kg)	Failure load (N)
1	2.5	2		
2	5.0	3		
3	7.5	4		
4	10.0	5		
5	12.5	6		

This data can now be explored to see what patterns might emerge, and this is easiest to do using graphical methods.

Activity 15.4

(a) Complete Table 15.3 by adding in the failure masses and the failure loads (take $g = 10\,\mathrm{m\,s^{-2}}$) .

(b) Plot the data on a graph, with the thickness in mm on the x-axis, and the failure load in N on the y-axis.

(c) What patterns, if any, do you think there might be?

There seems to be an interesting relationship between the thickness of the test shelf and the amount of load it can take before catastrophic failure (note that the relationship may have been different if the layers had been glued, or pinned together in some way). To explore this relationship further you need to know a bit more about the maths of lines and graphs, which you will look at in the next section.

15.2   Interpreting graphs: gradients

In this section you'll revise the mathematics of straight lines and learn how the properties of lines can provide useful information about real situations.

Even if you are confident about using this maths, go through this section to make sure you have a good understanding of how it can be applied in practice. It's the application that is of interest here, not just the maths. As always, the online study resources provide additional chances to practise.

15.2.1   Gradients of straight lines

The **gradient** of a straight line is a measure of how steep it is. To understand what gradient means, imagine tracing your pen tip along a straight line. The gradient (or slope) of the line is the number of units that your pen tip moves up for every *1 unit* that it moves to the right. For example, the line in Figure 15.9(a) has gradient 2.

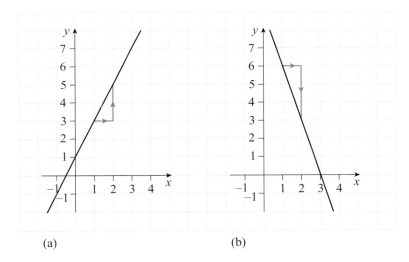

(a)   (b)

Figure 15.9   Straight lines with gradients (a) 2 and (b) −3

If you imagine tracing your pen tip along the line in Figure 15.9(b), you can see that it will move down, rather than up, as it moves to the right. It will move down by 3 units for every 1 unit that it moves to the right. A movement of 3 units down can be thought of as a movement of −3 units up. So your pen tip moves up by −3 units for every 1 unit that it moves to the right, hence the gradient of this line is −3.

It's helpful to remember the following:

- A line that slopes up from left to right has a positive gradient.
- A line that slopes down from left to right has a negative gradient.

Activity 15.5

By thinking about moving your pen tip along each of the lines below, and counting how many units it would move up or down for each unit it moves to the right, write down the gradients of the following lines.

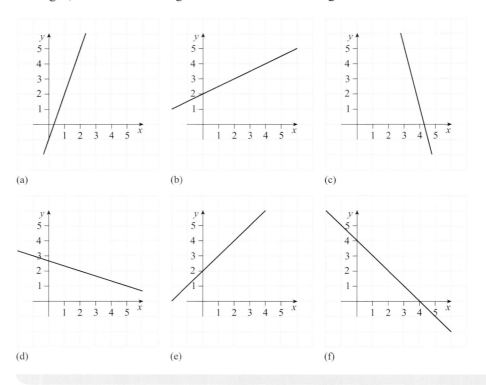

(a) (b) (c)

(d) (e) (f)

Lines with large positive or negative gradients, such as 10, 50, −10 or −50, are steeper than those with smaller positive or negative gradients, such as 1, 0.5, −0.5 or −1. This fact can be expressed more neatly by using the idea of the magnitude of a number, which is its value without any minus sign, if it has one. (You encountered this idea before when dealing with vectors.) For example, the magnitudes of 5 and −5 are both 5. The magnitude of a number is often referred to as its size, **modulus** or **absolute value**. The greater the magnitude of the gradient of a line, the steeper the line.

A horizontal line has a gradient of 0, but you can't calculate the gradient of a vertical line, so it is said to be 'undefined'.

When the coordinate axes have equal scales (that is, when the distance representing one unit is the same for both the horizontal and vertical axes), a line with gradient 1 or −1 makes an angle of 45° with the horizontal axis, as shown in Figure 15.10. So a line whose gradient has magnitude greater than 1 makes an angle of more than 45° with the horizontal axis, and a line whose gradient has magnitude less than 1 makes an angle of less than 45° with the horizontal axis. Remember, this is only true if the coordinate axes have equal scales.

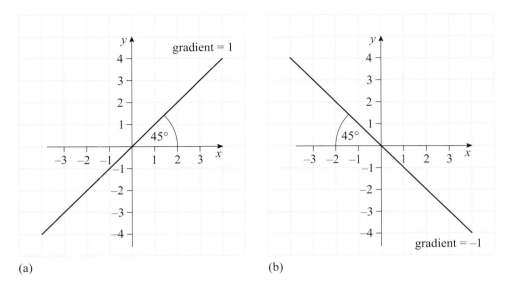

(a)   (b)

Figure 15.10   Lines with gradient (a) 1 and (b) −1

15.2.2   Calculating gradients

You can calculate the gradient of a straight line by choosing any two points on the line, and proceeding as follows.

1   Choose one of the two points (it doesn't matter which) to be the 'first point', and the other point to be the 'second point'.

2   Find the number of units by which x increases as you trace your pen tip from the first point to the second point. This is known as the **run** from the first point to the second point.

3   Find the number of units by which y increases as you trace your pen tip from the first point to the second point. This is known as the **rise** from the first point to the second point.

4   If x or y (or both) actually decreases as you trace your pen tip from the first point to the second point, then the run or rise (or both) is negative.

5   Once you have found the run and rise from the first point to the second point, you can calculate the gradient as follows:

$$\text{gradient} = \frac{\text{rise}}{\text{run}}.$$

For example, in Figure 15.11(a) the run is 4 and the rise is 2, whereas in Figure 15.11(b) the run is −1 and the rise is 3.

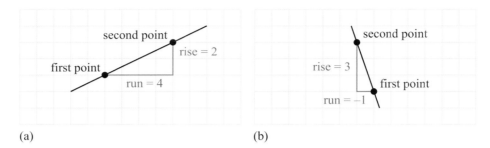

(a)   (b)

Figure 15.11   (a) and (b) are two examples showing the run and rise from one point to another

You can calculate the gradient of the line in Figure 15.11(a) as

$$\frac{\text{rise}}{\text{run}} = \frac{2}{4} = \frac{1}{2},$$

and the gradient of the line in Figure 15.11(b) as

$$\frac{\text{rise}}{\text{run}} = \frac{3}{-1} = -3.$$

This method for calculating the gradient of a line can be expressed as a formula in terms of the coordinates of the two points on the line. Here, the first and second points will be referred to as (x_1, y_1) and (x_2, y_2), respectively.

Using this notation,

$$\text{run} = x_2 - x_1 \quad \text{and} \quad \text{rise} = y_2 - y_1.$$

So

$$\text{gradient} = \frac{\text{rise}}{\text{run}} = \frac{y_2 - y_1}{x_2 - x_1}.$$

As you have seen previously, subscripts are being used here to indicate particular values of variables. So x_1 and x_2 represent particular values of x, and y_1 and y_2 are particular values of y. Be careful not to confuse x_2 with x^2, for example.

Although it doesn't matter which point on the line you choose to be (x_1, y_1) and which to be (x_2, y_2) when you use the formula above, it is important to take them the same way round in both the numerator and the denominator.

Activity 15.6

Consider the following diagram.

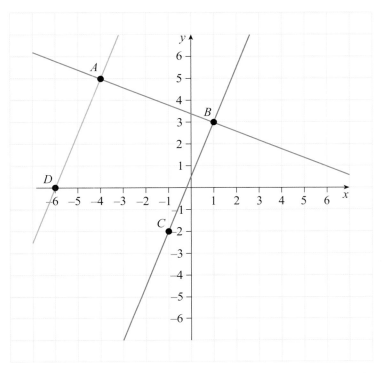

(a) Write down the coordinates of the points A, B, C and D.

(b) Use the formula for gradient to calculate the gradients of the lines that pass through the following pairs of points:

(i) A and B; (ii) A and D; (iii) B and C.

Just as it doesn't matter which points you choose in order to calculate the gradient, the units of measurement do not matter either *as long as they are consistent*. For example, you could be looking at the gradient of a line that shows the relationship between mass and length, in which mass is in kilograms and length is in millimetres. As long as the units are consistent (i.e. you don't mix millimetres with metres on the same axis), the gradient can be calculated.

What this also means is that the gradient itself will have units – in this case derived units (which you first came across in Chapter 3). The units are shown in the following calculation to demonstrate this. As you have seen before, it is often helpful to include units in your calculations, but in general it's not essential as long as you state them (carefully!) in the final answer.

Example 15.1 The gradient of a line using units

Calculate the gradient of the line shown below.

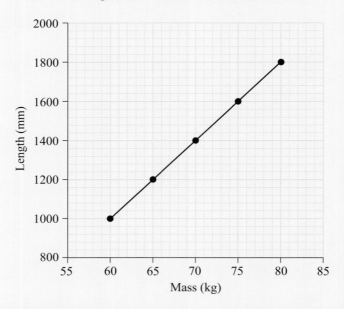

Figure 15.12 Graph showing relationship between mass (kg) and length (mm)

Solution

The gradient can be calculated using $\text{gradient} = \dfrac{\text{rise}}{\text{run}}$ as follows:

$$
\begin{aligned}
\text{gradient} \;&= \frac{(y_2 - y_1)}{(x_2 - x_1)} \\[2mm]
&= \frac{(1800 - 1000)\ \text{mm}}{(80 - 60)\ \text{kg}} \\[2mm]
&= \frac{800\ \text{mm}}{20\ \text{kg}} \\[2mm]
&= 40\ \text{mm kg}^{-1}.
\end{aligned}
$$

The gradient of the line is $40\ \text{mm kg}^{-1}$.

In this example the gradient has been calculated using the endpoints of the line. It isn't essential to choose these points, but it is a good idea to include as much of the line as possible when calculating the gradient, as this will usually give a more accurate result.

Now try the next activity.

Activity 15.7

A passive thermometer reports temperature by measuring the wavelength of electromagnetic radiation. Such a device was used to obtain the values in the graph below. What is the gradient of the line shown?

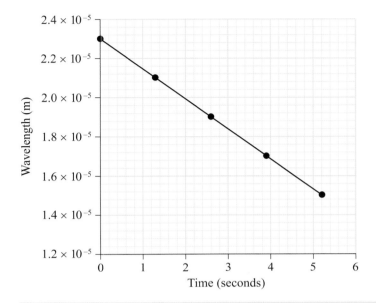

Here is a summary of the key points.

Finding the gradient (slope) of a straight line

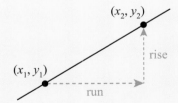

Figure 15.13   Finding the gradient of a straight line

Choose two points (x_1, y_1) and (x_2, y_2) on the line. Then use

$$\text{gradient} = \frac{\text{rise}}{\text{run}} = \frac{y_2 - y_1}{x_2 - x_1}.$$

The gradient of a vertical line is undefined.

A line that slopes up from left to right has a positive gradient.

A line that slopes down from left to right has a negative gradient.

A horizontal line has gradient 0.

If the axes have units that are different, then the gradient also has units. For example, if the units on the horizontal and vertical axes are seconds and metres, respectively, then the units for the gradient are $m\,s^{-1}$.

The setting out of your calculations is really important for this type of calculation. When you are working in design engineering, the numbers can often be very messy indeed so you have to be exceptionally careful to ensure you keep track of units, powers and operations.

If you find yourself making mistakes, then try to use more steps (don't try to do too much in one line of calculation). It's far better to have more correct steps than fewer incorrect ones.

15.2.3   Interpreting gradient

In every area of engineering the interpretation of gradients can be useful and very often vital. When there is a relationship between two quantities (and especially a linear one), you can use a set of very useful methods and tools to say things about that relationship.

For example, Figure 15.14 shows a gauge used to measure water depth in a river or reservoir. The way water levels change over periods of time is vital information in the design of water systems, large structures or flood management systems.

Figure 15.14   A gauge used to measure the depth of a river

The graph below shows the depth of a river over a 6-hour period after heavy rainfall. Notice that the y-axis does not start at 0; there is no need to include lower values if the data does not require it. (An alternative convention is to start at 0 but to 'break' the axis; this is not generally recommended for engineering applications.)

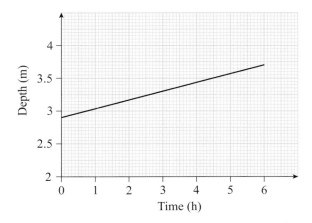

Figure 15.15   Graph showing the depth of a river over time

Being able to quickly read graphs such as this can be very useful. Looking at this graph you can immediately see that the line is rising to the right. By checking the horizontal and vertical scales (on the x- and y-axes) you should see that the information is presented in the usual way – lower values at the bottom left, higher values at the top right.

But it is also possible to be more precise about this by calculating the gradient. The points (0, 2.9) and (6.0, 3.7) lie on the line, so its gradient is

$$\frac{3.7 - 2.9}{6.0 - 0} = \frac{0.8}{6.0} = 0.13 \text{ m h}^{-1} \quad \text{(to 2 s.f.)}.$$

It is now possible to say something about this gradient and therefore about the water level: the gradient in this example measures the number of metres by which the river *changes* per hour. This specific example shows a positive gradient, with the river rising.

Activity 15.8

Graph (a) shows the distance travelled by a car plotted against the amount of fuel used. Graph (b) shows the distance travelled plotted against the time taken. For each graph, find the gradient and explain what it measures.

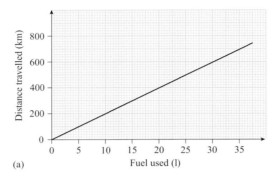

(a)

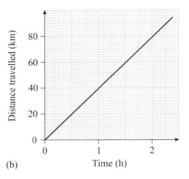

(b)

Activity 15.9

The figure below is an example of a real-life graph with a negative gradient. It shows the depth of the river in Figure 15.15 over an earlier 10-hour period.

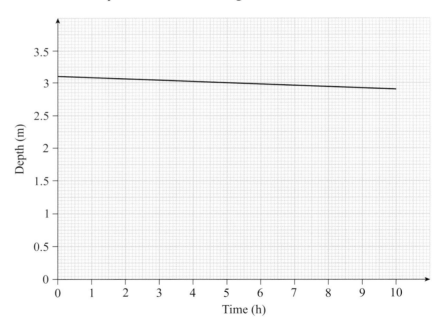

(a) Looking at the graph, describe what is happening to the river.

(b) Calculate the gradient of the line, and state what the gradient shows.

The following summarises what the sign of the gradient of a graph tells you.

Interpreting the sign of the gradient of a graph

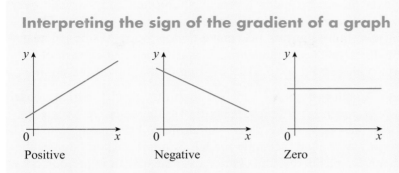

Positive   Negative   Zero

Figure 15.16 Diagrams of basic gradients

- A positive gradient indicates that the quantity on the vertical axis increases as the quantity on the horizontal axis increases.
- A negative gradient indicates that the quantity on the vertical axis decreases as the quantity on the horizontal axis increases.
- A zero gradient indicates that the quantity on the vertical axis remains constant as the quantity on the horizontal axis increases.

Sometimes when you want to model a situation, it is helpful to use a graph that consists of more than one straight line. For example, consider the graph in Figure 15.17. It shows the depth of the river in Figure 15.15, over an extended period.

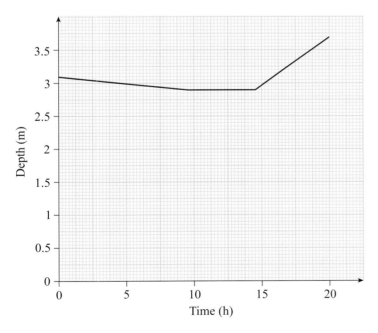

Figure 15.17 The depth of a river over a 20-hour period

The graph shows that in the first 9 hours the depth of the river fell from 3.1 m to 2.9 m, over the next 5 hours it remained constant at 2.9 m, and over the final 6 hours, after some heavy rain, its depth increased to 3.7 m. The gradients of the three line segments that make up the graph can be calculated in the usual way. Each of these gradients indicates the rate of change of the depth of the river with respect to time during one of the three time periods.

It is likely that the graph in Figure 15.17 is a simplified model, perhaps based on only four measurements, at 0 hours, 9 hours, 14 hours and 20 hours. If more measurements had been taken, then it might have been possible to use a curved graph to provide a more accurate model. Similarly, when large-scale groundwater design is considered, the change over several time periods is considered. For example, in the UK, surface water drainage design has to consider several time period cycles (e.g. 1, 10, 30 and 100 years) in order to make effective design decisions. Being able to quickly and accurately interpret gradients visually and analytically is a very efficient way of communicating such complex information.

15.3 Modelling materials

In addition to gradients, line graphs have several other useful features. So far you have focused on the measured data representing the *x* and *y* values. But the line itself is also a useful object that can be used to say something beyond the measured data. The lines drawn using these methods are geometrical *and* algebraic, meaning that they can represent more than just individual data points.

As you will see in the next chapter, this is one of the foundations of modern maths and is also one of the most important concepts in all fields of engineering. Essentially, if you can draw a defined shape, you can create some maths to model it. In other words, if you can draw it, you can work it out!

Of course, a bit of care is required to make sure that you know how to apply this. The chapter ends by looking at using these methods to complete the analysis of the cardboard shelf and consider the limitations and conditions that allow you to be confident in knowing something about the material.

15.3.1 Intercepts and checking points

The value of *x* where a line crosses the *x*-axis is called its **x-intercept**, and the value of *y* where it crosses the *y*-axis is called its **y-intercept**. For example, in Figure 15.18 the *x*-intercept is −3 and the *y*-intercept is 2.

Some mathematicians use the word 'intercept' to describe the point at which a line crosses an axis, rather than the value of the *x*- or *y*-coordinate there. They would say that the *x*- and *y*-intercepts in Figure 15.18 are (−3, 0) and (0, 2).

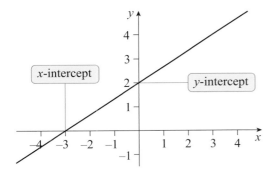

Figure 15.18 The *x*- and *y*-intercepts of a line

Using intercepts can be useful if there is confidence about the relationship revealed in the data. For example, it is often useful to consider what would happen if a straight line were extended, taking the relationship beyond what was actually tested or known. Doing this can reveal other useful aspects of linear relationships.

This technique can be especially useful for some physical properties where negative and positive values are required, such as temperature – something that has a significant effect on the performance of structures and mechanical systems. Measuring temperature in Celsius also gives us a very convenient zero point (freezing point of water) that can be used as a common reference point in practical situations.

As an example, consider the deflection of the Forth Road Bridge pictured in Figure 15.19. The bridge deck also changes height according to temperature: when it is warm, the bridge deck expands and this has a slackening effect on the whole structure, which in turn lowers the height of the deck above the water. Conversely, when the temperature reduces, the bridge deck contracts and raises the height of the deck above the water.

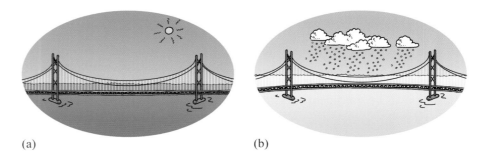

(a)   (b)

Figure 15.19   Exaggerated diagram showing how the Forth Road Bridge deforms at different temperatures: (a) when it is warm, the metal expands and the bridge deck lowers; (b) when it is cold, the metal contracts and the bridge deck is raised

The following table shows two measurements of the height of the bridge deck and the temperature when this height was measured. This height is the surveyed height above sea level in the UK, measured in the middle of the main span.

Table 15.4   Deflection on the Forth Road Bridge

Temperature (°C)	Bridge deck height above mean sea level (m)
9	64.6
4	64.8

Assuming this relationship is linear, these points can be plotted and the line extended to find out the height at freezing point. This freezing point will also occur at an x- or y-intercept because the temperature is 0 at this point. See Figure 15.20.

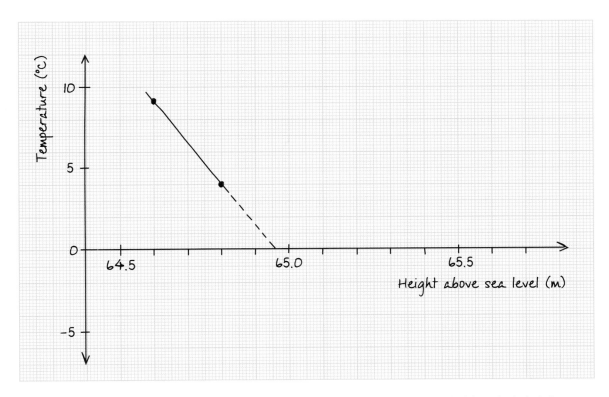

Figure 15.20 Graph showing the relationship between temperature and bridge deck height

Extending the line gives a result of about 64.95 m at 0 °C. That is, the height of the bridge deck rises by about 0.35 m or 350 mm when the temperature reduces by 9 °C. Try extending this data further to consider another temperature range in the next activity.

Activity 15.10

Have a look at Figure 15.20 and extend this relationship further to determine the bridge deck height when the temperature is −10 °C.

This line now represents an overall temperature difference of 19 °C. What is the overall difference in height?

On average, a temperature difference of 25 °C can represent a height change of over 1.0 m for the midpoint of the Forth Road Bridge, an incredible variation when you consider the other dynamic and static loads that it also has to deal with. Clearly, bridge design engineers need to think about a lot of movement.

Of course, you have to be very careful that this sort of extension of a graph makes sense. For example, if this were the relationship between the height and mass of a child, then it makes no sense to have length of 0 mm or even negative values! But because the bridge is a physical object, and how it operates is understood, the negative values (and the 0 value) make sense in terms of displacement. In other words, the application of extending this line has been checked and it is fine to do this, at least over the limited temperature range considered here.

Similarly, it is very easy to be fooled by apparently linear relationships – most relationships in engineering are not so simple. For example, the real relationship between height and mass in people is partly curved and partly straight. But where even part linear relationships are found, using the methods presented here can be very useful to begin to understand the overall relationship.

15.3.2   Modelling shelves

Returning to the cardboard shelf, what more can be said about it with these new techniques? You saw that in this case there seemed to be a linear relationship between the thickness and the failure load, and it is now possible to make a quantitative statement about that.

Activity 15.11

(a) Calculate the gradient of the graph you created for the data in Table 15.3 (in Activity 15.4).

(b) What does the gradient tell you about the shelf?

From the shelf experiment, there appears to be a linear relationship between the thickness and failure load of the shelf. As the thickness of the shelf is increased, the failure load also increases. These increases seem to be proportional to one another; that is, for an increase of 1 mm shelf thickness, there is a corresponding increase in the failure load of 0.8 N.

This is very useful information to know about this material and it can be applied in a range of different contexts. It is also possible to extend the line further and imagine how stacked sheets of this material would behave beyond the specific circumstances tested.

Activity 15.12

Assume that the relationship between thickness and failure load is linear. Extend your graph of the data in Table 15.3 to go up to 10 sheets of cardboard. You can either extend your existing graph or redraw it.

What is the predicted failure load of 10 sheets of cardboard?

Extending the line in this way allows you to extend the relationship between the thickness and failure load. But great care has to be taken when you do things like this – you have to be very careful about what you can know.

15.3.3 Being careful with knowing

The extension of the line in the previous section made two huge assumptions: that the relationship was perfectly linear; and that this relationship continues indefinitely. This might not be entirely true since only a limited number of shelves have been tested.

At a practical level this information might be useful under those conditions provided that they are stated and applied carefully. In other words, as long as the shelf thickness is between 2.5 mm and 12.5 mm and the layers are not fixed together, it would be acceptable to relate this to the failure load. **Interpolation** is the name given to the process of using a set of paired data to estimate a new data point within the range of the known data points. Beyond these limits it is less certain, but only because this has not been tested.

But there is a second use this data could be put to – it could set the *conditions* of tests to see if a theory about a relationship is correct. For example, the graph could be extended further to extrapolate what the failure load of a shelf of 50 mm would be, as shown in Figure 15.21. **Extrapolation** is the process of using a set of paired data to estimate a new data point that is *outside* the range of the known data points.

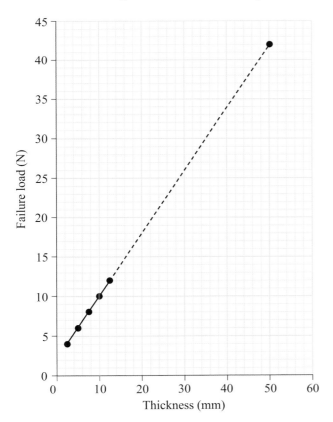

Figure 15.21 Extended graph showing point at 50 mm thickness

This could then be tested to see whether or not the value measured was the same as that extrapolated. For example, if the failure load measured for

50 mm thickness was 42 N, then that would support the idea that the linear model can be extended.

Activity 15.13

What might you conclude if the failure load values measured for a 40 mm shelf were (a) 30 N, (b) 34 N, (c) 72 N?

Modelling and tests such as these are carried out under very careful conditions for some of the most common materials and material products. The rigour required for advanced materials testing is beyond most companies, and may be carried out in collaboration with universities or specialist research centres, as you saw in the previous chapter. The information gained from such testing is readily available from a range of sources, such as British Standards (see Chapter 9). Without such knowledge the uncertainty would be too great and the risks of failure unacceptable.

Even for materials that are quite varied and complex, such as timber, there has to be some way of understanding their properties analytically. For example, there is a British Standard for timber strengths and performance (see box). Through years of testing and experience, sets of conditions for the use of timber have been developed, and this continues as new products and uses appear.

The knotty problem of timber

The material properties of timber can be found in a number of British Standards covering a range of subjects and properties, starting with BS EN 14081-1:2005 *Timber structures. Strength graded structural timber with rectangular cross section.* These Standards represent the general performance of certain timber types based on decades of testing and knowledge.

The basic strength of any timber depends on its density and hardness, which in turn depend on its species. Gradings for species of structural timbers are given in BS EN 1912:2012 *Structural timber. Strength classes. Assignment of visual grades and species.*

Timber is a natural material so it will exhibit significant variation, making it difficult to predict behaviour accurately. However, using statistical methods and allowing suitable margins means that usable information can still be obtained.

For example, using this information, suppliers can visually grade timber and the Standards provide guidance on how the main 'defects' in timber can affect the structural performance. Defects include: fissures; warp and wane; soft rot and dote; size and locations of knots; and the slope wood grain. Figure 15.22 shows some common defects in timber.

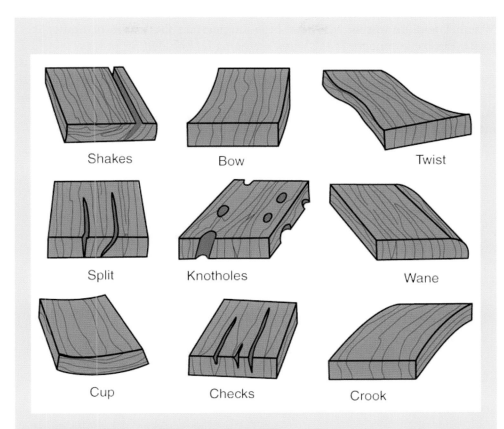

Figure 15.22 Common defects in timber

All these criteria can then be collected to give an overall strength grade that can be used by designers – a good example of using different types of knowledge and the techniques you have come across in the module so far.

The shelf experiment shows how material choice in design can be considered quantitatively. The conditions under which a material works depends on what you want it do and how its failure will be judged. But aspects of what you want it to do can be altered as part of the design process itself. In some ways, there is a trade-off, or negotiation, between what you want a material to do and what can be (realistically) achieved with it.

Of course, it is rarely the case that such a simple design decision can be made in isolation. In this particular example many other criteria might be more important than the material thickness – the aesthetics, recyclability, workability, etc. For example, a shelf product, such as one you might find in a furniture or DIY shop, would have aesthetics, buildability and manufacturing costs as some of the other key factors in its design.

Whether you are testing advanced high-temperature fan blades or timber joists, the basic process is the same mathematical modelling process introduced in Section 14.3 in the previous chapter. Starting with observations, you can develop and then test a model. Doing so allows you to be much more confident about what you 'know', and it is this process of knowing that is central to the use of standards in engineering. You will continue this modelling process in the next chapter.

Solutions to activities in Chapter 15

Solution to Activity 15.3

(a) The failure loads (in cans) are: 2, 2, 3, 1, 2.

The numbers in order are: 1, 2, 2, 2, 3, making the median 2.

The average is

$$\frac{2 + 2 + 3 + 1 + 2}{5} = 2 \text{ cans.}$$

(b) 2 cans have a mass of $2 \times 0.2 \text{ kg} = 0.4 \text{ kg}$.

(c) To find the failure load in N, the mass needs to be converted to weight. Failure load $= 0.4 \text{ kg} \times 10 \text{ m s}^{-2} = 4 \text{ N}$.

(d) From this data, the failure load is about 2 cans, which corresponds to a mass of 0.4 kg, and a weight of 4 N.

(e) The real value is actually somewhere between 1 and 2 cans, or 2 N and 4 N, if you look at the notes. It is probably closer to 2 N (perhaps 3 N?), but without more tests it would hard to be accurate about this. Some more tests with smaller increments of mass would help.

Solution to Activity 15.4

(a) The completed table is shown below.

Table 15.3 (solution)

Number of sheets	Card thickness (mm)	Failure load (number of cans)	Failure mass (kg)	Failure load (N)
1	2.5	2	0.4	4
2	5.0	3	0.6	6
3	7.5	4	0.8	8
4	10.0	5	1.0	10
5	12.5	6	1.2	12

(b) Your graph should look something like this:

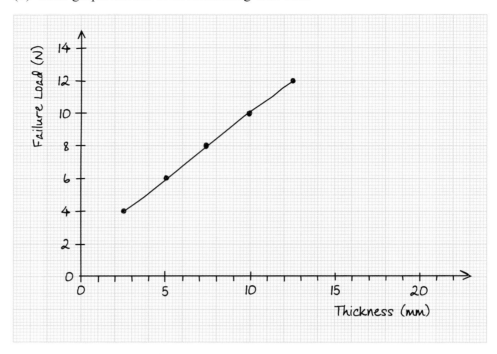

(c) When this data is plotted, a pattern seems to emerge – as the thickness is increased, the failure load also increases. In fact, it seems that these both increase together – in other words, there seems to be a linear relationship, so the failure load is directly proportional to the thickness.

Solution to Activity 15.5

(a) For every unit moved to the right, the pen tip moves up 3 units, so the gradient is 3.

(b) For every unit move to the right, the pen tip moves up $\frac{1}{2}$ unit, so the gradient is $\frac{1}{2}$.

(c) For every unit moved to the right, the pen tip moves down 4 units, so the gradient is -4.

(d) For every unit moved to the right, the pen tip moves down $\frac{1}{3}$ unit, so the gradient is $-\frac{1}{3}$.

(e) For every unit moved to the right, the pen tip moves up 1 unit, so the gradient is 1.

(f) For every unit moved to the right, the pen tip moves down 1 unit, so the gradient is -1.

Solution to Activity 15.6

(a) A is $(-4, 5)$; B is $(1, 3)$; C is $(-1, -2)$; D is $(-6, 0)$.

(b)

(i) For the gradient of the line through A and B, take A to be the first point and B the second:

$$\frac{y_2 - y_1}{x_2 - x_1} = \frac{3 - 5}{1 - (-4)} = \frac{-2}{5} = -\frac{2}{5}.$$

(ii) For the gradient of the line through A and D, take A to be the first point and D the second:

$$\frac{y_2 - y_1}{x_2 - x_1} = \frac{0 - 5}{-6 - (-4)} = \frac{-5}{-2} = \frac{5}{2}.$$

(iii) For the gradient of the line through B and C, take B to be the first point and C the second: $\dfrac{y_2 - y_1}{x_2 - x_1} = \dfrac{-2 - 3}{-1 - 1} = \dfrac{-5}{-2} = \dfrac{5}{2}.$

Solution to Activity 15.7

The gradient can be calculated as follows. Using the endpoints of the line to calculate the gradient is not essential, but is likely to give the most accurate result:

$$
\begin{aligned}
\text{gradient} &= \frac{(y_2 - y_1)}{(x_2 - x_1)} \\
&= \frac{(1.5 \times 10^{-5} - 2.3 \times 10^{-5})\,\mathrm{m}}{(5.2 - 0)\ \mathrm{s}} \\
&= \frac{-0.8 \times 10^{-5}\,\mathrm{m}}{5.2\ \mathrm{s}} \\
&= -1.54 \times 10^{-6}\ \mathrm{m\ s^{-1}}.
\end{aligned}
$$

Solution to Activity 15.8

(a) The points $(0, 0)$ and $(30, 600)$ lie on the line, so its gradient is

$$\frac{600\,\mathrm{km} - 0}{30\,\mathrm{l} - 0} = \frac{600\,\mathrm{km}}{30\,\mathrm{l}} = 20\ \mathrm{km\ l^{-1}}.$$

The gradient measures the number of kilometres travelled per litre of fuel. In other words, the gradient is the rate of fuel consumption.

(b) The points $(0, 0)$ and $(2, 80)$ lie on the line, so its gradient is

$$\frac{80\,\mathrm{km} - 0}{2\,\mathrm{h} - 0} = \frac{80\,\mathrm{km}}{2\,\mathrm{h}} = 40\ \mathrm{km\ h^{-1}}.$$

The gradient measures the number of kilometres travelled per hour. In other words, the gradient is the speed.

Solution to Activity 15.9

(a) The river depth is decreasing as time increases. Alternatively, over the past 10 hours the river depth has decreased.

(b) The points (0, 3.1) and (10, 2.9) lie on the line, so its gradient is

$$\frac{2.9\,\text{m} - 3.1\,\text{m}}{10\,\text{h} - 0} = \frac{-0.2\,\text{m}}{10\,\text{h}} = -0.02\,\text{m}\,\text{h}^{-1}.$$

The gradient measures the number of metres by which the river *changes* per hour, as before. This specific example shows a negative gradient and the water level in the river falling.

Solution to Activity 15.10

If you extend the line to $-10\,°\text{C}$, the height is approximately $65.35\,\text{m}$.

The overall height difference is $65.35\,\text{m} - 64.6\,\text{m} = 0.75\,\text{m}$.

Solution to Activity 15.11

(a) In the calculation below, the highest and lowest points have been used. Because the relationship is linear, you should get the same value for the gradient whichever points you choose. The gradient is

$$
\begin{aligned}
\text{gradient} \;&= \frac{(y_2 - y_1)}{(x_2 - x_1)} \\
&= \frac{(12 - 4)}{(12.5 - 2.5)} \\
&= \frac{8}{10} \\
&= 0.8.
\end{aligned}
$$

The units of the gradient will be (units of y) (units of x)$^{-1}$, which is $\text{N}\,\text{mm}^{-1}$.

(b) There are a few ways you might have phrased this, so check that you were close to one of these answers. Essentially, you should have linked the change in load (or weight) carried to the shelf thickness.

- The gradient represents the load a thickness of shelf can carry before failure. For every 1 mm, the shelf can carry 0.8 N.
- The gradient represents the fact that, as the thickness of the shelf increases, so does the load it can take before failure.

Solution to Activity 15.12

10 sheets of cardboard will be 25 mm thick (10 × 2.5 mm), so the graph has to be extended to cover at least this value. It should look something like this:

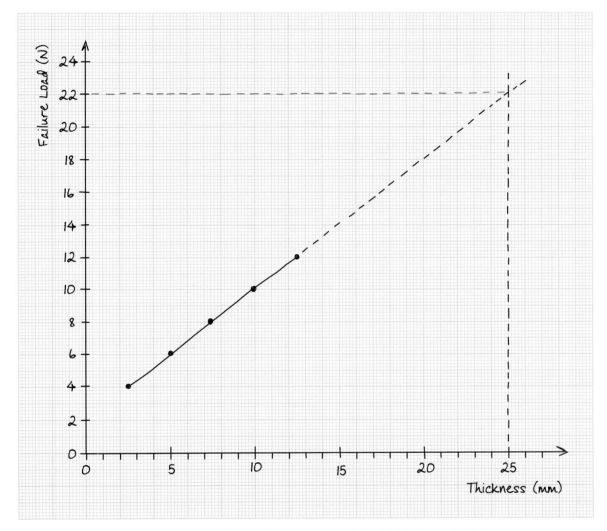

From this graph, the failure load for 10 layers (25 mm) is 22 N (though if the layers were glued or fixed together a different result might be expected).

Solution to Activity 15.13

(a) Measuring 30 N would suggest that the linear model does not extrapolate this far and that the failure load starts to decrease with thickness at some point.

(b) Measuring 34 N would suggest that the linear model is valid for this thickness of shelf.

(c) Measuring 72 N would again suggest that the linear model does not extrapolate accurately this far. In this case the failure load seems to increase at some point.

Part 2: Chapter 16   Design methods

Introduction

In this final chapter you will extend the exploration of analytical methods started in the previous chapter. Section 16.1 starts by completing an overview of straight lines in graphs and maths – this time by looking at how they can be understood and applied using algebra. This link between geometry and algebra provides the engineer with a vital tool when modelling design engineering situations.

This is continued in Section 16.2, which looks at how a generalised model of a material can be developed through understanding the technical definition of strength. This analytical knowledge of materials can then be applied to any situation in which the material is used, an exceptionally powerful general method in engineering.

Section 16.3 concludes the chapter by looking at the future of engineering and how new technologies and methods at all stages of the process are changing the way we design, make, use and reuse our material world.

16.1   Material analysis

You saw in the previous chapter that there are useful things that lines and graphs can reveal about relationships between quantities, such as how water levels might change with time, or how the failure load on a shelf could relate to the thickness of the shelf. You considered how graphs could be used practically – by extending lines or reading values from measuring. Using these methods, however, can lead to mistakes or errors through poor drawing or misreading a scale.

There are more rigorous ways to approach graphs that avoid relying only on measurement or observation. By linking the geometry of lines to algebra, you gain a whole range of interchangeable maths tools that can be applied in either domain. In this section you'll see that certain equations can be represented by straight-line graphs, and how to sketch such graphs from their equations.

16.1.1   Straight-line equations

All equations can be represented graphically in some way. The straight-line graphs you have come across so far are examples of this where the underlying equations include two variables that relate to one another. For example, the cardboard shelf thickness is a variable that can be related to failure load, another variable.

This relationship between lines and equations is an important and general result in mathematics, first demonstrated by René Descartes (1596–1650). The shapes of curves and surfaces can be studied using algebra. This also means the opposite is true – algebra can be studied using shape and geometry. So bear that in mind if you need another way to think about a mathematical problem – pictures might work better for the problem.

To explore this further, start by considering which equations relating a variable x to another variable y might be equations of straight lines. For example, consider the equation $y = 2x$. The points that satisfy this equation are those whose y-coordinate is twice their x-coordinate. These are the points that lie on the straight line through the origin (the point (0, 0)) with gradient 2, as illustrated in Figure 16.1(a).

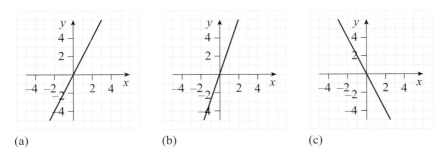

(a) (b) (c)

Figure 16.1 Lines through the origin with gradient (a) 2, (b) 3, (c) −2

Similarly, the points (x, y) that satisfy the equations $y = 3x$ and $y = -2x$ are the points that lie on the straight lines through the origin with gradients 3 and −2, respectively, as you can see in Figure 16.1(b) and Figure 16.1(c).

In general, for any value of a multiplier m, the points (x, y) that satisfy the equation $y = mx$ are the points that lie on the straight line through the origin with gradient m.

Now consider the equation $y = 2x + 1$. Note that if a point satisfies $y = 2x$, then adding 1 to its y-coordinate gives a point that satisfies $y = 2x + 1$.

So the points that satisfy the equation $y = 2x + 1$ are all the points on the line that is obtained by moving the line in Figure 16.1(a) vertically up by 1 unit, as shown in Figure 16.2. Moving the line up by this amount changes its y-intercept, the place where the line crosses the y-axis, from 0 to 1.

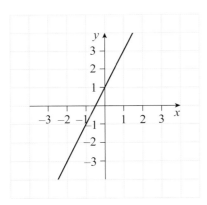

Figure 16.2 The line with equation $y = 2x + 1$

In general, for any constant c, the graph of the equation $y = mx + c$ is obtained by moving the graph of the equation $y = mx$ vertically by c units. This leads to a general equation that can (with suitable choice of m and c) be used to describe any straight-line graph that relates values of y to values of x.

Graphs of equations of the form $y = mx + c$

The graph of the equation $y = mx + c$ is the straight line with gradient m and y-intercept c.

It follows from this that the graph of any equation that can be rearranged into the form $y = mx + c$ is a straight line.

An equation of the form $y = mx + c$, or that can be rearranged into this form, is called a **linear equation** in the variables x and y. You were first introduced to linear equations in Chapter 6, and will by now have constructed, rearranged and solved many examples of a linear equation.

For example, the graph of the equation $3x + 2y - 4 = 0$ is a straight line, since this equation can be rearranged as $y = 2 - \frac{3}{2}x$, which is of the form $y = mx + c$.

When the equation of a line is written in the form $y = mx + c$, it is straightforward to 'read off' the gradient and the y-intercept. The gradient is the coefficient of x, and the y-intercept is the constant term. For example, the line $y = -\frac{3}{2}x + 2$ has gradient $-\frac{3}{2}$ and y-intercept 2.

To find the x-intercept of a line, you need to find the value of x for which $y = 0$ (satisfy yourself that this is the case by looking at the point where the line crosses the x-axis in Figure 16.2). Here is an example.

Example 16.1   Finding the x-intercept of a line from its equation

Find the x-intercept of the line with equation $y = 4x - 3$.

Solution

The x-intercept is the value of x when $y = 0$.

Putting $y = 0$ gives $4x - 3 = 0$.

Solving this equation gives

$4x = 3$

$x = \frac{3}{4}$.

Hence the x-intercept is $\frac{3}{4}$.

Leave the answer as a fraction.

(*Check*: substituting $x = \frac{3}{4}$ into $y = 4x - 3$ gives $y = 4 \times \frac{3}{4} - 3 = 0$, as expected.)

As illustrated in the example, if the x-intercept, y-intercept or gradient of a straight line is a fraction, then there is no need to change it to a decimal.

Activity 16.1

Find the gradient, and x- and y-intercepts of each of the following lines.

(a) $y = -4x + 3$

(b) $3y - x + 2 = 0$

Equations of horizontal and vertical lines

You saw in the previous chapter that the gradient of a horizontal line is 0. So the horizontal line with y-intercept c has equation $y = 0x + c$; that is, $y = c$. For example, the horizontal line in Figure 16.3(a) has y-intercept 3, so its equation is $y = 3$.

An alternative way to think of this fact is to notice that every point on the line in Figure 16.3(a) has y-coordinate 3, so the equation $y = 3$ describes each point on the line. It is therefore the equation of the line.

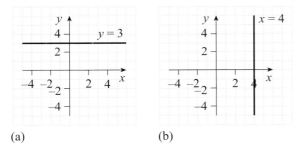

(a)   (b)

Figure 16.3   (a) A horizontal line; (b) a vertical line

What about vertical lines? A vertical line has no gradient, so it doesn't have an equation of the form $y = mx + c$. Vertical lines are the only straight lines that do not have equations of this form.

However, every point on a vertical line has the same x-coordinate, so the line has an equation of the form $x = d$. The constant d is the x-intercept. For example, consider the vertical line shown in Figure 16.3(b). Every point on this line has x-coordinate 4, so the equation $x = 4$ describes each point on the line and is therefore the equation of the line.

Equations of horizontal and vertical lines

The horizontal line with y-intercept c has equation $y = c$.

The vertical line with x-intercept d has equation $x = d$.

In particular, the equation of the x-axis is $y = 0$, and the equation of the y-axis is $x = 0$.

16.1.2   Drawing a line from its equation

One way to plot the graph of an equation is to find several points that satisfy the equation, and to draw a smooth line or curve through them. If you can recognise an equation as the equation of a straight line, then to draw this line you need to find only two points that satisfy the equation, and draw the straight line through them.

You could find two suitable points by choosing two values of x, and use the equation to find the corresponding values of y. You should try to choose values of x that are reasonably far apart and that lead to simple calculations. For example, if the equation is $y = \frac{1}{3}x + 2$, then you might choose $x = 0$ and $x = 3$, to avoid fractions. An alternative way to find two suitable points is to find the x- and y-intercepts.

Drawing a horizontal or vertical line from its equation is quite straightforward. To draw the line with equation $y = c$, mark the y-intercept c and draw the horizontal line through it. Similarly, to draw the line with equation $x = d$, mark the x-intercept d and draw the vertical line through it.

Activity 16.2

Draw the straight lines with the following equations.

(a) $y = \frac{1}{3}x + 2$

(b) $y = -2x + 4$

(c) $y = \frac{7}{2}$

(d) $x = -3$

16.1.3   Finding the equation of a straight line

Every straight line that you can draw in a plane, with the exception of any vertical line, has a gradient and a y-intercept, and hence has an equation of the form $y = mx + c$.

If you know the gradient and the y-intercept of the line, then you can write down the equation of the line. For example, the line with gradient 3 and y-intercept -5 has equation $y = 3x - 5$.

Sometimes, however, you might know different information about a line. The next example demonstrates a method for finding the equation of a line when you know its gradient and a point on it.

Example 16.2   Finding the equation of a line from its gradient and a point on it: method 1

Find the equation of the line that has gradient -6 and passes through the point $(-1, 4)$.

Solution

A straight line has an equation of the form $y = mx + c$, where m is the gradient.

So this equation is of the form $y = -6x + c$.

The point $(-1, 4)$ lies on the line, so this point must satisfy the equation.

Substituting $x = -1$ and $y = 4$ into the equation gives

$$4 = -6 \times (-1) + c$$
$$4 = 6 + c$$

Solve this equation to find c:

$$-2 = c.$$

So the equation of the line is $y = -6x - 2$.

(*Check*: substituting $x = -1$ into the equation $y = -6x - 2$ gives $y = -6 \times (-1) - 2 = 4$, so the point $(-1, 4)$ lies on the line, as expected.)

Here's an alternative way to find the equation of a straight line from its gradient and a point on it. Suppose that the gradient is m and the point is (x_1, y_1). If (x, y) is any other point on the line, then, using the formula for the gradient from Chapter 15,

$$m = \frac{y - y_1}{x - x_1}.$$

Rearranging this equation gives

$$y - y_1 = m(x - x_1).$$

The equation for gradient does not hold when $(x, y) = (x_1, y_1)$, since that would require division by 0, but it does hold for all other points (x, y) on the line. However, the rearranged equation holds for all points (x, y) on the line, including $(x, y) = (x_1, y_1)$, since for this point both sides are equal to zero. So the rearranged equation is the equation of the line. This is summarised as follows.

Finding the equation of a line from its gradient and a point on it

The equation of the straight line with gradient m that passes through the point (x_1, y_1) is

$$y - y_1 = m(x - x_1).$$

Example 16.3   Finding the equation of a line from its gradient and a point on it: method 2

Find the equation of the line that has gradient -2 and passes through the point $(1, 4)$.

Solution

Substitute $m = -2$, $x_1 = 1$ and $y_1 = 4$ into the equation $y - y_1 = m(x - x_1)$, and simplify it.

The equation of the line is

$$y - 4 = -2(x - 1).$$

It can be simplified as follows:

$$y - 4 = -2x + 2$$
$$y = -2x + 6.$$

So the equation of the line is $y = -2x + 6$.

(*Check*: substituting $x = 1$ into $y = -2x + 6$ gives $y = -2 \times 1 + 6 = 4$, so the point $(1, 4)$ lies on the line, as expected.)

Sometimes you might want to find the equation of a line from the coordinates of two points on it. If the two points have the same x-coordinate or the same y-coordinate, then you can immediately write down the equation of the horizontal or vertical line that they lie on. Otherwise, you can use the coordinates of the two points to calculate the gradient of the line, and then apply either of the methods above.

Activity 16.3

Find the equations of the following lines.

(a) The line through the point (2, 1) with gradient 3.

(b) The line through the points (2, 3) and (4, 5).

(c) The line with y-intercept 3 and gradient 2.

(d) The line with x-intercept 2 and gradient -3.

(e) The vertical line that passes through the point (1, 0).

(f) The line through the points $(-2, 3)$ and (4, 3).

16.1.4 Applications and practice

The relationship between two real-life quantities can often be modelled by an equation in two variables. If the equation representing this relationship is of the form $y = mx + c$, and hence has a straight-line graph, then you can say that the model is linear.

In this section, you'll look at some examples of linear models, and practise working with them.

First, consider the graph in Figure 16.4, which represents the journey of a car along a road. It shows the relationship between the time that has elapsed since the car began its journey, t (h), and the distance that it has travelled since the start of the journey, s (km). A graph like this, in which distance is plotted against time, is known as a distance–time graph.

As you have seen before, the variables s and t are often used for distance and time, respectively, so you need to be careful to avoid possible confusion if the unit s (seconds) is used for time.

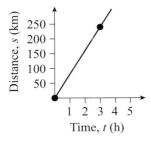

Figure 16.4 A distance–time graph for the journey of a car

This graph includes only positive values of t and s, as the times elapsed and the distances travelled since the start of the journey cannot be negative.

You can calculate the gradient of the graph in Figure 16.4 by choosing two points on it in the usual way. The two points marked on the graph have coordinates (0, 0) and (3, 240), so

$$\text{gradient} = \frac{(240 - 0) \text{ km}}{(3 - 0) \text{ h}} = 80 \text{ km h}^{-1}.$$

Remember, because the numbers on the axes of the graph have units, the gradient also has units. Since the rise is measured in kilometres (km) and the run is measured in hours (h), the units of the gradient are kilometres divided by hours, that is, kilometres per hour (km h^{-1}). In general, the units of the gradient of a graph are the units on the vertical axis divided by the units on the horizontal axis.

The fact that the gradient of the graph in Figure 16.4 is 80 km h^{-1} tells you that the distance travelled by the car changes by 80 kilometres for each hour of the journey. That is, it tells you that the car travels 80 kilometres in each hour, or, in other words, that the speed of the car is 80 kilometres per hour.

In general, if a graph is a straight line, then it means that the quantity on the vertical axis is changing at a constant rate with respect to the quantity on the horizontal axis. The gradient of the graph tells you how many units the quantity on the vertical axis changes for every one unit that the quantity on the horizontal axis changes. In other words, the gradient of the graph is the *rate of change* of the quantity on the vertical axis with respect to the quantity on the horizontal axis. So, for example, the gradient of a distance–time graph is the rate of change of distance with respect to time, which is speed.

Distance–time graphs

The gradient of a graph of distance against time is a measure of speed. If the graph is a straight line, then the speed is constant.

If the motion is in a constant direction, then a graph of displacement against time would have a gradient equal to the velocity.

When you're working with a linear model, it's usually helpful to use the equation of the associated straight-line graph. You can often find the equation using the methods that you practised earlier in this section – you use the variables that represent the real-life quantities in place of the standard variables x and y. For example, for the distance–time graph in Figure 16.4, the variables on the horizontal and vertical axes are t and s, respectively, so you use t in place of x and s in place of y. The gradient of this graph is 80 km h^{-1} and the y-intercept is 0 km, so the equation of the graph is

$$s = 80t.$$

You might recognise this as an example of the equation you have used before for motion at a constant speed:

distance = speed × time.

When you use relationships like this, it's important to remember that they're valid only if the units in which the quantities are measured are consistent. For example, for the relationship above, the units in which time is measured must be the same as the units of time contained within the derived units in which speed is measured. The units in that example are consistent since the number 80 represents the speed of the car in $km\,h^{-1}$, the variable t represents time in hours, and the variable s represents distance in km.

Activity 16.4

The figure below shows a graph of velocity ($v\,m\,s^{-1}$) plotted against time (t s) for a car.

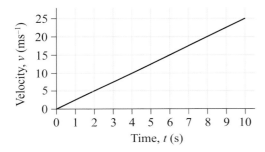

(a) Calculate the gradient of the line, including the units.

(b) Explain what the gradient of the line is telling you.

(c) The line passes through the origin so $c = 0$ in this case. What does this tell you?

(d) Write an equation in the form $y = mx + c$ relating v and t for this situation.

Velocity–time graphs

The gradient of a graph of velocity against time is a measure of acceleration. If the graph is a straight line, then the acceleration is constant.

Activity 16.5

In Chapter 8, Section 8.1, you looked at the equation for converting temperatures from Celsius (°C) to Fahrenheit (°F). The equation you used was

$$T_f = 1.8T_c + 32.$$

Can you see that this is another example of a linear relationship?

Sketch a graph of this relationship, from −20 °C to 40 °C, making sure you show the y-intercept clearly.

In the next activity, you're asked to find and interpret the gradients of two more straight-line graphs.

Activity 16.6

For each of the graphs below, find the gradient in appropriate units and explain what the gradient represents.

Graph (a) represents the relationship between the number n of people attending a meeting and the cost C (in £) of hiring the meeting room (including lunch and refreshments for the attendees).

Graph (b) represents the relationship between the price p (in £ kg^{-1}) charged for building sand and the quantity q (in kg) purchased by a customer.

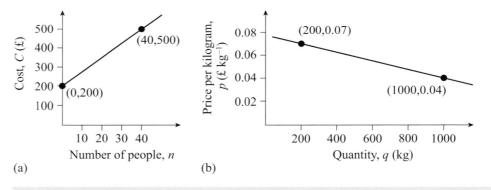

(a)   (b)

The intercepts of real-life graphs often have practical interpretations, as you have seen previously.

Activity 16.7

Look back at the graph in Activity 16.6(a). State the vertical intercept, and explain what it means.

The intercepts of real-life graphs don't always have useful meanings. For example, look back at the graph in Activity 16.6(b). Notice that it has been drawn as a line segment that doesn't cross either of the axes. This is because the model isn't valid for the values of q and p that don't correspond to points on this line segment. In particular, it isn't valid when $q = 0$ and $p = 0$, so the intercepts have no meaning in this case.

Activity 16.8

For this activity, use the graphs and your answers from Activity 16.6.

(a)

    (i)   Find the equation of graph (a) in Activity 16.6.

    (ii) Calculate the maximum number of people that can be accommodated in the meeting room, if the maximum budget for the meeting is £560.

(b)

    (i)   Find the equation of graph (b) in Activity 16.6.

    (ii) Calculate the price per kilogram of building sand that corresponds to a quantity of 500 kg.

16.1.5 Modelling the shelf

To complete this section you will return to the cardboard shelf and complete the mathematical model that you started in the previous chapter. In Activity 15.11 the gradient was calculated, and this can be used with one of the points on the graph to calculate the final equation.

Activity 16.9

Using the data from the completed table in Activity 15.4, the gradient from Activity 15.11 and your graph in Activity 15.4, find the equation of the line that relates the shelf thickness to the failure load.

Write this in the form $y = mx + c$, substituting suitable values for m and c.

Since y corresponds to the failure load (call this L_f) and x corresponds to the thickness (call this d), the cardboard shelf material's performance can be modelled using the following formula relating the failure load and thickness:

$$L_f = 0.8d + 2.$$

This final formula allows much easier calculation of the material's performance. It is now possible to calculate thickness based on load failure, or load failure based on thickness.

Activity 16.10

(a) Use the cardboard shelf equation (and a calculator) to calculate the shelf failure load for 13, 27 and 1835 sheets.

(b) What thickness of shelf would be required to support 40 kg?

In the last few activities you were asked to calculate some rather unrealistic situations.

First, the equation derived in Activity 16.9 allows you to calculate the failure load of a shelf with zero thickness. In terms of material engineering this is physically impossible. But this was necessary to complete the equation – it may not be possible in practice, but it is necessary for the equation.

Second, in Activity 16.10 you calculated the failure load for a shelf of 1835 sheet thickness, which is over 4.5 metres in depth! This was to demonstrate the usefulness of having the equation instead of the graph – it's easier to calculate this than it is find a piece of paper big enough.

Finally, you also have to remember the conditions under which this formula was created. If you recall, the mass was applied in 200 g increments, meaning that the results were not particularly detailed in some key respects. In reality, the straight line for the shelf isn't perfectly straight – it bends at either end. No material relationship is *infinitely* linear since there are always basic limitations to the physical universe. Remember too that the sheets were not fixed together in this particular shelf; you may have seen different behaviour if they had been.

The main point to remember here is that maths is a theoretical tool to use in design engineering – using it appropriately matters just as much as understanding the techniques themselves. In engineering it's important to understand the conditions under which knowledge like this is derived, and the usefulness of these types of relationship. This is what you will look at in the next section.

16.2   Analytical methods

In the previous chapter you saw how experiential knowledge can be used to say something specific about the use of a material. This information can then be applied using experimental methods to generalise this knowledge further. With the shelf example this was done in quite a basic way: a specific material was varied using a single parameter (its thickness) to see how it behaved. This focused on the superficial behaviour of the material – mainly whether it failed or not. But it did not really tell us anything about the material itself or give us a model that can be generalised in other ways.

In order to go beyond specifics, other techniques are required to obtain a more sophisticated method of 'knowing' – using mathematical models. In fact, the material itself has to be modelled in such a way that it can be analysed in any 'shape' to simulate a design proposal. To build this model, a few words and definitions and their application need to be introduced.

16.2.1   Words and definitions in engineering

In Chapter 13 you saw how important it is to be careful about the use of specific words in order to avoid miscommunication. In engineering certain words are used in very precise ways simply because if everyone in a team knows *precisely* what a particular word means, there is less chance of it being used incorrectly. You have come across many examples already in this module.

When you read about the design and development of a jet engine for an aeroplane in Chapter 14, you saw that this was one part (albeit a vital one) of the overall design project. There are a number of key technologies, business relationships and supplier industries that come together to make an aircraft: electrical and hydraulic systems, structures, materials, aerodynamics and engines. In order to do this successfully, the people involved would not only have had an excellent shared understanding of specific engineering terms, but they would also have good experience of how these terms relate to the projects they work on.

For example, Figure 16.5 shows the dominating design requirements at different points in an airframe.

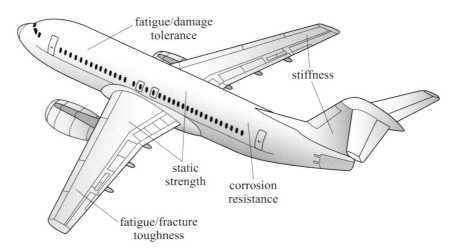

Figure 16.5   Dominating design requirements for an airframe

Very specific terms are used in this diagram, and each has a particular meaning in an analytical and design sense.

Fatigue, for example, is a very important concept in designing for the operating life of a product. Fatigue describes the tendency of a material to break when subjected to repeated loading and unloading. The extent to which fatigue will occur in a particular design depends on how the product is used – the operating conditions. The long-term effects of this fatigue are difficult to predict without extensive testing. A lot of the knowledge gained about fatigue is a mix of experiential and experimental. These are combined to create analytical models (see the box below).

Fatigue

Metal fatigue is an extremely common cause of material failure. Fatigue is a very subtle process, the onset of which can go unnoticed until the fatigued component fails. Fatigue can occur at stresses much below the strength of the material, so it may cause failure in a condition that was originally considered safe by a designer.

Fatigue occurs when the stress in a component oscillates with time. If the oscillations are sufficiently great, they can lead to the initiation and growth of cracks within the material. These cracks can grow until the component fails, often quite catastrophically (Figure 16.6).

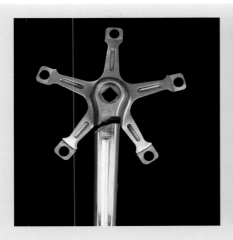

Figure 16.6   Failure of a bicycle crank due to the growth of a fatigue crack

The existence of fatigue has been recognised for over 100 years, but it is only in recent decades that the process has been understood thoroughly to the point where it can be designed against successfully. Failures such as the loss of three Comet airliners in the 1950s, the Markham Colliery disaster in 1973, the Hatfield rail crash in 2000 and the grounding of the fleet of A380s in 2012 were all caused by fatigue. The lessons learned in each case mean that designers are progressively better equipped to prevent such problems occurring in future. Analytical models have been developed in response to increases in information.

There are other ways to model some of the other properties shown in Figure 16.5. One of these – strength – will be considered here to complete your exploration of knowledge of materials in design engineering. The word 'strength' has a very particular meaning in mechanical and structural engineering, and it can be used in creating a purely analytical model to consider the strength of materials. A formal definition will be provided shortly, but first the relationship between strength and stress needs to be examined.

16.2.2   Strength under stress

Mechanical designs need to bear loads in order to work – they must be strong, but not over-designed (or over-engineered) so they are too strong because this would add wasteful material and mass. You encountered examples of designing for strength in Chapter 12 where different paper geometries were used in different ways to generate strength.

In that activity you were using your own physical and experiential knowledge. If the paper looked (or felt) as if it was collapsing (perhaps it started to sag or deform), then you assumed it was not strong enough. It will not be much of a surprise that you can't only rely on such hunches when it comes to real bridges and structures. To go beyond this kind of knowing, more rigorous approaches and methods have to be adopted.

Such a process starts with the realisation that material properties are directly related to structural or mechanical properties of an object or system. This may seem an obvious statement but it allows you to begin analytically modelling the material properties and then applying that to the structural and mechanical properties.

To start, consider a simple structure – a rod of material of constant cross-section, or, more familiarly, a long cylinder. This might be used as a bolt to keep two components together; for instance, to fix a wheel to a vehicle. Or it could be the spokes in a bicycle, the cables supporting a tent structure, or the electrical cables that make up the UK power grid (Figure 16.7). The approach about to be considered can be applied to any and all of these as well as countless others – that's why it's such an important and useful concept.

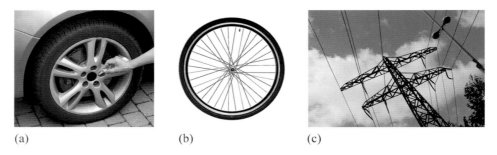

(a)   (b)   (c)

Figure 16.7   Examples of cylinders in engineering: (a) bolts are used to connect a wheel to a vehicle; (b) bicycle wheel spokes; (c) high-voltage suspended electrical cables

A key question is how large the diameter of each of these components should be. For example, for the car wheel bolts it depends on the forces trying to pull the wheel away from the axle. It also depends on what material the bolt is made from: stronger materials will require smaller diameter bolts. The design of the shape of a component depends on the external conditions (i.e. the force applied) and on internal properties (i.e. the material from which the bolts is made).

Strength is an important mechanical property of any material. It is related to the amount of force that can be applied to the material before it fails. Material failure generally means fracture: the material breaks into two or more pieces. There are other types of failure, though, such as permanent deformation, where a material's shape has not actually broken but has changed shape permanently.

The form of strength discussed here is a *material* property. You cannot change the inherent strength of a material by cutting it into a different shape. But the strength of an object made from a material depends directly on how much of that material there is.

Return to the simple rod example and consider a real application of this: a rope used to pull a load. Given a choice between a thicker or thinner rope of the same material and wound in the same way, which would you choose? To haul a heavy load you would probably choose the thicker rope. The reason you might give would be that the thicker rope 'looks stronger' (experiential knowledge). The actual measurable difference (experimental knowledge) is that the thicker rope can carry a greater force before breaking.

Why is this? Clearly the size of the rope does have a critical bearing on whether or not it will break when it is loaded. A thinner rope can't carry as much force. What you find is that the cross-sectional area of rope that is carrying the force is important. A rope with twice the cross-sectional area of material can carry twice the force (Figure 16.8).

Figure 16.8   Two diagrammatic ropes of different diameter. The one on the right has twice the cross-sectional area of the one on the left, hence it can take twice the force before failure. You can think of each arrow as representing the same amount of force per square millimetre: the force per unit area is the same in both so the stress is the same in both.

This special relationship between force and area can be used in engineering to say something important about any material. In fact, force and area are used to define the **stress** in the material. The stress is the force per unit area in the material and is found by dividing the force by the cross-sectional area.

Stress

Stress can be defined as follows:

$$\text{stress} = \frac{\text{force}}{\text{area}}.$$

Mathematically, this is

$$\sigma = \frac{F}{A}$$

where σ (the Greek letter 'sigma') is stress, F is the force and A is the area over which the force is acting. The SI unit of stress is $\mathrm{N\,m^{-2}}$, which is the same as the unit for pressure, Pa.

It is now possible to say that it is stress that controls whether a material will fail. Greater stress means greater force per unit area. Stress is a more useful general property to work with than strength because, by normalising for area, it can be applied to many different geometries.

The SI unit of stress is newtons per square metre, $N\,m^{-2}$, and is also called a Pascal, Pa. However, for practical purposes stress expressed in terms of $N\,m^{-2}$ turns out to be a very small number. For this reason, stress is often measured in other units, such as of newtons per square millimetre ($N\,mm^{-2}$) or meganewtons per square metre ($MN\,m^{-2}$).

Suppose there is a mass of 5.0 kg suspended on a thin rope of 5.0 mm diameter, and you wish to know the stress being applied to the rope (Figure 16.9).

Figure 16.9   A mass of 5.0 kg suspended on a 5.0 mm diameter rope

The stress will be:

$$\sigma = \frac{F}{A}$$

So you need to identify the force being applied (F) and the area (A) to which it is being applied.

For the force, you convert the mass (5.0 kg) to weight (in N) by multiplying by $g = 9.8\,m\,s^{-2}$:

5.0 kg × 9.8 m s^{-2} = 49 N.

Figure 16.10   Rope with circular cross-section of radius r

For the area, you can calculate the cross-sectional area A (shown as a shaded area in Figure 16.10), by using the formula for the area of a circle.

Area of a circle

The area of a circle can be calculated by multiplying the constant π (the Greek letter 'pi') by the radius squared.

Area of a circle $= A = \pi r^2$

where r is the radius and π is a constant with value approximately $\pi = 3.14$.

Your calculator will have a button marked π, and it is always better to use this (the full number) rather than the approximation (3.14) and then round appropriately at the end of the calculation.

For the 5.0 mm thick rope, the radius is half the diameter, so $r = 2.5$ mm:

$$
\begin{aligned}
A &= \pi r^2 \\
&= \pi \times 2.5^2 \ \text{mm}^2 \\
&= 6.25\,\pi \ \text{mm}^2.
\end{aligned}
$$

Now that you have the values of force and area, you can go back to the equation for stress and substitute $F = 49$ N, and $A = 6.25\,\pi$ mm^2 as follows:

$$
\begin{aligned}
\sigma &= \frac{F}{A} \\
&= \frac{49 \ \text{N}}{6.25\,\pi \ \text{mm}^2} \\
&= 2.5 \ \text{N mm}^{-2} \quad \text{(to 2 s.f.)}.
\end{aligned}
$$

The stress in the rope material is 2.5 N mm^{-2}. To put it another way: each square millimetre in the cross-section of the rope will be subject to a force of about 2.5 N.

Activity 16.11

Two ropes have diameters of 10 mm and 20 mm. What is the stress in N mm^{-2} in each rope if the same force of 500 N is applied to each rope separately? Give your answers to 2 s.f.

Note that the thick rope will fail at the same stress as the thin rope. This is because the overall force required to achieve that stress is much higher for the thicker rope (it has more area so it takes more force).

Another point worth remembering is that the only area that matters is that which the force is transmitted through. In this case it is the cross-sectional area of the rope. The paper bridges in Chapter 12 made use of this principle by trying to distribute the stress across as much of the material as possible. The shapes that distribute stress more evenly tend to be stronger.

Note also that this can be applied to any shape of material, provided that the material properties are consistent. A similar approach can also be used when considering the compressive strength of a material, such as a concrete column supporting a bridge, or bricks in a wall supporting a roof.

This provides a definition for the strength of a material.

Strength

The strength of a material is the maximum stress the material can withstand before it fails.

- **Tensile strength** (also known as ultimate tensile strength) is the maximum stress a material can withstand under tension.
- **Compressive strength** is the maximum stress a material can withstand under compression.

As stress varies depending on the area, a piece of material with smaller area will fail under a smaller force. However, the stress to cause failure for a given material will always be the same.

This type of knowledge can be applied in many situations and its value is in allowing the engineer to consider the shape and size of any material under any loading conditions, whether this is the steel tie in a suspension bridge or a mass of concrete in a large dam. Exactly the same method and approach will apply to any situation where you are working with a known, consistent material:

1   Identify the forces acting on the structure.
2   Calculate the maximum forces the structure can withstand.
3   Make sure that the latter are far greater than the former!

Activity 16.12

(a) Calculate the stress in a 300 mm by 300 mm square concrete column if it is subject to a compressive load of 100 kN. Give your answers to 2 s.f.

(b) The compressive strength of the concrete used is 20 N mm^{-2}. Confirm that the column will be able to support this load.

What you have considered in this activity is the point at which catastrophic failure takes place; this is a type of failure often associated with plastic deformation, as you saw in the previous chapter. It turns out that a very important relationship between stress and deformation can be useful when modelling materials.

16.2.3 Take the strain

What happens when a tensile or stretching force is applied to a rope? As long as the stress created is not greater than the maximum stress, it will stretch a bit – technically, it will deform. This specific type of deformation is described by the strain (which you met previously in Chapter 2), and it is often barely perceptible, unless you are pulling something like a rubber band.

Remember, the strain resulting from applying a force is defined as the extension of the sample divided by its original length (Figure 16.11):

$$\text{strain} = \frac{\text{extension}}{\text{original length}}$$

Strain is represented by the Greek letter epsilon ε, and mathematically is

$$\varepsilon = \frac{\Delta l}{l_1}$$

where Δl is extension and l_1 is original length.

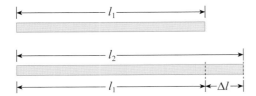

Figure 16.11 Stretching a piece of material

Strain has no units; it is just a number. This is because it is the ratio of two lengths, the extension and the original length, so provided both lengths are measured in the same units, the units will cancel.

Strain may be expressed as a percentage, and you will see this used in Figure 16.12 below. Strain (as a percentage) is calculated as extension divided by original length multiplied by 100%:

$$\text{strain \%} = \frac{\text{extension}}{\text{original length}} \times 100\%.$$

Mathematically, this is

$$\varepsilon\% = \frac{\Delta l}{l_1} \times 100\%$$

where ε is strain, Δl is extension and l_1 is original length.

Activity 16.13

Calculate the strains for the following two examples, and express your answers as percentages.

(a) A 1 m rod that is extended by 1 mm.

(b) A 10 m rod that is extended by 1 cm.

Remember always to use the same units of length for extension and for original length when calculating strain.

There are now two measures, stress and strain, which allow a comparison of materials *independently* of the size and shape of any sample used for testing. Stress relates how much force is being applied, and strain describes the physical change that happens to a material as a result of that force.

Together, these terms can be combined to further refine the definition of material strength. As stress increases, strain will increase, but for different materials strain may increase at different rates with increase in stress. You can see a picture of this by plotting graphs for stress against strain for different materials. In Figure 16.12, the stress/strain relationships for three different materials are considered:

- a strong carbon fibre reinforced plastic (CFRP)
- aluminium
- polystyrene.

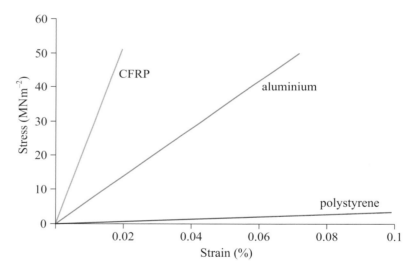

Figure 16.12   Graph comparing stress and strain for carbon fibre reinforced plastic (CFRP), aluminium and polystyrene

These graphs are all straight lines over the range of values shown. This means, for example, that as the stress on a sample is doubled, the strain also doubles (and the sample stretches twice as much). The gradients of these lines represent stress divided by strain:

$$\text{gradient} = \frac{\text{stress}}{\text{strain}}.$$

Notice that the x axis values need to be converted into a numerical strain by dividing by 100 to remove the percentage in order to calculate the Young's modulus from the gradient.

Young's modulus

The ratio of stress divided by strain is a constant for a material – it does not depend on the size and shape of a sample – and is called its **Young's modulus**. This can be shown mathematically where Young's modulus is represented by E and σ is stress and ε is strain.

$$\text{Young's modulus} = \frac{\text{stress}}{\text{strain}}$$

$$E = \frac{\sigma}{\varepsilon}$$

Young's modulus measures the **stiffness** of a material.

Any bar can be stretched more and more by applying greater force. At some point the material in the bar starts to change its microstructure. Now it won't return to its previous length and is permanently deformed – a plastic deformation. This point of no return is effectively the maximum stress that a material can take without being deformed permanently out of shape. This stress is taken as a measure of the **yield stress** of the material. The point at which this happens is called the **yield point**. Applying a force that induces a stress greater than the yield stress of a material will lead to plastic deformation. Some materials (e.g. glass) will break at, or soon after, this point, while others (e.g. thermoplastic polymers like HDPE) can be plastically deformed to a large extent before breaking.

Figure 16.13 shows a typical stress strain curve for a polymer such as HDPE. You can still measure a value of Young's modulus for this material from the initial, approximately linear, part of the graph, but it will apply for only low values of strain. Once plastic deformation has begun, the graph no longer follows a straight line.

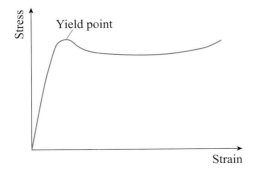

Figure 16.13 Stress–strain graph for a polymer

Activity 16.14

The figure below shows stress–strain graphs for three different materials, A, B and C, up to their breaking points.

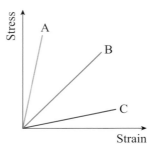

(a) Which material has the lowest strength? How do you know?

(b) Which material has the highest stiffness? How do you know?

So you now have a general model relating the forces acting on a material, the stresses they create in the material, and how that material will react to those stresses. This model is based only on the basic properties of the material and its geometry, meaning that it can be applied in a very broad range of situations.

This really is the value of being able to work with mathematical models as well as design processes – both can be used together to generate the best possible solutions. You have just seen how a material's physical properties relate to its shape. It is not only the design and shape that matters, it's the physical properties too; similarly, the physical properties cannot be isolated from the shape. As a design engineer you manipulate both to come up with creative *and* efficient solutions that you are confident will work.

16.3   Engineering the future

The future is difficult to predict, and when it comes to technology and innovation it is easier to get it wrong than it is to get it right. Take a look back at any old technology programmes or magazines, and futuristic films and novels, and you will see that what people thought the future would become is rarely what happens. Strangely enough, this does not seem to stop future thinkers constantly predicting flying cars (Figure 16.14)!

Figure 16.14   Flying cars feature heavily in most visions of the future featuring technology

One of the reasons why predictions of the future are regularly inaccurate was introduced right at the start of this book – people. The way people use a design is not necessarily the purpose for which it was designed. Most of us own devices that would have been classed as supercomputers only five years ago and yet we use them primarily for very human reasons – to connect with other people, entertain ourselves, and assist us in certain tasks.

This is one thing that has not changed for thousands of years – people attach themselves to technologies that fit their needs and desires. This particular relationship between people and technology can be seen throughout the history of design engineering, and it is one worth remembering in all areas of engineering.

Similarly, the relationship between designers and *their* technologies is also an important one. In Chapter 13 you came across several examples of digital prototyping, computer-aided design (CAD) and building information modelling (BIM). These were presented as ways of both communicating and designing, often at the same time. The growth of these digital methods has been one of the most significant developments in design engineering over the last decade.

But it has also been quite difficult to implement these methods successfully – again, because of the relationship between people and technology. In the late twentieth century, computing and design software focused on what the technology could do without fully considering how it would work *with* people. This has started to change in recent years, with a return to user-centred software design. For example, digital design prototyping software is now designed in a way that makes sense *conceptually* to designers, rather than as abstract elements in a computer (Figure 16.15). Using computers to simply draw is now being seen as less efficient than using them to analyse and design *at the same time*.

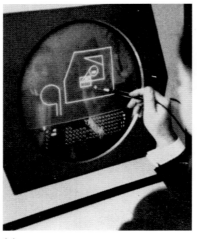

(a)

(b)

Figure 16.15   Advances in technology for design engineering: (a) early CAD system; (b) augmented reality on a building site

In fact, new ways of designing are leading to new designs by blending human and digital processes. For many designers the sketch is still the quickest way to think through several ideas at the same time, and it is possible to blend this form of thinking with the latest modelling methods. For example, procedural design and modelling is an extension of sketching using mathematics and allows the designer to abstract the most important aspects of a design through a sketch and then model using variables and numbers (see Figure 16.16) – a very efficient and effective design process.

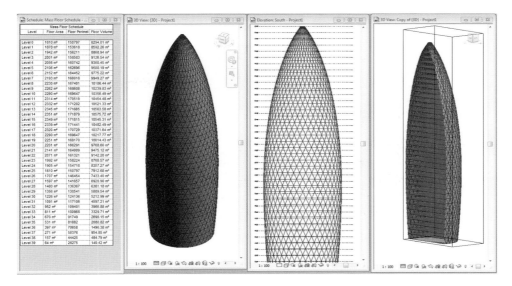

Figure 16.16   Building information model software procedurally modelling a building using surface geometry rules to create a shape

The lesson here is simple – people and technology have a particular relationship, but if one is considered without the other, there tends to be an imbalance that leads to less effective solutions. Achieve the right balances and incredible things are possible.

At the same time, new technologies, materials and processes are emerging at an increasing rate. Any designer should be interested in the world around them and constantly looking for anything to generate ideas. Emerging and future technologies are such an area of inspiration and also part of the ongoing professional development of a design engineer.

For example, rapid prototyping and 3D printing are new and emerging methods of physically making objects (Figure 16.17). Some 3D printers work in a similar way to 2D printers by laying down rows of material in layers to build up a 3D object. Others use a fixing method where a volume of powder is exposed to lasers, which intersect at points in 3D space causing the powder to solidify at that point. Yet other devices use flat material that can be cut very quickly using templates to generate 3D shapes.

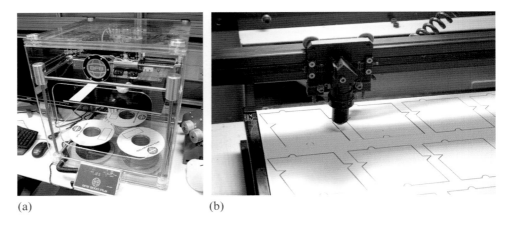

(a)   (b)

Figure 16.17   (a) A 3D printer showing the 'cables' of plastic used to print; (b) a laser cutting machine for rapid panel production

There are many different forms and methods of 3D printing, but all have the common aim of being able to quickly model shapes and objects (Figure 16.18). These resources can be especially useful when creating prototypes for testing during the design stages. As you saw in Chapter 13, having a physical prototype or model can be a significantly useful tool to support communication and reduce errors.

Figure 16.18   Samples of 3D printed materials and shapes

For a design engineer, having access to very quick physical modelling can allow new ideas to emerge at different points in the design process. The idea of the rapid prototyping 3D printer has even been scaled up to print with concrete to make buildings and larger structures (Figure 16.19).

Figure 16.19 3D printing using concrete

These technologies are now starting to blur the boundaries between design and manufacture. For example, the advance of technology is now allowing different materials to be used in the printing process, greatly increasing the range of objects that can be created quickly. Some writers suggest that a new age of local manufacture might be emerging through community design and technology events such as 'hack spaces' and maker labs, allowing almost anyone to experiment and prototype ideas (Figure 16.20).

Figure 16.20 An electronic game prototyped using 3D printing, modular electronics components and controllers, and visual programming software

Of course, new materials are constantly being developed and brought into commercial use. Paper made from rocks, fabric made from ceramics, electrically conductive inks, biological building materials, dye-free colouring from material structures – any of these materials or techniques could contribute to a new innovation in design engineering (Figure 16.21).

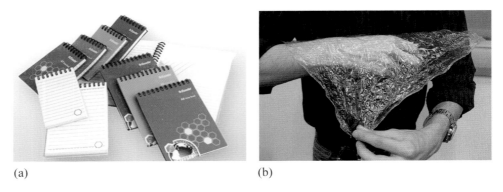

(a)   (b)

Figure 16.21   (a) Paper made from crushed stone waste; (b) biodegradable, strong, protein-based film called shrilk

In fact, 3D printing may be the best way to build on the Moon when we decide to go there permanently (Figure 16.22). The surface of the Moon is covered in a very fine silicate powder (regolith) that has tiny impurities that give it a very special property – when it is compacted and exposed to certain sound waves, it turns to concrete!

Figure 16.22   3D printing on the Moon – what might we build …?

Whatever does happen, it will be human drivers that will determine it. And it will be design engineers who will imagine it and then turn it into a reality.

Solutions to activities in Chapter 16

Solution to Activity 16.1

(a) The coefficient of x is -4, so the gradient is -4.

The constant term is 3, so the y-intercept is 3.

To find the x-intercept, put $y = 0$, which gives
$0 = -4x + 3$.

Solving this equation gives $4x = 3$, so $x = \frac{3}{4}$.

Hence, the x-intercept is $\frac{3}{4}$.

(b) Rearranging the equation in the form $y = mx + c$ gives $y = \frac{1}{3}x - \frac{2}{3}$.

The coefficient of x is $\frac{1}{3}$, so the gradient is $\frac{1}{3}$.

The constant term is $-\frac{2}{3}$, so the y-intercept is $-\frac{2}{3}$.

To find the x-intercept, put $y = 0$, which gives $0 = \frac{1}{3}x - \frac{2}{3}$.

Solving this equation gives $\frac{1}{3}x = \frac{2}{3}$, so $x = 2$.

Hence the x-intercept is 2.

Solution to Activity 16.2

(a) Putting $x = 0$ gives $y = \frac{1}{3} \times 0 + 2 = 2$, so $(0, 2)$ lies on the line. (You might also notice that this point lies on the line since the y-intercept is 2.)

Putting $x = 3$ gives $y = \frac{1}{3} \times 3 + 2 = 1 + 2 = 3$, so $(3, 3)$ lies on the line.

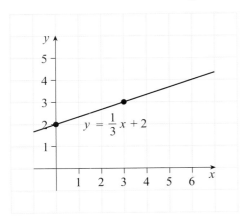

(b) Putting $x = 0$ gives $y = -2 \times 0 + 4 = 4$, so (0, 4) lies on the line.

Putting $x = 4$ gives $y = -2 \times 4 + 4 = -8 + 4 = -4$, so (4, −4) lies on the line.

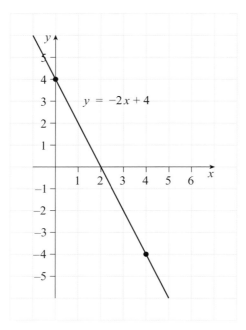

(c) This is a horizontal line, with y-intercept $\frac{7}{2}$.

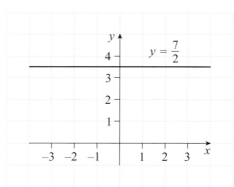

(d) This is a vertical line, with x-intercept -3.

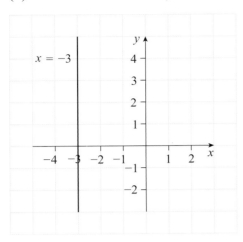

Solution to Activity 16.3

(a) Using the equation $y - y_1 = m(x - x_1)$ with $m = 3$, $x_1 = 2$ and $y_1 = 1$ gives

$$y - 1 = 3(x - 2).$$

Expanding the brackets and rearranging gives the equation of the line as

$$y = 3x - 5.$$

(b) The gradient of the line is given by

$$\frac{5-3}{4-2} = \frac{2}{2} = 1.$$

Using the equation $y - y_1 = m(x - x_1)$ with $m = 1$, $x_1 = 2$ and $y_1 = 3$ gives

$$y - 3 = x - 2.$$

So the equation of the line is $y = x + 1$.

(c) Using the equation $y = mx + c$ with $m = 2$ and $c = 3$ gives the equation of the line as $y = 2x + 3$.

(d) The point at which the line crosses the x-axis is $(2, 0)$. Using the equation $y - y_1 = m(x - x_1)$ with $m = -3$, $x_1 = 2$ and $y_1 = 0$ gives

$$y - 0 = -3(x - 2).$$

So the equation of the line is $y = -3x + 6$.

(e) Each point on a vertical line has the same x-coordinate, so the equation of the line is $x = 1$.

(f) The y-coordinates of the two points are the same, so the line is horizontal with equation $y = 3$.

Solution to Activity 16.4

(a) Using the points (10, 25) and (0, 0) to calculate the gradient:

$$\text{gradient} = \frac{(y_2 - y_1)}{(x_2 - x_1)}$$

$$= \frac{(25 - 0) \ \text{m s}^{-1}}{(10 - 0) \ \text{s}}$$

$$= \frac{25 \ \text{m s}^{-1}}{10 \ \text{s}}$$

$$= 2.5 \ \text{m s}^{-2}.$$

(b) The graph is telling you the rate at which the velocity changes over time. This is the acceleration of the car (you may have recognised m s^{-2} as the unit for acceleration). So this car has a constant acceleration of $2.5 \ \text{m s}^{-2}$.

(c) The velocity is 0 at $t = 0$. So the car started from rest.

(d) For this straight-line graph, $y = v$, $x = t$, $m = 2.5$, $c = 0$. So the equation represented by the line is

$$v = 2.5t.$$

Solution to Activity 16.5

Your graph should look something like this:

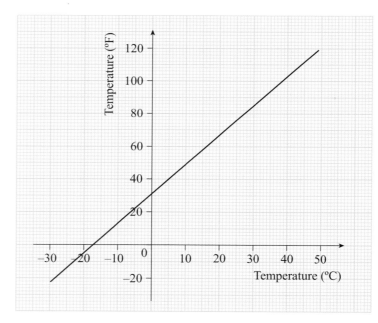

There are lots of possible ways to approach this. Spotting (from the equation) that the y-intercept must be at 32 is a good start, then you could substitute any value of x and find the corresponding value of y to get a second point. Once you have two points, you can join them together and extend the line to cover the required range, since you know that the relationship is linear.

Solution to Activity 16.6

(a) The line passes through the points (0, 200) and (40, 500), so its gradient is

$$\frac{500 - 200}{40 - 0} = \frac{300}{40} = 7.5 \text{ £ per person.}$$

The gradient is the rate of increase of the cost of the room with respect to the number of people attending the meeting. Each additional person attending raises the cost by £7.50.

(b) The line passes through the points (200, 0.07) and (1000, 0.04), so its gradient is

$$\frac{0.04 - 0.07}{1000 - 200} = \frac{-0.03}{800} = -\frac{3}{80\,000} \frac{\text{£/kg}^{-1}}{\text{kg}}.$$

The units can be simplified to $£\,\text{kg}^{-2}$.

So the gradient is $-\frac{3}{80\,000}\ £\,\text{kg}^{-2}$.

The gradient is the rate of change of the price (in $£\,\text{kg}^{-2}$) with respect to the quantity (in kg). For each extra kg of sand, the price (per kg) decreases by $0.000\,0375\ £\,\text{kg}^{-1}$, or approximately $4 \times 10^{-5}\ £\,\text{kg}^{-1}$.

Solution to Activity 16.7

The y-intercept is £200. This represents the basic cost of the meeting room without the additional cost for each person attending.

Solution to Activity 16.8

(a)

(i)

The gradient of the graph of the cost of the meeting room is 7.5 £ per person. From the graph, the vertical intercept is £200. So the equation of the graph is

$$C = 7.5n + 200,$$

where C represents the cost (in £) of the meeting room and n represents the number of people attending.

(ii)

Using $C = 7.5n + 200$ with $C = 560$ gives

$$560 = 7.5n + 200$$

$$7.5n = 360$$

$$n = \frac{360}{7.5} = 48.$$

So the maximum number of people that can be accommodated is 48.

(b)

(i)

The gradient of the building sand graph is $-\frac{3}{80\,000}$ £ kg^{-2}. The graph passes through the point (200, 0.07), so its equation is given by

$$p - 0.07 = -\frac{3}{80\,000}(q - 200)$$

that is,

$$p = -\frac{3}{80\,000}q + \frac{600}{80\,000} + 0.07$$

$$p = -\frac{3}{80\,000}q + \frac{31}{400}.$$

(ii)

Using $p = -\frac{3}{80\,000}q + \frac{31}{400}$ with $q = 500$ gives

$$p = -\frac{3}{80\,000} \times 500 + \frac{31}{400} = \frac{47}{800}$$

so the price per kilogram is approximately £0.059.

Solution to Activity 16.9

The gradient was calculated in Activity 15.11 as $m = 0.8$, giving:

$$y = 0.8x + c.$$

Using the gradient and one point method, and substituting $y = 10.0$ and $x = 10.0$, gives:

$$y = 0.8x + c$$
$$10.0 = 0.8 \times 10.0 + c$$
$$c = 10.0 - 8.0$$
$$= 2.0.$$

Hence the equation of the line using $m = 0.8$ and $c = 2.0$, is

$$y = 0.8x + 2.$$

Solution to Activity 16.10

Units have been omitted from some of these calculations for clarity, but are shown at the end.

(a) The failure loads can calculated by substituting the shelf thickness in mm for d in the equation, as follows:

For 13 sheets: $d = 13 \times 2.5$ mm $= 32.5$ mm
$$L_f = 0.8 \times 32.5 + 2.0$$
$$= 28.0 \text{ N}$$

For 27 sheets: $d = 27 \times 2.5$ mm $= 67.5$ mm
$$L_f = 0.8 \times 67.5 + 2.0$$
$$= 56.0 \text{ N}$$

For 1835 sheets: $d = 1835 \times 2.5$ mm $= 4587.5$ mm

$$L_f = 0.8 \times 4587.5 + 2.0$$
$$= 3672.0 \, \text{N}$$

(b) A mass of 40 kg represents a load of 400 N. The thickness can be calculated by substituting the failure load (400 N) for y in the equation as follows:

$$L_f = 0.8d + 2.0$$
$$400 = 0.8d + 2.0$$
$$d = \frac{398}{0.8}$$
$$= 497.5 \text{ mm.}$$

Solution to Activity 16.11

For a 10 mm diameter rope the radius r is 5 mm:

Cross-sectional area is:

$$A = \pi r^2 = \pi \, 5^2 \, \text{mm}^2 = \pi \, 25 \, \text{mm}^2$$

thus

$$\text{stress} = \frac{\text{force}}{\text{area}} = \frac{500 \, \text{N}}{\pi \, 25 \, \text{mm}^2} = 6.4 \, \text{N mm}^{-2} \quad \text{(to 2 s.f.)}.$$

For a 20 mm rope the radius, r, is 10 mm:

Cross-sectional area is:

$$A = \pi r^2 = \pi \, 10^2 \, \text{mm}^2 = \pi \, 100 \, \text{mm}^2$$

thus

$$\text{stress} = \frac{\text{force}}{\text{area}} = \frac{500 \, \text{N}}{\pi 100 \, \text{mm}^2} = 1.6 \, \text{N mm}^{-2} \quad \text{(to 2 s.f.)}.$$

This illustrates that the stress is less in the larger rope when the same force is applied.

Solution to Activity 16.12

(a) The force applied is given as 100 kN, which is 100 000 N.

The area is 300 mm × 300 mm = 90 000 mm^2.

So the stress is

$$\sigma = \frac{F}{A}$$
$$= \frac{100\ 000\ \text{N}}{90\ 000\ \text{mm}^2}$$
$$= 1.1\ \text{N mm}^{-2} \quad (\text{to 2 s.f.}).$$

(b) Since the actual stress is far less than the compressive strength (by some margin), the column will support the load specified.

Solution to Activity 16.13

(a) You have

$$\text{strain}\ \% = \frac{\text{extension}}{\text{original length}} \times 100\%.$$

However, you need to convert both extension and original length into the same units. If this is mm, then

$$\text{strain}\ \% = \frac{1\ \text{mm}}{1000\ \text{mm}} \times 100\%$$
$$= 0.1\%.$$

(b) Here

$$\text{strain}\ \% = \frac{\text{extension}}{\text{original length}} \times 100\%$$
$$= \frac{10\ \text{mm}}{10\ 000\ \text{mm}} \times 100\%$$
$$= 0.1\%.$$

Solution to Activity 16.14

(a) Material C has the lowest strength, because it reaches the lowest value of stress before breaking.

(b) Material A has the highest stiffness, because its graph has the steepest gradient, and therefore the highest value of E.

Acknowledgements

Grateful acknowledgement is made to the following sources. Every effort has been made to contact copyright holders. If any have been inadvertently overlooked the publishers will be pleased to make the necessary arrangements at the first opportunity.

Chapter 9

Figure 9.1a: Ubergirl/ https://commons.wikimedia.org/wiki/File:Hoover_Dam, _Colorado_River.JPG. This file is licensed under the Creative Commons Attribution-Share Alike Licence http://creativecommons.org/licenses/by-sa/ 3.0/; **Figure 9.1b**: Richard Semik / www.shutterstock.co; **Figure 9.2a**: kavalenkava volha / www.shutterstock.com; **Figure 9.2b**: Taken from: http:// www.protostack.com/semiconductors/transistors/2n2907-general-purpose-pnp-switching-transistor; **Figure 9.2c**: Taken from: http://www.velcro.com/ products/adhesive-backed/900100__sticky-back; **Figure 9.3a**: © ironrodent / www.istockphoto.com; **Figure 9.3b**: Taken from: http://gigazine.net/news/ 20140915-maersk-triple-e/; **Figure 9.3c**: Taken from: http://www. technologytell.com/gadgets/27219/medion-delivers-biometric-technology-in-gps-sorry-thieves/; **Figure 9.4a**: Taken from: http://www.criticalgamers.com/ archives/cat_blogpire_news.php; **Figure 9.4b**: Taken from: http://lxo.hu/ megye/6-fejer; **Figure 9.4c**: Taken from: https://kz.jura.com/ru/homeproducts/ machines; **Figure 9.5**: Josh von Staudach / https://commons.wikimedia.org/ wiki/File:Forth_rail_bridge_head-on-panorama_josh-von-staudach.jpg. This file is licensed under the Creative Commons Attribution-Share Alike Licence http://creativecommons.org/licenses/by-sa/3.0/; **Figure 9.6a**: © Copyright Dr Richard Murray and licensed for reuse under this Creative Commons Licence. This file is licensed under the Creative Commons Attribution-Noncommercial-ShareAlike Licence http://creativecommons.org/licenses/by-nc-sa/3.0/; **Figure 9.6b**: © The National Grid; **Figure 9.6c**: http://quest.eb. com.libezproxy.open.ac.uk/search/substation/1/132_1343226/Electricity-substation/more; **Figure 9.6d**: Richard Thomas / www.123rfimages.com; **Figure 9.7**: Trunki - hello@trunki.com; **Figure 9.8**: https://www.flickr.com/ photos/45782447@N02/5957461446 This file is licensed under the Creative Commons Attribution-Share Alike Licence http://creativecommons.org/ licenses/by-sa/3.0/; **Figure 9.9**: Nightman 1965 / www.shutterstock.com; **Figure 9.10**: magnetcreative / www.istockphoto.com; **Figure 9.11a**: Taken from: http://www.langebergandashton.co.za/about/fruit-production-facilities. php; **Figure 9.11b**: Copyright unknown; **Figure 9.11c**: www.gettyimages. com; **Figure 9.12a**: © mbortolino / www.istock.com; **Figure 9.12b**: Taken from: http://www.lydogbilde.no/test/mobil-gadgets/samsung-galaxy-note-edge? replytocom=62789; **Figure 9.12c**: Taken from: http://www.digitaltrends.com/ mobile/best-student-services/; **Figure 9.16**: http://www.flickr.com/photos/ 83823904@N00/64156219/. This file is licensed under the Creative Commons Attribution Licence http://creativecommons.org/licenses/by/3.0/.

Chapter 10

Figure 10.1b: Brian Stansberry / https://commons.wikimedia.org/wiki/File:Tom-cassidy-house-tn1.jpg#/media/File:Tom-cassidy-house-tn1.jpg. This file is licensed under the Creative Commons Attribution Licence http://creativecommons.org/licenses/by/3.0/; **Figure 10.2**: Reproduced under the terms of the OGL, www.nationalarchives.gov.uk/doc/open-government-licence; **Figure 10.4**: Taken from: http://www.sustainablecitiescollective.com/donnellyb/1062226/speed-price-and-quality; **Figure 10.7**: © National Geographic; **Figure 10.11**: AGFA ISOLY © Gabriel Menashe; **Figure 10.12**: Taken from: https://www.mobiquityinc.com/insights/blog/author/jennifer-halloran; **Figure 10.13a**: Georges Jansoone / https://commons.wikimedia.org/wiki/File:Batalha47.jpg. This file is licensed under the Creative Commons Attribution-Share Alike Licence http://creativecommons.org/licenses/by-sa/3.0/; **Figure 10.14**: SBA73 from Sabadell, Catalunya / https://commons.wikimedia.org/wiki/File:Sagrada_Familia_nave_roof_detail.jpg. This file is licensed under the Creative Commons Attribution-Share Alike Licence http://creativecommons.org/licenses; **Figure 10.15a**: Taken from: http://o.nouvelobs.com/galeries-photos/voyage/20121115.OBS9627/le-triste-top-10-des-hauts-lieux-de-suicides-dans-le-monde.html; **Figure 10.15b**: www.gettyimages.com; **Figure 10.16**: © Unknown; Activity **Figure 10.3a**: © Courtesy Kacey Limited; Activity **Figure 10.3b**: © Courtesy Kacey Limited; Activity **Figure 10.3c**: © Courtesy Kacey Limited; Activity **Figure 10.3d**: © Courtesy Kacey Limited.

Chapter 11

Figure 11.2: Taken from: http://www.habiague.com/ouvre-boite/2636-ouvre-boite-a-anneau-popper.html; **Figure 11.4**: (left) Simon A Eugster / https://commons.wikimedia.org/wiki/File:Swiss_Army_Knive_opened.jpeg. This file is licensed under the Creative Commons Attribution-Share Alike Licence http://creativecommons.org/licenses/by-sa/3.0/; **Figure 11.4**: (top left) http://photo.torange.biz/2/2825/HD2825.jpg; **Figure 11.4**: (bottom right) Taken from: http://www.elitehealthcareltd.co.uk/product/one-handed-tin-opener/; **Figure 11.6b**: Taken from: http://www.hypeness.com.br/2012/02/video-mostra-o-melhor-manual-de-celular-ja-criado-ate-agora/; **Figure 11.7a**: Taken from: http://www.refold.co/#about; **Figure 11.7b**: Taken from: http://www.amazon.com/Hand-holder-tablet-electronic-reader/dp/B004EBBNP2; **Figure 11.9**: NLM/Science Source / Photo Researchers / Universal Images Group; **Figure 11.10**: © Spencer Nugent. This file is licensed under the Creative Commons Attribution-Noncommercial-NoDerivatives Licence http://creativecommons.org/licenses/by-nc-nd/3.0/; **Figure 11.12:** Taken from: http://www.youlearnsomethingneweachday.com/galleries/chindogu-art-useless-inventions-2/; **Figure 11.13**: © www.eucomed.org.

Chapter 12

Figure 12.2a: © IDEO; **Figure 12.2b**: © www.olympusmedical.com; **Figure 12.5**: © www.ketchu.org; **Figure 12.7a**: © Timothy Pike / Arcaid Picture Library / Universal Images Group /Britannica Image Quest; **Figure 12.7b**: shingopix / www.istockphoto.com; **Figure 12.9** Jürgen Matern / https://commons.wikimedia.org/wiki/File: Eden_Project_geodesic_domes_panorama.jpg. This file is licensed under the Creative Commons Attribution-Share Alike Licence http://creativecommons. org/licenses/by-sa/3.0/; **Figure 12.11**: Shizhao/ https://commons.wikimedia. org/wiki/File:Chimney-beijing.JPG. This file is licensed under the Creative Commons Attribution-Share Alike Licence http://creativecommons.org/ licenses/by-sa/3.0/; **Figure 12.13b**: © Brompton Bicycle Limited; **Figure 12.15**: Courtesy Richard Davidson; **Figure 12.17**: Courtesy Richard Davidson; **Figure 12.18**: Courtesy David Richardson; **Figure 12.20**: Courtesy Richard Davidson; **Figure 12.22**: fateson / www.istockphoto.com; **Figure 12.24**: Wikialine / https://commons.wikimedia.org/wiki/File: Brosen_windrose-fr_green.png; **Figure 12.27a**: mihalec / www.istockphoto. com; **Figure 12.27b**: Taken from: http://hds.leica-geosystems.com/en/Press-Releases_5604.htm?id=1329.

Chapter 13

Figure 13.3: Images courtesy of Keppie Design Ltd. www.keppiedesign.co. uk; **Figure 13.4**: Images courtesy of Keppie Design Ltd. www.keppiedesign. co.uk; **Figure 13.7b**: © Juwei Architectural Model; **Figure 13.9**: © United States Patent Office; **Figure 13.10a**: Copyright unknown; **Figure 13.10b**: Copyright unknown; **Figure 13.12a**: Paul Rautakorpi / https://commons. wikimedia.org/wiki/File:Microchip_PIC16C74A_die.JPG?uselang=en-gb. This file is licensed under the Creative Commons Attribution-Share Alike Licence http://creativecommons.org/licenses/by-sa/3.0/; **Figure 13.15**: Prof.DEH / https://commons.wikimedia.org/wiki/File:Architectural_drawing_001.png. This file is licensed under the Creative Commons Attribution-Share Alike Licence http://creativecommons.org/licenses/by-sa/3.0/.

Chapter 14

Figure 14.8: Imagecom / www.dreamstime.com; **Figure 14.9**: Taken from: http://www.its.kit.edu/; **Figure 14.10**: Taken from: http://www.facweb.iitkgp. ernet.in/~aguha/index.html?groovybtn1=Link+to+Personal+HomePage+of +Abhijit+Guha; **Figure 14.11**: Taken from: http://acidcow.com/pics/50864-very-interesting-photos-part-4-30-pics.html; **Figure 14.12**: © McLaren; **Figure 14.15**: Taken from: http://www.mechanicalengineeringblog.com/1757-finite-element-analysis-fea-list-of-fea-softwares-list-of-open-source-softwares-list-of-commercial-softwares/.
Tables:
Table 14.1a: Taken from: https://www.englishforums.com/media/p/588834. htm#,588834,78123,5; **Table 14.1b**: © www.airbus.com; **Table 14.1c**: ©

www.airbus.com; **Table 14.1d**: © www.airbus.com; **Table 14.1e**: © www.airbus.com.

Chapter 15

Figure 15.1: UserFir0002 / https://en.wikipedia.org/wiki/Emissivity#/media/File:Blacksmith_at_work02.jpg This file is licensed under the Creative Commons Attribution-Noncommercial-ShareAlike Licence http://creativecommons.org/licenses/by-nc-sa/3.0/; **Figure 15.4**: © www.forthroadbridge.com; **Figure 15.14**: Dolas / www.istockphoto.com; **Figure 15.22**: Taken from: http://garageplansandmore.com/garage-resources/articles/Choosing-Lumber-for-Framing-a-Garage.

Chapter 16

Figure 16.7b: Alfonso Cacciola / www.istockphoto.com; **Figure 16.7c**: P.J.L. Laurens / https://commons.wikimedia.org/wiki/File:High_Voltage_Cable.jpg. This file is licensed under the Creative Commons Attribution-Share Alike Licence http://creativecommons.org/licenses/by-sa/3.0/; **Figure 16.14a**: AMBLIN/UNIVERSAL/ Album / Universal Images Group; **Figure 16.15a**: © Computer History Museum; **Figure 16.15b**: Taken from: http://www.hetnationaalbimplatform.nl/actueel/nieuws/bimpraat-over-verdienmodellen-bim-en-augmented-reality/; **Figure 16.19** (left): Taken from: http://hackaday.com/2014/05/29/man-builds-concrete-3d-printer-in-his-garage/; **Figure 16.19** (right): © 'The Freedon Bench', Professor Richard Boswell, Professor Simon Austin and the School of Civil and Building Engineering at Loughborough University; **Figure 16.21a**: The Stone Paper Company Limited; **Figure 16.21b**: Alt979 / https://commons.wikimedia.org/wiki/File:Shrilksheet.jpg. This file is licensed under the Creative Commons Attribution-Share Alike Licence http://creativecommons.org/licenses/by-sa/3.0/; **Figure 16.22**: © NASA

Part 2: Chapters 9–16

INDEX

Page numbers in *italics* refer to diagrams and illustrations.

3D printing 315–18, *316*, *317*, *318*
5W and 1H approach 87–8, 98

A
A380 aeroplane 227–31, 242–3
absolute value 260
acceleration 199, 297, 322
acute angles 105
addition of vectors
    displacement vectors 158–61, 165, 187–9, 204
    dynamic systems 199, 201
    static systems 195-8, 201
adjacent side 109–10
aesthetics 5–6
agile design 225
Airbus A380 227–31, 242–3
aircraft
    cockpit *27*
    dominating design requirements 301–3
    forces acting on 200–1
    fuel consumption 227–31, 242–3
    jet engines *see* jet engines
algebra *see* equations
alternate angles 105
alternative energy project 176, 202–3
aluminium 144–5, 310
analysis 11, 59
    analytical and design processes 232–40
    communicating 186–201
    material analysis 288–300
analytical methods 141, 301–12
analytical solutions 238–40

angles 104, 105
    principles involving 105
    in triangles 106
    types of 105
anthropometric data 22
appearance 5–6
Apple 13
apps 15
arches 61
arccosine 111
arcsine 111
arctangent 111, 120–1
Arroyo Cangrejillo Pipeline Bridge *131*
assumptions 184, 203
augmented reality *314*
averages 20–1, 32
axonometric view *183*

B
baby buggy/pram design 44, 75–6
bar charts 22–6, *24*
basic creative design cycle 212–13, *212*, *232*
Batalha Monastery, Portugal *61*
Beauvais Cathedral 61, 248
bell crank *148*, 149
bespoke projects 226
bicycles
    Brompton folding bicycle *97*
    crank failure *302*
    frame strength *136*
    free-wheeling 200
    wheel spokes *304*
BIM (building information modelling) *173–4*, *186*, 313–14, *315*
biodegradable plastics 50

blades, turbine *221*, 222, *223*
BMW 225
book on table static system 195–6
bookshelves 136, 248–54
    see also shelves
boundaries of design 47–9
box on a slope 197–8
brake, stretcher carrier 146–9, *147*, *148*
brick tower chimney *134*
bridges 6
    cable stay 113, 120–1
    deck height 272–4, *272*, 282
    deflection *253*, *272*
    Forth Rail Bridge 6, 128, *129*
    Forth Road Bridge *see* Forth Road Bridge
    Palladio's design *170*
    suspension *62–3*, 130–1, *131*, 248, 257
British Standards
    BS 3939 182
    BS 7671:2008 42
    for timber 276
British Standards Institute (BSI) 22, 42
Brompton folding bicycle *97*
bronze 65
Brown, Tim 64
Brunel, Isambard Kingdom 62–3, 248
buildability 226
building information modelling (BIM) *173–4*, *186*, 313–14, *315*
Building (Scotland) Act 2003 40, 41

Building (Scotland) Regulations
    2004 40, 41–2
bus shelter options 53–5, *54*, 127
butter stick *96*
buttresses, flying 60, *61*

C
C section *69*, 71
cable stay bridge 113, 120–1
calculation sheet 102
calculators 110–11
can opener lifter *83*
can openers 82–3
cantilevers 6, 129
carbon fibre reinforced plastic
    (CFRP) 310
cardboard shelf
    modelling 274–6, 282–3, 299–
        300, 324–5
    testing 255–6, 279
    thickness and failure load
        257–8, 274, 275–6, 279–80,
        282–3, 299–300, 324–5
cars 22
    design for manufacture 224, 225
    flying *313*
    forces on a car 196, 206
    McLaren MP4-12C *180*, *225*
    Mercedes-Benz SLR McLaren
        180, 225
    Mini 224, 225
    wheel bolts *304*
catastrophic failure 255–6, *256*,
    308–9
cathedrals 60–2
challenge, setting a 98
change 11
    responding to 13, 15, 29
characteristics of design 5–11
checkpoints 217–19, 241–2
chimney, tower *134*
Chindogu *96*
circle, area of a 306–7
circular cross-section columns
    133–4, *133*, 137
circular hollow section (CHS) *69*
Clifton Suspension Bridge 62–3,
    62, 248
coded values 20
coffee cup 139–40, 163
coffee machines *5*

communication 140, 167–207, 215,
    216
    of analysis 186–201
    design prototyping and 128–9
    failure to communicate 184–5,
        203
    methods 177–85
    need for 168–76
compass bearings, full 156
compass points 154–5
complex (ill-defined) problems 82,
    84, 118
complexity 37, 38, 58–9
    and communication failures 184
    iteration and complex models
        239–40
    uncertainty and 58–73
    visual thinking 64–73
components of vectors 189–94
    free body diagrams 198–9,
        206–7
compound interest 235–7, 238,
    239, 244
compressive forces 60–1
compressive strength 308, 326
computer-aided design (CAD) 186,
    233, 313–14, *314*
concept design stage 126–37, 138,
    141, 215, 216
concepts
    developing into detailed design
        138–50
    development and analysis of
        170, 173–4, 202
concertina structure 131–2
concrete *317*
    curing 68–9
    mixing ratios 64–9
conditions 38–42, 45–6, 143, 215,
    216, 257
    design evaluation 138, 140, 141,
        163
confirmation of proposals 170,
    175–6
congruent shapes 106
considerations 38, 44–6, 138, 141,
    215, 216, 257

constraints 20, 38, 43–4, 45–6,
    75–6, 215, 216, 257
    developing concepts into
        detailed design 138, 141, 143,
        149
continuous data 20, 32
convergent thinking 84, 85
Conway's Game of Life 239, *240*
cooling channels 222, *223*
corresponding angles 105
corrugated cardboard *132*
    shelf *see* cardboard shelf
cosine 110–11, 191, 192, 193
cosine rule 114–15, 116
cost 43–4
creative design cycle 212–13, *212*,
    232
creativity 11, 215, 216
    creating solutions 81, 92–100,
        119
    getting stuck 99–100
    nature of 95–7
    sketching and thinking creatively
        92–5
    techniques and methods 98–9
creep 237–8
Crick, Sir Francis *93*
Cross, Nigel 9
cross-sectional area 304–5
    calculating 306–7
    structural steel sections 69,
        70–2, 77–8
culture of innovation 64
curvature 132–3, 137
cylinders *304*

D
Data Protection Act 1998 40
datasets 19–21, 22, 32
Davidson, Rob 144
decision making 123–50
    developing concepts into
        detailed design 138–50
    developing ideas into concepts
        126–37, 138, 141, 215, 216
    recording and confirming
        proposals 170, 175–6
decision tables 53–7
decision tree *116*
decommissioning 217
defects in timber 276, *277*

definitions 301–3
deflection 252, 256–7
  bridges *253*, *272*
deformation 252, 308–9
  elastic *252*
  plastic *252*, 256, 304, 308–9,
    311
  strain 309–12, 326
demands 13
Descartes, René 288
design concepts 126–37, 138, 141,
  215, 216
design drivers 12–15, 26, 29–30,
  45, 46, 82, 142–3
design evaluation 138–42, 215
design for manufacture 224–6
design for service 227–31
design immersion 85–6
design lifecycle 47–53
design limits 38–46
  see also conditions;
    considerations; constraints
design precedents 179–80, 224
design problems *see* problems
design process management 220–
  31
  design for manufacture 224–6
  design for service 227–31
  incremental innovation 220–3
design processes 209–44
  basic 212–19
  checkpoints 217–19
  iteration 212–13, 241
  limitations of design process
    models 231
  phases 214–17
design prototyping 18–19, 30–1,
  128–35, *128*, 141–2
desires 13, 14, 29
desk height problem 18–19, 25–6,
  27, 30–1, *90*, 141
  problem statements 89–90
desktop computers 242
detailed design 215, 216
  case study 142–50
  developing concepts into 138–50
details 8

diagrams 101–4, *101*, *103*
  problem solving with
    trigonometry 111–13
  stretcher carrier 143, 144
  stretcher carrier brake 147–9
  see also sketching/sketches
diamond-frame bicycle *136*
different perspectives 88, 98, 176,
  202–3, 254
digital models 178
digital prototyping 173–4, 313–14
direction 151, 153, 154–6
Disability Discrimination Act
  1995 39
discrete data 20, 32
displacement vectors 151–7, *152*,
  153, *155*, 158, 164
  adding 158–61, 165, 187–9, 204
  direction and magnitude 154–7
  representing 153–4
disposable hypodermic needle *3*
distance measuring machine 111,
  157
distance–time graphs 268, 281,
  295–7
distributed load 132–3, 250, 251
distribution and transport *4*, 56–7
divergent–convergent model of
  problem exploration 84, *85*
DNA structure *93*, *95*
documents 179
domestic appliances *5*, 224–5, 242
drag (air resistance) 200, *201*
drawings *177*
  see also sketching/sketches
drivers, design 12–15, 26, 29–30,
  45, 46, 82, 142–3
dubious data 20
dynamic loads 250, 251
dynamic systems 199–201

E

Eden Project *133*
edge strengthening 133, 134, 137
Edison, Thomas 126
effective depth 131, 132, 135, 136,
  137
elastic bands 237–8
elastic deformation *252*
electrical cables *304*
electrical safety 41–2

electrical sockets and plugs *7*
electrical symbols *182*
electricity supply system 6–7, *7*, 15
electronic distance measuring
  device (EDM) 111, *157*
electronic theodolite *157*
electronic toy battery storage 84,
  118
elevations *175*, *177*, 180–1, *180*,
  183
embodied (experiential) knowledge
  58–9, 248–54
emergency services stretcher
  carrier 142–50, *143*, *144*
end of life 48, 49, 217
  MET matrix 56–7
  waste plastics 49–51
energy 56–7
Energy Act 2013 40, 75
Engineering Council 42
Environmental Protection Act
  1990 40
equal vectors 157
equations
  straight-line 288–300, 319–25
  visualising 69–73, 77–8
equilateral triangles 106
ergonomics 22, 26
ethnographic studies 86
evaluation
  checkpoints 217–19, 241–2
  design 138–42, 215
existing objects 179–80
experiential knowledge 58–9,
  248–54
experimental knowledge 257–8,
  279–80
exploration 216
  problem exploration 84, 85–6
extrapolation 275–6, 283, 284
extreme environments *10*

F

failure
  catastrophic 255–6, *256*, 308–9
  cathedrals 61
  of communication 184–5, 203
  learning from 61, 126–7, 129,
    134–5
  performance 256–7
  of a shelf 251–2
  types of material failure 304
failure load
  shelf thickness and 257–8, 274,
    275–6, 279–80, 282–3,
    299–300, 324–5
  testing a shelf 255–6, 279
'fast, good, cheap' triangle 43–4
fatigue 302–3
finite element model *233*
fire evacuation simulation *234*, 239
floor plans *183*
flying buttresses 60, *61*
flying cars *313*
focusing, problem 84, 87–8
folded structure 132
food can openers 82–3
food production systems *14*
forces
  components 192, 193, 194, 205
  compressive 60–1
  dynamic systems 199–201
  free body diagrams *see* free
    body diagrams
  loads *see* loads
  static systems 194–9, 201
  strength by design 135–7, 163
  stress *see* stress
  tensile 60–1, 194, 198–9, 205,
    206–7
  vector representation 187
Forth Rail Bridge *6*, 128, *129*
Forth Road Bridge
  deflection *253*, *272*
  replacement *68*, *226*
  temperature and bridge deck
    height 272–3
fractions 64–9
fracture 304
framing problems 46, 84–91
Frederick, Matthew 213

free body diagrams 102, 103,
  194–201
  dynamic systems 199–201
  static systems 194–9, 201
free-wheeling bicycle 200
friction 130, 197–8, 200
front elevations *177*, *183*
fuel consumption 268, 281
  aircraft 227–31, 242–3
  per passenger 229–31, 243
full compass bearings 156
future, the
  designing for 52–3
  predicting 313–18

G

geometric doodles *95*
geometry 104–16
  angles 104, 105, 106
  lines 104, 105, 107
  triangles *see* right-angled
    triangles; triangles
getting stuck 99–100
Goldberg, Rube *139*
good problems 82, 83, 88
Google 13
gradients 259–70, 280–2
  calculating 261–6
  distance–time graphs 268, 281,
    296
  finding the equation of a straight
    line from the gradient and a
    point on it 292–5, 321
  interpreting 267–70
  straight-line equations 289–91,
    298, 319, 323
  velocity–time graphs 297, 322
graphics 177
  communication techniques
    180–3
graphs
  checking points 271–4
  gradients *see* gradients
  intercepts *see* intercepts
  modelling materials 271–6
  straight-line equations 288–300,
    319–25
gravity 195

H

hand holder for tablet computer/e-
  reader *90*
hard checkpoints 217–18
headphone ear buds *94*
Health and Safety Executive (HSE)
  22
height variation 16–17, 21, 23,
  25–6, 30, 32, 33
high density polyethylene (HDPE)
  51, 311, 312
high-performance engine testing
  laboratory 44, 75
histograms 22–6, *23*
Hoover Dam *3*, 69
horizontal lines 260
  equations 291–2, 320
houses *38*
human factors 26–7
human variation 16–17, 21, 23,
  25–6, 30, 32, 33
hydroelectric dam *7*
hypodermic needle, disposable *3*
hypotenuse 107–8, 109–10

I

I section *69*, 71
ideas 96
  creation and development of
    170, 171–3, 215, 216
  developing into concepts
    126–37, 138, 141, 215, 216
  implausible 98
  quantity not quality 99
  sketching and thinking creatively
    92–5
  thread of 98
IDEO 126, 128, 135
ill-defined (complex) problems 82,
  84, 118
images 177
implausible ideas 98
improvement 13, 15, 29, 30
inclusive (universal) design 26
incremental design 13, 96–7
incremental innovation 60, 64, 76,
  96–7, 137
  design process management
    220–3
incubation 98
information sources 85–6

innovation 48
  culture of 64
  incremental 60, 64, 76, 96–7,
    137, 220–3
  radical 60, 64, 76
  uncertainty and risk 60–4
intercepts 271–4, 289–91, 298–9
  x-intercept 271, 290–1, 319
  y-intercept 271, 289–90, 291,
    298, 319, 323
interest calculation 235–7, 238,
  239, 244
International Space Station *3*
interpolation 275
inverse cosine 111
inverse sine 111
inverse tangent 111, 120–1
iron reinforcing bars 61
isometric view *183*
isosceles triangles 106
iteration 27–8, 138, 171
  basic process 233–4
  creative design cycle 212–13,
    241
  as mathematical process 232–40
  project design phases 214–15
  using numbers 235–8, 244
  versus solving 238–40

J
jet engines
  design for service 227–31
  turbofan and incremental
    innovation 220–3
'John's Phone' *88*
'just because' design driver 13–14,
  15
just-in-time manufacture 225

K
kitchen appliances *5*, 224–5, 242
knowledge 247,
  248–58
  experiential (embodied) 58–9,
    248–54
  experimental 257–8, 279–80
  from testing 254–7, 279

L
L section *69*, 70–2, *70*, *71*, 77–8,
  77
laser cutting machine *316*
laser scanner *157*

legislation 39–40, 41–2, 75
Leonardo da Vinci 92–3, *93*
lifecycle
  design 47–53
  project 56–7
lift force 200
light bulbs *15*, *126*
limits, design 38–46
  see also conditions;
    considerations; constraints
line segments 104
linear equations 288–300, 319–25
linear models 295–300
linear processes 215
lines 104, 105
  perpendicular 107
loads
  on a bridge 253
  distributed 132–3, 250, 251
  failure load *see* failure load
  on a shelf 250–1
London Millennium Footbridge *63*,
  257
low density polyethylene (LDPE)
  51
low-volume design and
  manufacture 47, *48*

M
Mach number 227
maintenance
  and upkeep phase 217
  and use 56–7
making and production phase 216
manufacturing
  boundaries of design 47–8
  design for manufacture 224–6
  MET matrix 56–7
maps 182, *183*
Mars Climate Orbiter 184
mass manufacture 224–6
material analysis 288–300
material properties 144–5, 245–84
  creep 237–8
  knowledge of 58–9, 247, 248–
    58, 279–80
  modelling 271–8
  strength by design 135–7, 163
  strength under stress 303–9
materials, energy and toxicity
  (MET) matrix 56–7

mathematical model creation cycle
  232
mathematics
  equations *see* equations
  geometry 104–16
  iteration as a mathematical
    process 232–40
  statistics 19–21
  triangles *see* right-angled
    triangles; triangles
  trigonometry *see* trigonometry
  vectors *see* vectors
  visual thinking 64–73, 77–8
maximum landing weight 227–8
maximum take-off weight 227–8,
  229, 242
McLaren MP4-12C car *180*, *225*
mean 21, 32
median 21, 32
medical instrument prototyping
  128, 129
Mercedes-Benz SLR McLaren *180*,
  225
merging ideas 98
MET matrix 56–7
microchips *181*
Millau Viaduct *3*
mind mapping *86*, 87
Mini cars 224, 225
missing data 20
mobile phones *15*, 60, 88, *152*
  problem framing 87–8, 91,
    118–19
mock-ups 178
modelling 59
  design evaluation 141–2
  digital models 178
  materials 271–8
  mathematical model creation
    cycle *232*
  physical models *178*
  shelves 274–6, 282–3, 299–300,
    324–5
modulus (absolute value) 260
monocoque racing bicycle *136*
Moon, the 317–18, *318*
multiple representations 182–3

N
name-frame-move-evaluate cycle 212–13, 232
NASA 184
needs 215, 216
    meeting 13, 14, 29
negative gradients 259–60, 261, 269
negative vectors 161, 165
new materials *317*
Newton's laws of motion
    first law 194
    second law 199
    third law 195
non-linearity 217
normal 195
normal forces *see* reaction forces
numerical variation 19–21

O
obtuse angles 105
offshore drilling rigs *10*
    pumping station 44, 75
online services 15
opportunities 49–52
opposite side 109–10
'Out of the Box' concept *88*
outliers 20

P
Palladio, Andrea *170*
paper *317*
    prototyping a paper support structure 129–35
paperback book lifecycle 57
'particle' simulations *234*, 239–40
passenger capacity 228, 229–30
patents 179
peg crank *148*, 149
pendulum 194, 205
people
    asking other people for ideas 99
    designing for 16–28
    relationship with technology 313, 314–15
    and variation 16–17, 21, 23, 25–6, 30, 32, 33
performance failure 256–7
performance specifications 139–40, 144, 163
permanent deformation *252*, 256, 304, 308–9, 311

perpendicular lines 107
Phillips Lighting 52–3
physical models *178*
plan representations (plans) 180–1, *181*, 182–3
planes 104
planned obsolescence 48
planning permission 175
plastic deformation *252*, 256, 304, 308–9, 311
plastic water bottles *12*, 29–30
plastics 49–52
    stress–strain graphs 310, 311, 312
point loads 250, 251
points 104
pollution 50
polyethylene terephthalate (PET) 51
polypropylene 51
polystyrene 51, 310
polyvinyl chloride (PVC) 51
positive gradients 259–60, 261, 269
practical knowledge 58–9, 248–54
practical variation 18–19, 30–1
pram design 44, 75–6
precedents 179–80, 224
precision, spurious 20
preparation 92, 216
presentations 178
prioritisation 45, 46
problem exploration 84, 85–6
problem focusing 84, 87–8
problem framing/reframing 46, 84–91
problem solving 8–9, 82
    basic creative design cycle and 212–13, 232
    design driver 13, 14, 29, 30
    iteration vs 238–40
    tools 58
problem statements 84, 85, 89–91, 118–19, 141, 142–3
problems 81, 82–91, 215, 216
    good 82, 83, 88
    ill-defined (complex) 82, 84, 118
    well-defined 82, 84, 118
procedural design and modelling 314–15

processes 7–8
    design as process 11
    design processes *see* design processes
product development 221–3
product families 97, 224–6, 242
product platforms 224–6, 242
products 6–8
    boundaries of design 47–51
    design drivers 12–15
profiled metal *132*
project design phases 214–15, 241
project lifecycle 56–7
project management triangle *43–4*
projection 180–2
proposals, recording and confirming 170, 175–6
prosthetic limbs 96, *97*
prototyping *178*
    design 18–19, 30–1, 128–35, *128*, 141–2
    digital 173–4, 313–14
    rapid 315–18
pylons *7*
Pythagoras' theorem 107–8, 112, 113, 115–16, 119, 120, 188, 204

Q
qualitative information 19
quality
    cost, time and 43–4
    quantity rather than quality of ideas 99
quantitative information 19

R
radical innovation 60, 64, 76
rail mounted stretcher carrier 142–50, *143*, *144*
random input 99
range
    aircraft fuel consumption 228, 229
    of a dataset 19, 21, 32
rapid prototyping 315–18
ratios 64–9, 77
    calculating a quantity from a ratio 67
    comparing 67
    finding a ratio equivalent to a given ratio 67

reaction force 195–6, 197–8, 200, 206
recording proposals 170, 175–6
recycling 49
    plastics 50, 51–2
reflex angles 105
reframing problems 46, 84–91
regolith 317–18
regulations 40–2
reinforced edges 133, 134, 137
repairability 48
representation methods 177–85
repurpose 49
    repurposing and reusing phase 217
Res-Q-Rail 142–50, *143*, *144*
research and development (R&D) 221–3
resolving a vector 189–94
    see also components of vectors
resources 47
resultant vector (resultant) 159–60, 188, 189, 190, 204
reuse 49, 217
right-angled triangles 106, 107–13, 114, 116, 119–21
    trigonometry *see* trigonometry
right angles 104, 105
ring pull cans 82–3, *83*
ring-weight-strings static system 198–9, 206–7
rise 261–2
risk 90
    balancing uncertainty and 63–4
    uncertainty and 59–63
river depth 266–7, 268, 269–70, 282
Rolls-Royce 220–3
run 261–2

S
Sagrada Familia, Barcelona 61, *62*
satellite navigation (satnav) system *4*
scalars (scalar quantities) 152, 161
scale 180–2, 203
scallop shell structure 131–2, *131*, 134, 137, 141–2
section AA *183*
self-operating napkin *139*
service, design for 227–31

services 7–8
    design drivers 15
shape 145
    strength by design 135–7, 163
shelves 136, 277
    experiential knowledge and building 248–54
    modelling 274–6, 282–3, 299–300, 324–5
    testing 254–7, 279
shrilk *317*
side elevations *183*
silver 68, 77
similar shapes 106, *107*
    triangles 107, *109*
simple suspension structure 130–1, *130*, 137
sine 110–11, 120, 191, 192, 193
sine rule 114–15, 116, 121
sketching/sketches 101–2, *101*, 127, 314
    creating and developing ideas 171–3, 174, 202
    creative solutions 100, 119
    good habits and tips 171
    stretcher carrier brake 147–9
    and thinking creatively 92–5
    visualising equations 69–73, 77–8
    see also diagrams
smartphones *152*
soft checkpoints 217–18
soft landings process model 218, 242
SOH CAH TOA 110
solder 68, 77
solutions 83
    analytical 238–40
    creating 81, 92–100, 119
specifications 7, 42, 139–40
    performance 139–40, 144, 163
    technical 139–40, 144, 163
specifying and procurement phase 216
speculative design 13–14, 15
speed 281, 296–7
spurious precision 20
square hollow section (SHS) *69*, 72, 78
stage-gate process model 218, 241

stakeholders 176, 202–3
standard recycling symbols 51
standard structural steel sections 69–72, 77–8
standardisation *4*, 59–60
standards 39, 41–2, 179
starting point 216
statement, problem 84, 85, 89–91, 118–19, 141, 142–3
static loads 250, 251
static systems 194–9, 201
statistics 19–21
steel cable 112–13, 120–1
steel structural sections 69–72, *69*, 77–8
stiffness 311, 312, 326
stone 60–1, 317
story-telling 87–8, 99
straight angle 105
straight-line graphs
    drawing a line from its equation 292, 319–21
    equations 288–300, 319–25
    finding the equation from its gradient and a point on it 292–5, 321
    gradients 259–70, 280–2
strain 309–12, 326
strength 312, 326
    by design 135–7, 163
    compressive 308, 326
    tensile 63, 308
    under stress 303–9
stress 233, 325–6
    defining 305
    and fatigue 302
    and strain 310–12, 326
    strength under 303–9
stretcher carrier 142–50, *143*, *144*
strong concrete 65
substations *7*
subtracting vectors 161–2, 165
suspension bridges *62–3*, 130–1, *131*, 248, 257
sustainability 48, 49, 52–3
symbols 182
synthetic wood replacement 52, *76*

systems 7–8, 49
  design drivers 15
  dynamic 199–201
  static 194–9, 201

T
tablet computers *14*
  hand holder for *90*
tangent 110-11, 120–1, 189, 193, 204
teams, communication in 173–4
Technical Handbook 2015 Domestic 42
technical specifications 139–40, 144, 163
television transmitter masts 112–13
Telford, Thomas 62–3
temperature 272
  and bridge deck height 272–4, 282
  converting from Celsius to Fahrenheit 298, 322
  and curing concrete 68–9
tensile forces 60–1, 194, 198–9, 205, 206–7
tensile strength 63, 308
testing 59, 151
  knowledge from 254–7, 279
  materials testing and extending graphs 275–8, 284
  stretcher carrier *146*, 150
Tetra Pak *9*
text 94, 179
thickness of a shelf 257–8, 274, 275–6, 279–80, 282–3, 299–300, 324–5
thinking around the object 10
thread of ideas 98
three-frame cartoon 87, *88*
thrust force 200
ticket machines *17*
timber 52, 276–7
  defects 276, *277*
time 43–4
tin 68, 77
tolerance 25
Tongzhou city, China *181*
toothpaste tube metaphor 45, *46*
tower chimney *134*
toxicity 56–7
traffic lights *14*

transistor *3*
transmitter masts 112–13
transport and distribution *4*, 56–7
triangle law for vector addition 159
triangles 106–16, 187
  angles in 106
  general rules 113–15
  right-angled *see* right-angled triangles
trigonometric identities 193
trigonometric ratios 110–11, 115–16
  see also cosine; sine; tangent
trigonometry 108–13, 120–1
  problem solving with 111–13
  using a calculator 110–11
  use with vectors 187–9, 191–3, 204
Trunki *8*
tub 225
turbofan jet engines 220–3, *221*, *223*

U
UK government legislation website *39*, 40
UK-SPEC 42
uncertainty 58–73, 90
  balancing risk and 63–4
  design process 213, 241
  and risk 59–63
  uncertain structures 60–3
United States (US)
  maps *183*
  patent application *179*
units 297
  gradient 263, 264
universal (inclusive) design 26
Universal Serial Bus Implementers Forum (USB-IF) 42
USB 3.0 42
use and maintenance 56–7
use and operation phase 217
usefulness 96
user-centred design 26–7
user perspective 88
uses 249–50

V
variation 16–21
  design variation and people 26–8
  numerical 19–21
  people and 16–17, 21, 23, 25–6, 30, 32, 33
  practical 18–19, 30–1
vaulted structure 132–3, *132*, 134, 137
vectors 151–62
  adding *see* addition of vectors
  applications 201
  communicating analysis 186–201
  components of 189–94, 198–9, 206–7
  displacement *see* displacement vectors
  free body diagrams 102, 103, 194–201
  representing 153–4
  special 157
  subtracting 161–2, 165
  using trigonometry with 187–9, 191–3, 204
Velcro *3*
velocity 190, 193, 205
velocity–time graphs 297, 322
vertical lines 260
  equations 291–2, 321
view types *183*
visual mapping 53, 57
visualisation 64–73, *178*
  equations 69–73, 77–8
  fractions 64–9
Volkswagen Golf 224

W
waste plastics 49–51, *50*, *51*
water depth gauge *266*
water bottles, plastic *12*, 29–30
weak concrete 65
weight
  aircraft maximum landing weight 227–8
  aircraft maximum take-off weight 227–8, 229, 242
  free body diagrams 195–6, 197–8, 200, 206–7
  see also loads

well-defined problems 82, 84, 118

wheel bolts *304*

whole service product 52–3

wood

   synthetic wood replacement 52, *76*

   timber properties 276–7

words 301–3

writing 94, 179

X

x-intercept 271, 290–1, 319

Y

y-intercept 271, 289–90, 291, 298, 319, 323

yield point 311, 312

yield stress 311

Young, James Webb 58, 92

Young's modulus 311

Z

zero gradient 269

zero vector 157, 160